Higher Education in Europe

also in the Higher Education Policy Series

Graduate Education in Britain
Tony Becher, Mary Henkel and Maurice Kogan
ISBN 1 85302 531 3
Higher Education Policy Series 17

Public Expenditure on Higher Education
A Comparative Study in the Member States of the European Community
Frans Kaiser, Raymond J.G.M. Florax, Jos B.J. Koelman, Frans A. van Vught
ISBN 1 85302 532 1
Higher Education Policy Series 15

University and Society
Essays on the Social Role of Research and Higher Education
Edited by Martin A. Trow and Thorsten Nybom
ISBN 1 85302 525 9
Higher Education Policy Series 12

Evaluating Higher Education
Edited by Maurice Kogan
ISBN 1 85302 510 0
Higher Education Policy Series 6

The Use of Performance Indicators in Higher Education
A Critical Analysis of Developing Practice 2nd edition
Martin Cave, Stephen Hanney and Maurice Kogan
ISBN 1 85302 518 6
Higher Education Policy Series 3

Innovation and Adaptation in Higher Education
The Changing Conditions of Advanced Teaching and Learning in Europe
Edited by Claudius Gellert
ISBN 1 85302 535 6
Higher Education Policy Series 22

Higher Education in Europe

Edited by Claudius Gellert

Jessica Kingsley Publishers
London and Philadelphia

First published in the United Kingdom in 1993 by
Jessica Kingsley Publishers Ltd
116 Pentonville Road
London N1 9JB

Copyright © 1993 the contributors and the publisher

British Library Cataloguing in Publication Data

Higher Education in Europe. - (Higher
Education Policy Series; v.16)
I.Gellert, Cladius II. Series
378.4

ISBN 1-85302-529-1

Printed and Bound in Great Britain by
Bookcraft Ltd., Avon

Contents

Preface

The volume *Higher Education in Europe* is the outcome of a collective effort of leading European researchers in the field of comparative higher education. It addresses major institutional and structural changes which have occurred in European universities and other tertiary institutions in recent years. Besides descriptive accounts of new developments in the organisational patterns of the respective systems, the authors attempt to show in which ways quantitative expansion new demands from the labour market and socio-political expectations have led to the emergence of modified roles and purposes in higher education. Since one of the most significant influences in the recent past has been the process of European integration, the system of higher education in the European Community is also considered in its development as a whole, by the inclusion of investigations of related problem dimensions from outside the Community. It is hoped that the contributions in this collection will help not only to understand the ongoing transformation of the European system of higher education in times of rapid economic and technological change, but will also assist the further integration process within the European Community and beyond.

The authors of the volume came together at the end of 1990 to discuss the developments of higher education which are described and analysed here. This was possible within a research project which the European University Institute in Florence is undertaking with the help of a research grant from the Commission of the European Communities. In the meantime, a second conference on 'Innovation and Adaptation in Higher Education' has taken place, the results of which will also be made available to the public.

My thanks for enabling me to pursue these matters go first of all to the European University Institute, and in particular to its President Emile Noël, and to the Commission of the European Communities, and here especially to Hywel Jones, Director of the Task Human Resources, Education, Training and Youth, for having opened up the opportunity for this research project. Their permanent encouragement and interest have been overwhelming and are highly appreciated. But there are also numerous other persons to whom I am grateful. On the one hand, a research undertaking like this one would not be possible without the contributions, discussions, suggestions and criticisms of colleagues in the scientific community. Those who are represented in this volume, deserve my particular gratitude. One of them, Maurice Kogan, I would like to single out as someone who not only helped me enormously, including during some difficult times, but who also assisted me a great deal with the preparations for this publication. There are also all those who were, in varying degrees and at different times, of immense help here in Florence. Here I would like to mention in particular my secretary, Dorothea Detring, and the former and present research assistants Inger Stokkink, Hans Kraft and Annemarie Sprokkereef. But also the members of the Academic Council of the European University Institute, who gave me their frequent support, must be mentioned here. Finally, and by no means least, I wish particularly to thank Roger Morgan, the Chairman of the steering committee for the project, who, together with the other members, constantly accompanied the project-work in all its phases with never-ending advice and support.

In his address to the participants of the above-mentioned conference, the Principal of Institute, Emile Noël, stressed the importance of higher education remaining the first and foremost prerogative of the national states, without losing sight of the importance it has for the European Community. To that effect he maintained it was important to reach common guidelines, in order to make student exchange and the recognition of diplomas easier. If the present volume does not only serve as a contribution to academics and others interested in research on comparative higher education, but also helps to provide 'common guidelines' for the growing-together of the European system of higher education, in that as it makes its diversity more transparent, then it will have fulfilled its purpose.

Dr. Claudius Gellert
Research Director
European University Institute, Florence

Changing Patterns of European Higher Education

Claudius Gellert

Socio-Economic Transformations and Advanced Training

In most industrialised countries, the recent decades have been times of rapid socio-economic and political modifications, even if we disregard the most dramatic transformation of Central and Eastern Europe during the last few years. Particularly in Western societies, the speed and range of economic, technological and cultural change have been enormous, and have encompassed all spheres of public and private life. One of the key sectors in this revolutionary process has been science and technology, since the massive increase in fundamental knowledge and applied technologies has been a major determinant for this socio-economic progress. Thus, the institutional sphere of research and training became of central importance for this development. This, in turn, put growing pressure on the universities and other forms of higher education to cope with ever-increasing student numbers, while remaining responsible for a large part of the research output upon which societies and their economies depended.

However, not only the productive sectors have been in need of larger potentials of highly qualified manpower, but also the expanding service industries and multiple segments of public administrations (the latter, in order to cope, for instance, with unintendend by-products of the industrial process). In consequence, not only science and engineering subjects expanded, but also e.g. law, the social sciences and the humanities. New and better trained personnel was not only needed for the production of goods, but also for organising, counselling, catering, advising and, not least, education and training purposes.

But besides industry and commerce, on the one hand, and the service sector and administration, on the other, there was a third major driving force behind the expansion of higher education in Europe. Related to the other socio-economic developments, there emerged increasing political demands for the advancement of educational opportunity for larger segments of the population. This growing 'social demand' for improved education and training, including higher education, was part of an overall process of democratisation of societies. In any case, it turned out to be a decisive challenge to outmoded elite concepts of the 'gifted few' in education and related traditional organisational patterns of advanced professional training.

As a result of this all-embracing socio-economic transformation, the numbers of students in higher education exploded. Most European countries, like other advanced Western societies, have seen an unprecedented expansion of their institutions of higher education over the last 30 years, and contrary to many predictions, this process of growth has not yet stopped in several systems. In many of them the number of post-secondary students quadrupled over that period. Staff in universities and other institutions of higher education, as well as government funds for teaching and research, increased at a similar rate.

But the changes were not only of a quantitative kind. In many areas the very concepts of higher education were being modified. New disciplines or sub-disciplines emerged. Outdated structures of institutional authority and government were being challenged. Admission to tertiary levels of education and training in most national systems changed from a restrictive elite-mode to varied patterns of mass higher education. And, most importantly, the equation that higher education meant university training was radically challenged and turned into an historical assumption. New types of universities or altogether new institutional forms of advanced learning were set up in most countries.

The overall picture, for several years, has in most European countries been rather confusing. The traditional organisational and conceptual features in higher education have become fluid. While in earlier times, universities and similar institutions may have been fairly stable providers of clearly circumscribed social goods, they are now definitely bound into the constantly changing flow of societal and political processes. It is therefore now much more difficult than in the past to know what exactly the phenomena are that we are dealing with, what purposes they serve and how they are related to their respective environments.

In which ways, then, is it possible to make sense of these emerging new patterns of European higher education? How can we adequately describe them, what are the driving forces behind change and persistence, what indeed are the characteristics of institutional and structural modifications which we can observe in Europe and elsewhere? Are we above all dealing with new institutional forms of higher education, or is the traditional university sector also changing, and if so, in which ways and under what kind of influences? The contributions in this volume represent a collective attempt to identify major developments and modifications in European higher education. Let us, in the following, summarise the individual outcomes of this joint effort.

Contributions to this Volume

The articles are grouped together in three sections. The first one, *Structural Modifications of the Major Models*, comprises broad structural and institutional developments in the larger European systems of higher education, i.e. those in Germany, Great Britain, France, Italy and Spain. The second section, *Adaptation and Distinctiveness: Diversification in European Tertiary Training Systems*, deals with adaptive processes to new socio-economic needs and challenges in the Mediterranean countries of Portugal and Greece, as well as with functional differentiation and movements towards more accountability in Ireland, The Netherlands, Belgium (and Luxembourg), and Denmark. And the final part, *Policy Impacts and Institutional Change*, addresses transnational legal and policy issues in the course of higher education reforms, including observations from outside the European Community, as well as some theoretical considerations on the notions of structures and functions in research on higher education.

Structural Modifications of the Major Models

Ulrich Teichler (Comprehensive University of Kassel and Northwestern University), in his paper 'Structures of Higher Education Systems in Europe', opens up the discussion with an overview of the history of the debate on structures of higher education in Europe and America. He sees a clear distinction in the way structural issues have been addressed over the years. In the 1960's and early 1970's, structural issues were in the middle of political and policy attention. Most of the relevant literature on the matter of structural change was written in the early 1970's (e.g. Trow, OECD report on short-cycle higher education). After that, the matter became less important in discussions on higher education. A main explanation for this is, according to Teichler, the fact that structural changes go hand in hand with circumstances of educational and economic expansion. This expansion made it socially, economically and politically possible to undertake projects on a large scale. In times of economic contraction, however, there is a tendency to be content with what is available. A critical account of Teichler's conceptualisation of structures in higher education is contained in Gellert's contribution (see below).

Einhard Rau (Free University of Berlin), in 'Inertia and Resistance to Change of the Humboldtian University', traces the still very influential ideas of Humboldt (such as institutional autonomy, and the freedom of teaching and research) with regard to the reform of German universities after the expansionist phase. In his opinion, these ideas remained relatively intact during the years of change, and this has made them dysfunctional and ideological: ideas orientated towards a small and socially homogeneous student body had to operate in a massively expanded and heterogeneous environment. The continuing strong emphasis laid on the research function of university training, for instance, has led to long study-durations and a neglect of the teaching function. The ideal of a 'unity of research and teaching', i.e. the concept of utilizing topical research results directly for the process of student training (with the students being conceived of as 'co-researchers') could perhaps be maintained during the 1950's, when participation rates at universities were around five per cent of the respective age-cohorts. But in present times of mass higher education, professional training of large numbers becomes the primary aim, and research evolves into an activity quite separate from the teaching function. Humboldtian ideas helped to strengthen the power of the professoriate, and thus helped to neglect necessary tasks such as reforms of curricula, student counselling etc. What has made the 'Humboldtian university' successful is not so much the ideas behind it, but rather the fact that during the last few decades sufficient resources were available to cover up the mistakes.

Maurice Kogan (Brunel University) asks in 'The End of the Dual System? The Blurring of Boundaries in the British Tertiary Education System' whether there are so-called 'educational essentials', i.e. values and relationships which could be defined as almost naturally given tasks of higher education. In contrast to such essentials, higher education changes in Britain, according to Kogan, do not follow the logic of academic organisation, but the needs and expectations of educational policy-making and governments. On the basis of this conceptual framework he analyses the British higher education system which until recently could be described as dual or binary: with the universities and the polytechnics sector. This binary divide has virtually collapsed; not by law (legislation on higher education came only in 1988, when other changes were already in full force), but through a complex interplay of various influences, such as budget cuts, change in the organisation of funding (the English 'bidding'-system), strategic funding from the side of the government, academic drift processes in the polytechnics sector, imposed managerial measures because of the 'cult of efficiency', and the subordination of higher education to overall social policy.

All this came about in an *ad hoc* way: government had no clear ideas about what a university should be like. Yet its measures led to the closing of the gap between polytechnics and universities and to an erosion of close bonds between research and teaching. It seems that next to purely academic objectives, economic and vocational objectives have gained ground in British higher education policies. Kogan fears the emerging of a second-class higher education system: the rich and famous institutions will get richer and more famous (for instance, through privileged access to research resources), whereas other institutions will find it difficult to survive.

Kogan's paper raises a number of interesting questions of evaluation and assessment processes, what their criteria should be, and the influence of these on the position of academic staff and their power in relation to the government (cf. Kogan 1989). Furthermore, it draws attention to the ambivalent merits of strategic funding, and the vulnerability of so-called 'weaker' institutions to the 'whimsical labour market': the more vulnerable they are, the more they will want to meet vocational requirements. But it may be pointed out that there is also the opposite tendency of institutions which, once they are fairly safe and well-established in the non-university sector, show a tendency to imitate universities, thereby sometimes endangering their successful identity and profile. (On the problem of 'academic drift' and 'blurring of boundaries', see also OECD 1991.)

Jean-Pierre Jallade, Jean Lamoure and Jeanne Lamoure Rontopoulou (European Institute of Education and Social Policy, Comité Nationale de la Gestion, École Nationale Supérieure d'Enseignement Technique, Paris, respectively) begin their account of 'Tertiary Diversification in France and the Conditions of Access' with a description of the various forms of higher education at bachelor level (in the French system the *'premier cycle'*). Here we see two types of technical vocational training, next to the preparatory classes for the *grandes écoles* and the university. Only universities have unlimited access, whereas the other forms of higher education can make selections. They also emphasise the importance of the features and contents of secondary education as influencing the organisation of higher education on the *'premier cycle'* level.

The paper raises questions concerning the position of research in French higher education. Universities have to compete with other institutions which focus mainly on vocational training and offer short-term courses, whereas university courses in practice become 'socially useful' only after a long-term course. Does competition, therefore, make universities vocationalise the content of university courses to the detriment of research? What are the prospects of research, if other institutions have the possibility of selecting students and universities have not? Even if such questions remain partly unanswered, the framework for further analysis is clearly given.

Roberto Moscati (University of Milan) perceives the Italian higher education system as moving from a highly centralised towards a decentralised system, as the title of his paper indicates: 'Moving towards Institutional Differentiation: The Italian Case'. After decades of centralisation, based partly (apart from the Napoleonic heritage) on the idea of using education as a means for culturally unifying Italy, consensus on this matter seems to have disappeared. Decentralisation as an answer to the growing call for diversification has become *en vogue*. To the extent that such a development would still be enhanced by the government, it is, however, opposed by people who would like to leave it to the market to regulate what is important. Centralisation is still supported by those who see it as a tool to bring the 'poorer' regions and universities to an acceptable level.

The same antagonism characterises curricula reform and the organisation of research funding. Regionally based political motivations and vested interests in academia (i.e. strong professorial powers) until now have blocked any meaningful reform. It is hoped that European integration will put politicians and universities alike under pressure to come to a working solution. Meanwhile, reality catches up on planning. On post-*laurea* level (*laurea* being the usual undergraduate degree), private schools are flourishing, especially in the field of business studies.

This paper has partly to be seen in the context of the Italian discussion on the pros and cons of short courses within universities, which recent legislation is intending to bring about. So far, it is an open question whether short-cycle courses will have a chance for survival within the university framework, since most academics are against them, despite a strong backing by politicians. And it may well be asked, considering the relative lack of non-university (short) courses, how Italy satisfies its need for professionals of this type.

Emilio Lamo de Espinosa (Complutense University, Madrid), in his contribution 'The Spanish University in Transition', offers a comprehensive and sociologically informed explanation of the role of student and academic cultures for the development of Spanish society and politics since Francoism. This, in turn, enables him to describe the reform process of the Spanish system of higher education during the last 15 years as a dependent variable as well as an influencing factor of the socio-political system. This reform affected all areas of tertiary education, from access and expansion to curricular reform and degree structures and to faculty selection (with a strong tendency towards inbreeding) and research funding. The situation is portrayed as a highly complicated and structurally antagonistic one, which, on the other hand, is also characterised by promising dynamics, not least with regard to recent competitive elements through the establishment of private universities.

Adaptation and Distinctiveness: Diversification in European Tertiary Training Systems

Eduardo Marçal Grilo (Fundaçao Calouste Gulbenkian, Lisbon), in his paper 'The Transformation of Higher Education in Portugal', pictures the Portuguese situation as radically different from the situation of the countries discussed until then. Portugal, recently having entered the European Community, sees itself put to the enormous double task of catching up with the other European Community member-states, by modernising a relatively underdeveloped country (18 per cent illiterates among the population above 15 years of age; only about 3.6 per cent of the over-15-year-olds with intermediary or higher education), and anticipating further modernisation due to the shaping of new higher education structures. In this process, the European Community is sometimes seen as the panacea to strengthen Portuguese higher education, in particular to build up and establish new research centres. Although this is vital for Portuguese higher education, it also might lead to great difficulties because of the sums that will be involved in the running costs of these institutions in later years, costs for which the government will have to be responsible. Furthermore, the paper gives an extensive view on the organisation and recent developments in higher education and its policies in Portugal, a system with a binary organisation with universities (private and public) at one end, and polytechnics at the other, whereby the polytechnics have only a low status, although the demand on the labour market for professionals from this institution is great, and whereby recent *numerus clausus* measures at public universities had a bolstering effect on the private universities.

Christos Saitis (Ministry of Education, Athens), in 'Main Features of Higher Education in Greece', gives a comprehensive account of the Greek higher education system. Striking characteristics of that system are the rigid centralisation, the *numerus clausus* for all studies, the (until recently) prohibition of private higher education, and the extent to which higher education policy is still a vehicle for political power-wielding of all groups involved. In contrast to most other Western systems which have been experiencing processes of overall institutional differentiation, the Greek development is characterised by the reverse trend towards more integration through the lifting of non-university sectors into university status. This is comparable only to the situation in

Australia (see Moses in this volume), since it is also a government-prescribed reform (and not, as in Great Britain, an assimilation from 'below').

Patrick Clancy (University College, Dublin), in his contribution 'Goal Enlargement and Differentiation: The Evolution of the Binary System in Ireland', gives a thorough account of recent developments in the Irish higher education system. One outstanding feature is the firm grip government has on the direction of higher education: techno-logical research, in particular, is boosted through strategic funding. Also the shaping of the higher education is heavily 'front-loaded' with short-cycle vocational training as a sign of this. Recently, however, criticism has been voiced that research has become too subordinated to vocationally orientated teaching. The paper clearly points to the dangers of too much emphasis on short-cycle and vocational courses. Also the migration of Irish students and academics is a concern. Business studies seem to have taken the place of teacher training: on top of quite specialised courses students tend to take another short-cycle business course in order to become more broadly orientated. This may be a sign of a still existing need for 'generalists' on the labour market.

Peter Maassen, Leo Goedegebuure and Don Westerheijden (University of Twente), in their paper on the Dutch higher education system 'Social and Political Conditions for the Emerging Tertiary Structures in the Netherlands', draw attention to the two 'dogmas' that have ruled higher education policy in the Netherlands since World War II: open access and equality. These notions stand in a somewhat strained relationship to the two principles that have shaped the drastic changes in higher education since the 1980's: efficiency and quality. Especially the call for quality in connection with diversification made it difficult to maintain that the non-university HBO-sector and universities were equal in quality. Also, recent moves in Dutch higher education attempting to bring university and non-university courses to the same level can be seen as another compli-cation of the same kind. For the Netherlands, Maassen and his colleagues see a tendency of a growing diversification of the system although accompanied by a force to make institutions at the same time more equal on the level of public recognition. This problem is obviously related to the issue of autonomy, which leads to a number of yet unresolved questions. How sound is the assumption of Dutch policy-makers that quality is related to autonomy? How autonomous can a system, heavily relying on State funding be, and what is the relationship between autonomy and processes of evaluation and assessment? To what extent does academic freedom presuppose institutional autonomy?

In their paper 'New Tasks and Roles for Higher Education in Belgium and Luxem-bourg', *Willy Wielemans and Johan Vanderhoeven* (Katholieke Universiteit, Leuven) point out that room for manoeuvering in the field of Belgian higher education has been scarce because of two major social issues: religion and language. The delicate balance between the interest groups of Catholics and 'latitudinarians', and between Flemish and French speaking communities, was not to be upset by higher-education policy. If one group asked for something, the other group got the equivalent of it as well. This restricted government in real, at first sight efficient retrenchment operations. It also restricted government in stimulating one university to the disadvantage of another university, if this university happened to be of the 'other' group. Apart from these aspects, the authors give a comprehensive account of the Belgian higher education situation and its quantitative as well as structural development.

This paper may lead to further considerations concerning the question what skills entrepreneurs ask of university graduates. Paradigmatic knowledge and the ability to embed one's discipline within broad categories of learning, is receiving less and less attention, although entrepreneurs say that what they need are generalists. In the authors' view, there is a dangerous development towards vocationalism. How can graduates be prepared for immediate labour market utilisation, if technical knowledge 'burns out' after five or six years, and if people change careers after roughly six years? In other words, what kind of generalist is being asked for?

Poul Bache (Ministry of Education, Copenhagen), in 'Reform and Differentiation in the Danish System of Higher Education', gives a detailed account of the characteristics of the system. One of the remarkable features is the age of Danish graduates: they are the oldest in Europe. This has to do with the fact that secondary education ends late (at 19); furthermore, it has become fashionable to wait before starting to study, and, for instance, to pass some practical training before-hand; and finally it takes a long time for students to get their degrees, because the first and only degree is a long-course degree. Recently, short courses have been introduced at university level; higher education policy is now emphasising the need to orient higher education to labour market requirements.

Policy Impacts and Institutional Change

Bruno de Witte (Limburg University), in his paper 'Higher Education and the Constitution of the European Community', gives an overview of the legal aspects connected with higher education in the Community. Although the European Community Constitution in the past has offered little opportunity to develop a Community policy on higher education, there exist several legal rights which, due to recent treaties and decisions by the European court, have far-reaching impacts on the field of higher education. These legal aspects concern equal treatment of EC citizens as regards:

- the right to work everywhere in the Community
- the right to provide training (i.e. to teach)
- the right to receive training
- the right to have one's diplomas recognised.

De Witte describes in detail how recent developments have resulted in the inclusion of education and higher education into the legitimate realm of European Community policy-making, as a result of changing definitions of the term 'training'. He also analyses the impact of various exchange and research programmes of the Community, which consist of financial incentives, without encroaching upon the prerogative of the Member States to establish the content of courses. Of course, one cannot separate these objectives of EC policies from the indirect influence they undoubtedly exert on national systems.

Concerning the relationships between national government policy, EC policy and the universities, a tendency can thus be observed in several countries to look to Brussels rather then to the national government as a source of expected and desired change (Denmark, Portugal, France, Italy, etc). And it may therefore be a matter of concern, where exactly the legitimacy of higher education policy of the Community is founded. The Maastricht summit of December 1991 has certainly clarified many of the vital issues in this area. The codification of European Community responsibility for education in the Maastricht treaty would however not have been possible without the gradual creation of factual arrangements at Community level through agreements on substantive issues. De Witte is providing a detailed account of this development and its legal implications.

Erich Leitner (Klagenfurt University), in 'Developments in European Community Politics of Higher Education – Observations from Outside', takes up some of the considerations with which De Witte was concerned. He relates them to an analysis of his home territory, by sketching the Austrian higher education system (which is, for instance, characterised by an almost total lack of a non-university sector), and by describing the international relations Austria already has in the field of higher education. He then outlines some problems and expectations concerning the future development of its system of higher education in connection with Austria's envisaged entry to the European Community. One of the problems consists in the possible consequences of the recent disappearance of barriers to East-European students who wish to study in the West. Because of its geographical location, Austria will in any case have to play a particular role in that respect. When it has become a member of the European Community, it will, more than most other member states, have to bear the crunch of the respective demands and expectations from Central and Eastern Europe.

Ingrid Moses (University of Technology, Sydney) rounds up the external observations with 'Against the Stream: Australia's Policy of Tertiary Integration', where she analyses and describes the government-led reform process of bringing about an integrated system of higher education. Most of the non-university sector which had been primarily engaged in technological fields, is being amalgamated with universities, thus turning former non-university diploma courses into university degrees, expanding and raising in status large groups of academic personnel, but, in turn, also getting traditional research-oriented universities to accommodate themselves to the more practical concerns of their new partners within a unified institutional setting. The difficulties arising from the prospect of integration are especially illuminating: has, for instance, formal uniformity impeded diversity in content? Furthermore, Moses describes a development which may still serve as an example for other Western systems, because the Australian government deemed it necessary to introduce performance indicators in the new integrated system, to allow for a differentiated system of research funding (cf. also the Dutch contribution in this volume). It remains to be seen how the application of performance indicators works in Australia, and what consequences the new system may have for the relationship of tertiary institutions with the national and State governments.

Claudius Gellert, in his final contribution on 'Structures and Functional Differentiation – Remarks on Changing Paradigms of Tertiary Education in Europe', attempts to clarify some theoretical issues related to higher education structures and institutions. Starting from the observation of overall differentiation in systems of higher education, he asks in which ways we can analytically account for these new structural patterns of European higher education? He suggests, above all, a *functional* approach (which is primarily concerned with roles and purposes) to the classification of higher education models as being useful for the understanding not only of the flagships of European higher education, i.e. the universities themselves, but also for a differentiated analysis of institutional variations as well as historical and political developments. The identification of the 'research model' in Germany, the 'training model' in France and the Mediterranean countries, and the 'personality model' in England, does not mean that there are such 'pure' systems. Rather, these models serve heuristic purposes, insofar as they make alternative developments within their own realms as well as differing structures and aims in other systems more transparent and easier to locate.

A major result from such considerations is the methodological need of putting less emphasis in future analyses of this research field on formal aspects of structural differentiation, and of concentrating more on functional, i.e. qualitative and historically informed features of tertiary education and research institutions. This implies, for instance, the need to get away from attempts of overall conceptualisations of systems of higher education. Although the necessity to analyse all segments of higher education is not in question, he argues that the need to analyse them in their distinctive features and respective modifications over time, requires a differentiated *functional* description and investigation of all the major sub-sectors.

Summary and Conclusions

The essential areas of change in European higher education in recent years have been the following:

Quantitative expansion, i.e. the transformation of small elite-oriented university sectors comprising some 5 per cent of the respective age-cohorts into a massive enterprise in most countries involving between 20 and 30 per cent; the tendency in most instances is still rising, despite intermediary phases of stagnation in some countries. Portugal in all this is a notable exception and is still expecting a major expansionist period.

Institutional differentiation, i.e. the development of new forms of higher education, like the *Fachhochschulen* in Germany, the polytechnics in Britain or the IUTs in France, or in some cases like recently in Italy, the establishment of short-cycle programmes within the university sectors (an experiment which was started by France in the early 1970's). Without these alternative institutional provisions the rapid quantitative expansion would not have been possible, since the universities in many countries displayed a large degree of inertia and unwillingness to adapt to emerging socio-economic needs and requirements.

European experience seems to support the hypothesis that in higher education systems in which universities are orientated towards vocationalisation, integration with non-university sectors tends to occur more easily 'under one roof', while the emergence of the non-university sector in systems with a stronger research orientation of the universities tends to happen outside the latter (as a kind of alternative to universities). This would underline a functional approach to institutions of higher education (as e.g. the case of Spain's intended integration of vocational short-cycle courses into the existing university system may well demonstrate in the near future), because, on the basis of a functional approach, it may be predicted that in this system there will either occur functional assimilation or institutional separation not before long.

Functional modifications, i.e. the emergence of new tasks and purposes in higher education. This phenomenon to a large extent was linked to the above-mentioned process of institutional differentiation, since the non-university sectors in most countries are characterised by a more practical orientation of teaching and learning, by more responsiveness to demands from industries and the labour market, and generally by a redefinition of higher education as not being any longer exclusively based on parallel processes of research and research training, but as science-based applied training for the professions. The main difference consists in the notion that students do not any longer, as in the university sector, have to be enabled to become researchers themselves, but that it suffices to base their training of practical skills and abilities on science and academic knowledge. But the universities did not remain totally untouched by this process of functional modification. The successful examples of the non-university sectors, together with growing pressures from economy, employment system and governments, made also the traditional academic institutions aware of the need to be more oriented to 'useful' professional knowledge or to practical ventures such as science-parks, centres for technology transfer and the like. Finally, new functional aspects occurred with respect to increasing social demands for 'second chances' and generally the need to open up restrictive tertiary structures in favour of better participation opportunities for larger segments of society.

New modes of teaching and learning, i.e. the trend in some countries, which in the past had been characterised by rather loose arrangements of teaching and learning, to introduce stricter and more transparent curricula, to abbreviate study periods by requirements of more frequent examinations or simply attendance in lectures and seminars. Here it was again primarily the non-university sectors which were the spearheads of higher education reform. While related experiments in some universities of the 1970's (sandwich-course etc.) were later given up again, the non-university sectors introduced a significant element of practical training into the regular curriculum. The universities, so far, in most cases are rather hesitant to follow such examples.

Access and educational opportunity. This aspect comprises on the one hand the already mentioned offerings in some systems of second chances to 'mature students' or others who during their former primary and secondary socialisation missed the chance to enter the route to higher education. On the other hand, it also refers to large-scale improvements of educational opportunity for the total population through massive expansions of school and higher education support systems, infrastructural and building programmes, by the introduction of means-tested grants and loans to significant proportions of the population and by a general, policy-influenced shift in the public culture which created a more liberal and encouraging atmosphere for education and advanced learning. While this process was interrupted in some countries due to conservative intervention, bringing about periods of stagnation in the area of educational changes, this trend practically all over Europe has again been replaced by a fresh and dynamic appreciation on the policy level of the merits and the socio-economic value of enlarged educational participation rates, including higher education.

Research and graduate training. To the same extent to which undergraduate education has again taken a rapid expansionist development, graduate education, and the training of future researchers in particular, has also become a focus of policy measures and institutional changes. There have been clear indications in the recent past of dangers that the funding base for fundamental research in the university sector was gradually shifting towards outside research organisations. The profitability of investments in pure research institutes seemed to be higher and the returns more promising. But this trend, despite the still existing overcrowding of institutions of higher education, may recently have come to a halt. New initiatives can be observed in some systems for a more systematic support for graduate training and the implementation of organisational frameworks, like the *Graduiertenkollegs* in Germany, which are meant to assure the future supply of highly qualified researchers and academics. During the 1980's, almost a whole generation of young academics has been prevented or at least discouraged from entering a sound and secure career in higher education. But now policy-makers as well as those responsible for the future of science and scholarship within the institutions of higher education attempt to rearrange the conditions not only for the reproduction of disciplinary and teaching requirements, but also for research processes which are vital for heavily export-oriented economies.

Government interventionism and accountability. The trend in recent years towards more efficiency and accountability in the field of higher education has within Europe probably been most noted in the Netherlands, and outside in Australia. In times of financial stringencies governments are seeking to economise in education and training, even while accepting the need for further investments and expansions. As a consequence, new efficiency criteria like performance indicators are experimented with, primarily as a possible means for more adequate distribution of research funds. The academic world in most European countries reacts with uneasiness to such tendencies and programmes, rightly putting disciplinary concerns and considerations of academic freedom first. Nevertheless, even if they concede the need to respect institutional and individual autonomy in academia, governments in many systems are displaying multiple measures of influence and interference. Financial incentives are the main steering mechanism by which certain disciplinary areas like engineering, computer sciences or business studies are particularly supported, while others, like some humanities and social sciences, have difficulties in surviving.

But again, as in many similar incidences in the recent past, the direction of change and public debate is not one-sided. Already there those, even among representatives from industry and the employment system, who warn that the interpretive academic disciplines are essential in societies characterised by rapid economic and technological change, because the fundamental social and economic restructuration which most highly industrialised societies are experiencing demands highly qualified experts to cope with these structural changes and to offer advice for policy-makers about the social and political costs and risks which are entailed in these transformations.

Europeanisation. This, finally, is perhaps the most far-reaching and comprehensive transforming mechanism of all. The process of European integration, after more than 30 years of concentrating on economic requirements, has at last also reached the field of education, and that of higher education in particular. Recent decisions of the European Court concerning the recognition of degrees, financial support for students from other EC countries, and the like, together with an extensive programme of exchange-initiatives for students and academics, undertaken by the Commission, have brought about a situation which is characterised by an ever increasing factual transparency within the European higher education system and a consequential development towards harmonisation and integration. Even though the principles of subsidiarity and national responsibility for the policy areas of education and culture are respected as necessary features of the historically grown cultural diversity of Europe, the permanent flow of persons and ideas within the realm of research and advanced training is bringing about unavoidable institutional and structural modifications in the national systems. The student exchange programme in itself and the envisaged credit transfer system make it necessary for individual universities to adapt their organisational features and course programmes to the experiences and qualifications gained by their students abroad. In this way, and perhaps this is the paradigmatic model which applies to all areas of cultural integration in Europe, it is not even necessary for national governments to interfere in order to implement EC measures, because it is the individual unit concerned, i.e. in our case the single institution of higher education, which reacts to grass-root needs and expectation of its clientele, thus changing its organisational pattern in favour of further advances towards European integration.

References

Commission of the European Communities (1991) *Memorandum on Higher Education in the European Community.* Brussels: Commission of the European Communities.

Cerych, L. and P. Sabatier (1986) *Great Expectations and Mixed Performance. The Implementation of Higher Education Reforms in Europe.* Trentham: Trentham Books.

Gellert, C. (1985) 'State Interventionism and Institutional Autonomy' in *Oxford Review of Education* Vol 11 No 3, 283–293.

Gellert, C. (1988) *Vergleich des Studiums an englischen und deutschen Universitäten.* Frankfurt: Lang (2nd edn.; 1st edn. 1983).

Gellert, C. (1989) 'The Limitations of Open Access to Higher Education in the Federal Republic of Germany' in *Higher Education Policy* Vol 2 No 1, 32–34.

Gellert, C. (1990) 'Academic Inquiry and Advanced Training. International Perspectives of a Changing Paradigm' in C. Gellert, E. Leitner and J. Schramm (eds) *Research and Teaching at Universities – International and Comparative Perspectives*. Frankfurt: Lang, 28–64.

Gellert, C. (1991) 'Higher Education: Changing Tasks and Definitions' in *Higher Education in Europe*. Vol XVI No 3, 28–45.

Gellert, C. (1991) 'Funktionswandel der Hochschulsysteme im internationalen Vergleich' in O. Zuber-Skerrit, R. Egger and H. Altrichter (eds) *Wie Studierende Forschen Lernen. Helping Students Become Researchers. Zeitschrift für Hochschuldidaktik* Vol 15 No 4, 367–379.

Gellert, C. (1992) 'Faculty Research' in B.R. Clark and G. Neave (eds) *The Encyclopedia of Higher Education*. Oxford: Pergamon, Vol. 3 *Analytical Perspectives*, 1634–1641.

Gellert, C. (1992) 'The Impact of United States Higher Education on Higher Education Reform and Innovation Debates in the Federal Republic of Germany' in U. Teichler and H. Wasser (eds) German and American Universities: Mutual Influences Past and Present, Kassel: Centre for Higher Education and Work, 45–56.

Gellert, C. (1993) *Wettbewerb und Leistungsorientierung im amerikanischen Universitätssystem*. Frankfurt: Lang.

Gellert, C. and Rau, E. (1992) 'Diversification and Integration: The Vocationalization of the German Higher Education System' in *European Journal of Education*, Vol 27 Nos 1/2, 89–99.

Goedegebuure, L.C.J. (1989) 'Institutional Mergers and System Change. Reconstructing the sector of higher vocational education' in Peter A.M. Maassen and Frans A. van Vught (eds) *Dutch Higher Education in Transition. Policy Issues in Higher Education in the Netherlands*. Culemborg: Lemma, 73–99.

Goppel, Th. (1991) (ed) *Kontinuität und Wandel. Perspektiven Bayerischer Wissenschaftspolitik*. Munich: Oldenbourg.

Kalamationou, A.G. et al. (1988) 'Technical Higher Education in Greece' in *European Journal of Education*, Vol 23 No. 3, 261–279.

Kogan, M. (1989) (ed) *Evaluating Higher Education*. London: Jessica Kingsley Publishers.

Moscati, R. (1988) 'Editorial: Higher education in Southern Europe: different speeds or different paths toward modernisation?' in *European Journal of Education* Vol 23 No 3, 189–194.

OECD (1973) *Short-Cycle Higher Education: A Search for Identity*. Paris: OECD.

OECD (1983) *Policies for Higher Education in the 1980s*. Paris: OECD.

OECD (1989) *Alternatives to Universities in Higher Education – Country Study Federal Republic of Germany*. Paris: OECD.

OECD (1987) *Universities under Scrutiny*. Paris: OECD.

OECD (1987) *Post-Graduate Education in the 1980s*. Paris: OECD.

OECD (1991) *Alternatives to Universities*. Paris: OECD.

Teichler, U. (1988) *Changing Patterns of the Higher Education System: The Experience of Three Decades*. London: Jessica Kingsley Publishers.

Trow, M. (1979) 'Elite and mass higher education: American models and European realities' in *Research into Higher Education: Processes and Structures*. Stockholm, National Board of Universities and Colleges, 183–219.

Part I

Structural Modifications of the Major Models

CHAPTER 1

Structures of Higher Education Systems in Europe

Ulrich Teichler

The Changing Emphasis on Structural Issues in Higher Education Policy

Patterns of the higher education system have been among the issues of higher education policy in industrialised societies which absorbed quite enormous attention during the last three decades. On the one hand, issues of financing of higher education were so much dictated by governments that institutions of higher education remained the happy beneficiaries or the unhappy victims. On the other hand, issues of curricula and of teaching and learning were so much shaped by academics that governments either claimed to respect autonomy of higher education or looked rather clumsy in their interventionist behaviour.

Patterns of higher education systems, however, obviously were at the crossroads of legitimate influence and interest on the part of governments, institutions of higher education and society at large, and thus became a major focus of debate. Debates on patterns of the higher education system, however, changed substantially over the last few decades – both in the degree of emphasis placed on structural issues as compared to other issues of higher education in the structural elements addressed (for example access, institutional types, duration of studies or stages of course programmes).

From about the late 1950s to the mid 1970s, patterns of the higher education system were clearly among the major policy issues in higher education. Structural issues were considered important, because whereas expansion of higher education was seen as desirable or a matter of course, experts seemed to believe that expansion could not be realised without a change of patterns or the character in general of either the total system of higher education or major parts of it (for example OECD, 1974). Substantial attention was paid to the establishment or expansion of a non-university sector of higher education (OECD, 1973). In addition, the concern about over-education in the early 1970s led to growing interest in matters of access and admission to higher education (UNESCO/CEPES, 1981; OECD, 1983).

From the mid 1970s to about the mid 1980s, patterns of higher education were not so high on the agenda in most European countries. Only in the Netherlands do we note substantial changes during this period. As will be discussed below, a variety of structural 'models' could be observed without indication of any convergent trend.

As will be explained below, structural policies are back on the agenda as from the late 1980s.

Changing Concepts and Research Approaches

The most influential concepts on structures or patterns of higher education systems were published during the 1970s. Among others, Trow's (1974) model of 'elite, mass and universal higher education', OECD's (1973) 'short-cycle higher education'... 'in search for identity', Burgess' and Pratt's 'academic drift' (Burgess, 1972), the debate on 'comprehensive universities' (Hermanns, Teichler and Wasser, 1983) refer to developments in the 1960s and 1970s. I argued – no doubt in a less influential way – at that time that structural changes were most strongly driven by a repeating cycle of bleeding to death and upgrading of second-rank institutions (Teichler, Hartung and Nuthman, 1980).

The period of the early 1970s was a relatively creative one in terms of experts' conceptualisation of issues of institutional patterns, even though we might consider them not appropriate and convincing any more. Experts could analyse interesting actual changes occurring in the preceding years. At the same time, this period was shaped by dramatic tensions due to a rapid shift from positive to negative assessment of educational expansion. During the 1980s, research on higher education paid less attention to structural issues than in the preceding decades. This is not to say that the topic did not play a role any more. For example, Clark (1983) published the concepts we developed during the 1970s in a comprehensive way in the 1980s. In Europe, various scholars focused on issues of diversification within institutional types (Neave, 1989; Gellert, 1984). Becher and Kogan (1991) discussed the internal structures and processes of higher education institutions in the context of issues of the overall patterns of the higher education system. I tried to summarise the debates in industrial societies (Teichler, 1988a) as well as describe and explain the variety of institutional patterns in Western Europe (Teichler, 1988b).

As will be discussed below, various collaborative activities are currently undertaken in analysing patterns of higher education systems. The revival of structural policies, thus, might be accompanied by a new 'wave' of hopefully interesting concepts.

An Attempt to Explain Structural Phenomena and Developments

A few years ago, I tried to summarise both academic analyses and policy debates on higher education focusing on 'structures' or 'patterns' of the higher education system (Teichler, 1988a). I take the liberty of recalling the major arguments, because the importance of the most recent debates referred to below might best be understood, if put in contrast to the preceding debates.

- Typical 'structural' issues dealt with are the following (Teichler, 1988a, 13):
- the definition of common features of higher education in terms of typical prerequisites for access or typical elements of institutions and course programmes;
- the degree of heterogeneity or homogeneity of students within sectors, institutions or individual departments;
- the degree of unity and variety of objectives and programmes within sectors, institutions and departments;
- the objectives of institutions (research versus teaching, academic versus professional thrust, personality development versus academic and professional training);
- the degree of 'vertical' differences perceivable in a higher education system in terms of 'quality', 'reputation' and graduates' prospective occupational status;
- the extent to which differences between higher education sectors are 'visible' or 'blurred'.

Most typologies of patterns of higher education were a mix of focusing on structural phenomena (institutional types, stages etc) and normative statements on the patterns and their functional implications (for example 'elite higher education'). As I argued in the overview of those typologies (Teichler, 1988a, 27–31), these typologies were based on different levels of categorisation. For example, Clark (1977) describes systems according to tiers (short-cycle, undergraduate, graduate, etc), control (public, private), and the number of major types of institutions. Trow (1984) referred to the underlying motives and attitudes in a matrix of 'meritocrats' versus 'egalitarians' and 'unitarians' versus 'pluralists'. In the context of OECD studies, models close to institutional types were chosen like 'multipurpose', 'specialised' and 'binary' models (Furth, 1973) or – in consideration of reform efforts – 'integrated comprehensive model', 'combined development model' and 'first cycle multipurpose model' (Cerych, Furth and Papadopoulos, 1974).

When the debate began around the 1960s, relatively extreme structural alternatives were posed. I argued that the multitude of models and major alternatives – in part claiming to analyse the systems currently existing, in part aiming to characterise reform concepts – could be reduced to four models of higher education systems. In summarising these models I did not aim to shift the conceptual framework of that debate characterised, as stated above, by a mix of describing structural phenomena and stating the functions of the structural model in a normative way. I called the models the 'elitist model', the 'vertical model', the 'unitary model' and the 'model of recurrent education' (Teichler, 1988a, 29–30). Over the years, a consensus seemed to have emerged that borderlines between various sectors of the higher education system should be blurred and that a certain degree of permeability of educational ladders should be ensured. The range of models discussed in the 1970s became smaller, whereby the 'extremes' of the continuum could be named 'the diversified model' on the one hand and on the other 'the integrated model' (Hermanns, Teichler and Wasser, 1983).

The vast variety of arguments found in the structural debates had – from my point of view – one element in common: from under the surface of various types of institutions, factors explaining structural change, etc arose the question of how students should be sorted, if learning in higher education was to be improved: should differences in quality, status and content be substantial or should they be kept in bounds? In this debate, the 'diversified' model, stressing vertical differences but also respecting to some extent horizontal diversity, became much more popular than an 'integrated' model, keeping vertical differences in bound. I argued that this popularity reflects the views and values of the majority of politicians, scholars in general as well as scholars of the domain of 'higher education' as a field of study. This popularity was so strong that experimentation with the 'integrated' model was so restricted from the very beginning that its potential was never tested validly.

Many analyses, however, aimed not only to provide systematic descriptions, but also to explain causes for the configuration viewed. Why are higher education systems shaped the way they are? Such explanations also imply assumptions as regards a possible emergence of converging trends or a continued variety of higher education systems. I argued that three major approaches – 'idiosyncratic', 'functional' and 'political' – to explanations can be observed as typical:

> In idiosyncratic approaches, emphasis is put on characteristics of the higher education system which – once they have emerged under certain historical conditions, due to the overriding influence of certain concepts or because of certain incidents – tend to remain fairly stable or to continue to put their stamp even on substantial innovations. (...) According to functional approaches, higher education systems in

all modern industrial societies are influenced by certain societal, economic, technological, cultural or educational factors more or less common at certain developmental stages of industrial societies. (...) Finally, political approaches put emphasis on
programmes and powers aiming to change systems of higher education and the
degree to which they succeed in changing the structures of higher education. The
question is raised in what way and to what extent deliberate options shape higher
education. (Teichler 1988a, 14–5)
No single conceptual framework – typology, prediction of trends, explanation of causes
for change – was generally accepted as suitable in explaining structural developments
of higher education, for obviously patterns of higher education systems did not remain
constant, did not become rapidly more alike and did not follow closely certain political
options. In spite of their weaknesses in explaining trends, various concepts turned out
to be useful in mapping and explaining higher education structures.

Certainly, the 'functional' approach was weakened by the lack of dominant convergent trends (Trow, 1979). We do not note, though, a revival of purely idiosyncratic or
purely political reasoning in structural debates. As will be discussed below, I argued that
structural policies in the 1980s seemed to be based on the belief that options can be
taken, which as a rule are influenced by a mix of underlying 'functional', 'idiosyncratic'
and 'political' assumptions.

Continuing Variety in the 1970s and 1980s
Structural developments during the period from the mid 1970s to the mid 1980s – i.e.
the period in which little emphasis was placed on structural issues – were analysed in
a study on 11 member states of the Council of Europe. The major findings of the
synthesis report (Teichler, 1988b), based on reports by the invidual countries, will be
summarised and presented here.

In more or less all the European countries analysed, we note a lower rate of
qualitative increase during the 1970s and 1980s than during the preceding years, when
the number of students in these countries almost doubled on average within a decade.
The mean increase of new entrant students was about 30 per cent from 1970 to 1975
and about 20 per cent each in the late 1970s and early 1980s. Among the countries
surveyed, the development from 1975 to 1985 ranged from almost a duplication of new
entrant students to zero growth.

Relatively short course programmes expanded in some countries, in others enrolment in long course programmes grew. If we exclude small countries not having a
'complete' higher education system, the percentage of students enrolled in relatively
short programmes varied among the countries surveyed in the mid-1980s between less
than 10 per cent to more than 70 per cent.

The composition of students according to field of study did not develop as similarly
as frequently stated. There were some countries in Europe where the proportion of
students in engineering declined and some countries where the proportion of humanities students increased. Notably, quantitative developments in the fields of medical and
agricultural work were divergent.

Few figures were provided on 'adult' students. Accordingly, the proportion of adult
students declined in Belgium and Sweden and remained constant in Norway. In some
other countries, the proportion was supposed to increase but no respective data were
presented.

In contrast, an almost consistent trend could be observed towards more or less equal
numbers of male and female students. By 1985, only 3 of the 11 countries analysed fell

short of more or less equal representation of women: Malta, the Netherlands and Germany.

Terminologies frequently used such as 'university-type' versus 'non-university type' higher education, 'universities and equivalent institutions' versus 'other tertiary education institutions' or 'other third-level institutions' suggest that the structural patterns of higher education in most societies to some extent share common features. The terminology assumes that as a rule two major types of institutions of higher education can be disentangled and that relatively long course programmes are provided at institutions at which teaching is linked to research, whereas short course programmes are offered at institutions not responsible for research. On the other hand, the range of fields provided by institutions – specialised institutions versus universities or other multidisciplinary colleges – is not significant for such a typology.

The countries analysed neither directly confirm nor challenge the view that institutions of higher education as such can be classified more or less into two types in most countries. It is not possible, either, to replace typologies based on the combination of 'university/long' versus 'non-university/short', by referring solely to the type of institution or solely to the required duration of course programmes. Rather, individual systems of higher education might be characterised according to various features, notably the distribution of students according to types of institutions; the duration of course programmes and their respective institutional bases; differences in the legal status and research functions of institutions; and the years of prior schooling required for various course programmes.

On that basis, we note almost as many 'types' as countries observed. They were characterised in the survey in the following way:

- Austria: The traditional predominance of the university;
- Finland: Move towards a relatively homogeneous university system;
- Spain: Incorporation of short programmes in universities;
- Federal Republic of Germany: Two distinct types of institutions and corresponding course programmes;
- Belgium: Distinct institutions with overlapping educational tasks;
- France: Diverse institutions and a stage structure;
- Sweden: Partially diverse tasks of formally equal institutions;
- The Netherlands: Distinct institutional types and entrance requirements but equal duration of studies;
- Norway: A multitude of degree levels and institutions;
- Cyprus: Exclusively non-university higher education.

Duration of Studies

Over the years, when borderlines between types of educational institutions got more and more diffused, the duration of studies in terms of the required length of study became the most important single indicator for the 'level' of education acquired. In all countries analysed a clear notion seems to be established as regards a minimum length of regular university-type or 'long' course programmes, though it varies among the countries analysed from three to five years. It is three years in France and Sweden, three and a half years in Norway, four years in Austria, Belgium, Malta and the Netherlands, somewhat more than four years in Finland and Germany, and five years in Spain. In two countries, we note two levels of university-type degrees where the higher level degree is not understood to be part of postgraduate education (*licence* and *maîtrise* in France, *cand. mag.* and higher level *cand.* after two additional years of study in Norway).

The European countries analysed also differ substantially in the extent to which the required duration of 'long' studies is standardised according to field of study. We note less of a general norm in the required length of study of short or non-university course programmes both between and within countries than can be noted in the sector of long studies. During the period observed, the required length of study was changed in some countries, whereby in many cases those changes referred only to some fields. As a consequence the average required length increased substantially in Finland, and increased somewhat in Austria, Germany, Spain and Sweden. In the case of France and Cyprus, no clear trend in either direction can be observed. Besides, some reduction in the average duration of studies seems to have taken place during the 1980s in Belgium, the Netherlands and Norway.

The actual length of study varies even more strongly due, in part, to practical periods required in some countries in certain fields, and notably due to prolongation of study. In some countries the actual length surpasses required duration only to a small extent, whereas in other countries, the average length is more than 150 per cent of the required length. The strongest efforts were made in the Netherlands both to reduce the standard period of study and to eradicate prolongation of studies at universities by two years or even more on average. In some countries, similar suggestions were made but not put into practice.

The drop-out quotas seem to vary between the countries analysed from less than 10 per cent (students in Sweden in regular course programmes) to more than 50 per cent (university students in Spain). The statistics available, however, are not very precise, as far as drop-out is concerned.

Higher education systems in Europe also vary substantially as regards the structures of the course programmes. Three elements are most important in this respect: the major stages of the course programmes, the examination systems and course programmes subsequent to regular degree programmes.

Major Stages of a Course Programme

As regards major stages of a course programme, we note four different models:

- No visible stages of a course programme can be found in Cyprus and Sweden.
- A propaedeutic year was introduced in the Netherlands in 1982 at universities and in 1986 at HBO institutions.
- Most frequently, a mid-course stage can be found: it is established in Austria, Belgium, France, Spain and partially in Germany. The first stage ends after one and a half or two years at German *Fachhochschulen*, after two years in Austria, Belgium, France and at German universities, and after three years in Spain. In Belgium and France, a title is conferred upon completion of the first stage.
- Finally a model of a multi-stage and multi-disciplinary course programme in some disciplines can traditionally be found in Scandinavian countries. It still exists in Norway and – with some modifications – in Finland and Denmark (sub-division according to 'basic subject', 'intermediate subject' and 'main subject').

However, there are two common features in the stage models observed: first, students in the European countries analysed enrol from the very beginning in a certain field of study (or one of the subjects in the case of the traditional Scandinavian model). Second, intermediate examinations are not officially claimed to be both transitional and preparatory for employment.

The Examination System

The examination system is another formal element in the structure of studies. We observe three major modes of examination in the European countries analysed.

- In the case of the major examination mode (for example in Austria and Germany), the grading assessment culminates at the end of a major stage or at the end of the whole course programme. No matter how previous examinations take place and how the completion of the required individual courses is assessed, the final grading depends predominantly on a thesis and final exams.

- In the case of an annual examination or a similar stage mode (for example in Belgium and to some degree in France), students have to progress through various stages. At each stage, achievement is comprehensively assessed, and completion of the annual or similar programme is essential for progression to the next year or other short stage.

- In a credit mode (most clearly established in Sweden), the course programme is conceived as an accumulation of short course units – no matter what stages are established and whether final assessments (thesis etc) are customary as well. The overall assessment at completion of studies is based on all credits awarded in the course programme.

Moves towards the organisation and assessment of studies according to credits were made in Sweden around 1970 and in France and Finland during the 1970s. This was followed by the Netherlands in 1982.

Postgraduate Studies

In various European countries, action started or continued during the 1980s for introducing formal structures of postgraduate studies and for delineating more clearly studies leading to a first degree from any kind of advanced and postgraduate study. In Norway, regular programmes leading to a doctorate degree in about four to five semesters, which had already existed in science and engineering, were introduced in the 1980s in the humanities and social sciences as well. In Austria and Germany, the system was phased according to the fact that students could progress to a doctoral dissertation and a doctoral degree in various fields without taking any prior degree. Finally, the two-stage structure was introduced in the Netherlands in 1982: the second stage comprised about two years of either advanced academic or professional studies.

The relationship between advanced professional programmes and first degree programmes at institutions of higher education in the European countries analysed does not seem to have changed significantly during the 1980s. Various models continue to coexist without substantial change.

Links Between Non-Degree and Degree Course Programmes

As regards links between open non-degree studies and degree course programmes, different philosophies – already emerged in the 1970s – continue to prevail in the 1980s. In various Scandinavian countries, a certain permeability between open studies in individual non-degree courses and degree programmes is emphasised. Both in Sweden and Norway, course units of half a year or of one year are conceived to be part of regular course provision, and students opting for these courses may be regularly enrolled. There are various opportunities for accumulation of these courses and for transfer to degree courses. In other European countries surveyed, a clear delineation exists between non-degree programmes and degree programmes. There are, however, mechanisms for the assessment of competences acquired outside higher education which would allow admission to degree programmes without the regular school prerequisites or mechanisms for recognition of qualifications as equivalent to some parts of a degree programme – again varying substantially in detail and in the chances they actually provide (OECD, 1988).

The status of relatively 'short' or 'non-university' higher education programmes to 'long' or university programmes is influenced by many factors. Of these, firstly, the mechanisms and practices concerning access and admission to the respective course programmes, and secondly, the rules and practices regarding transfer between the different types of course programmes, deserve most attention.

Access and Transfer

As regards formal prerequisites for access, persons wishing to enrol at German 'Fachhochschulen' and Dutch HBO institutions not only need one year less schooling, but also do not have to take the academic track of upper-secondary education. In Belgium and Norway, 12 years of schooling are expected for both sectors as a rule, but only those heading for 'long' higher education course programmes in Norway have, however, to complete academic secondary education, and those heading to 'long' programmes have to pass an additional aptitude examination. In two countries – France and Spain – formal prerequisites for short-cycle programmes are identical to those for 'long' course programmes. Finally, 'short' or 'non-university' programmes in various European countries are more readily accessible for applicants who do not hold the regular entry requirements.

Hardly any information on opportunities for transfer from 'short' to 'long' courses or from non-university higher education to universities was provided. From what is available, practices seem to vary substantially between European countries. From the mid-1970s to the late 1980s, conditions for transfer may have become more favourable in some areas in Norway and in the Netherlands. In a few other countries, however, opposite indicators are visible. For example, the change of legislation in Germany in 1985, according to which comprehensive universities are no longer viewed as a prototype for future development, but rather as exceptions, might indicate that mobility from 'short' to 'long' courses is not encouraged.

Trends

Altogether, we do not observe a general trend towards a European convergence of structural and organisational aspects of studies and their context. Striking differences are visible as regards total enrolment trends, the proportion of students in short programmes, the enrolment patterns according to the field of study. Also, the required lengths of study vary in most countries according to the specific field and do not seem to become more similar in Europe. There are no general moves, as expected by some experts in the past, towards a blurring of boundaries between 'higher' education and other kinds of post-secondary education or towards the establishment of a clear stage structure of course programmes. In almost all structural dimensions, there are some countries moving in one direction and other countries not implementing any significant change in this area, or even moving in the opposite direction. The only exception worth mentioning were moves in most European countries towards more formal structuring of course programmes, although the means adopted varied, and could be, for example, the introduction of visible stages within course programmes or the counting of courses and examinations partly according to a credit system (Teichler, 1988b, 171–173).

From a broader perspective, however, it is possible to recognise a certain number of common elements in the seemingly diverse trends and policies. For example, we observe in most European countries a move away from relatively consistent models of institutional types, which had been classified in the past as 'unitary', 'comprehensive', 'binary', etc, as well as from consistent models of stages of degrees. Also, overlaps of functions of various institutions of higher education seem to grow in some European countries without, however, leading to a systematic blurring of the sectors of higher education. Finally – this is certainly related to the previous two points – the organisation of studies in the majority of countries analysed followed to some extent a 'middle of the road' solution between a 'horizontal', 'open' or 'blurred' model on the one hand and a clearly segmented model on the other. Obviously, a further search for theoretical perspectives is needed helping to sort out the variety of phenomena.

Recent Issues and Debates

Based both on the analysis of developments of higher education systems in the late 1970s and during the 1980s and on most recent experiences, I note five challenges for future study of higher education structures.

First, we might seek for explanations of the low emphasis placed on structural issues from the mid-1970s to the mid-1980s or of the ups and downs of emphasis placed on structural issues in general. The available literature suggests for examination the following hypotheses:

- There is a functionally stronger need in changing patterns of higher education at times of high quantitative growth of education.

- There might be political efforts to change patterns of higher education during a period of stagnation or slow expansion as strongly as during a period of rapid expansion (see Windolf, 1990), but these efforts are less successful at times of stagnation, because a redistribution of resources is more painful than under conditions of growth.

- Previous claims about the need to change turned out to be exaggerations. The need was no longer felt strongly nor did national systems actually move towards a similar direction; subsequently, interest in structural issues as such might have declined.

- Higher education planning turned out to be less powerful and effective, as the turn toward 'implementation' issues (Cerych, 1980) showed; structural policies, therefore, might have been given up.

- Structural policies and structural changes became less visible, though possibly not less important and effective, when they turned from types of institutions and course programmes, sequences etc to diversification within the same institutional and course types.

Neither of the hypotheses presented is likely to be generally accepted as the most convincing one. This does not call into question the need to explain these experiences; for the most part, revival of structural debates will hardly be understood without explanation of the emphasis placed on this issue in preceding years.

Second, we might ask why higher education structures did not show any sign of convergent trends during the late 1970s and early 1980s. I argued, for example, that developments do not support 'functional', 'idiosyncratic' or 'political' explanation, but rather a mix. It is interesting to note that debates and efforts for innovation in the structural dimensions of higher education and the organisation of studies during that period were neither similar across most European countries nor specific to individual ones. It was rather a range of options which tended to be discussed and possibly realised, and countries with distinctive traditions in the higher education systems or distinctive societal conditions may have opted for similar solutions. International comparison no longer served as a tool for detecting convergent needs and trends but as an information base to 'test' the strengths and weaknesses of a range of possible solutions (Teichler, 1988b, 174–175). But there certainly might be different views as regards the causes of a lack of convergent trends.

Third, the notion presented above that European systems of higher education do not converge, is confronted with other perceptions of structural developments. Some other experts point at phenomena which according to their views indicate a growing similarity of higher education systems in Europe. For example, according to the recent OECD project 'Alternatives to Universities in Higher Education', structural developments in higher education partially follow similar routes and partially are distinct. I quote the respective paragraph of the report:

'The comparative perspective offered by the country studies is particularly valuable. They reveal many variations among countries, due to the particular national contexts, traditions, priorities and, especially, the structural differences between the different secondary and higher education systems. However, this perspective also reveals a number of common trends and problems, many of them deriving from shared pressures and concerns among governments to increase the social and economic role of higher education in meeting the requirements of advanced and rapidly changing industrialised societies.' (OECD, 1991).

In my emphasis on a growing variety between countries I did not at all want to exclude certain common elements. I only did not find any evidence that these common elements grew over the span analysed. In contrast to the widespread assumption according to which common elements grow, I considered it appropriate to point at the fact that systems did not become more similar rather than pointing at common elements remaining. I definitely disagree, however, with the OECD report's view that most variations can be explained 'idiosyncratically', whereas most common elements can be explained as outgrowth of 'functionally' oriented policies. Rather, I claim that political options intentionally make use of international comparison of national idiosyncrasies, assumed general functional needs and specific political models.

Also, Neave (1990) makes us aware of convergent political options taken in some European countries in view of future integration of the European community. Neave points at decisions already taken or under way to establish or extend degrees upon completion of three years of study in Denmark, Spain and France. This argument, however, does not challenge my observation that patterns of higher education systems in Western Europe did not become more similar between 1975 and 1987 – the period which I observed. It challenges, however, my predictive summary that Europe will settle with preserving and bridging the diversity rather than becoming more similar as far as patterns of the higher education systems are concerned.

Certainly, there are indications that the Commission of the European Communities favours a certain extent of convergence of higher education systems although the Commission is obliged to respect the cultural diversity in Europe. According to the Conclusions of the Siena Conference (Higher Education and 1992: Planning for the Year 2000, 1991), which might be viewed as an informal agenda of the EC higher education policy, the Commission should seek to establish 'measures of greater compatibility between the higher education systems in the different Member States'. These measures should ease academic mobility of students as well as occupational mobility of graduates. But it remains an open question whether a 'greater mobility' actually will emerge in this context. Apart from the existing forces in favour of varied systems, one might argue that study abroad is valuable exactly because it offers the opportunity of getting to know contrasting systems and that co-operation among European universities might lead to 'greater compatibility' within co-operation networks of universities rather than between higher education systems.

Fourth, we might observe recent developments contrasting those observed between the mid-1970s and mid-1980s. When I began to summarise trends and concepts regarding patterns of higher education in 1986, I assumed that the final text might be a postscript about structural developments which were politically overrated and lost their practical impact as well as about experts' writings which went too far in predicting trends on the basis of interesting, though incomplete explanations of those trends. In pointing at the constant instability of structures leading to revivals of debates, however, I noted at least that it was not certain whether the volcano was completely dead or might erupt again:

> It is justifiable to argue, though, that many of those approaches indicate a basic instability and vulnerability of structures. Any change in public funding of higher education, in employment prospects of graduates, in aspirations to enrol on the part of prospective students, or in policies of certain sectors of the higher education system to enhance their status seems to be quickly interpreted as a threat to the status quo of the structures of the higher education system – a system which does not in any case easily cope with the conflicting functions of disseminating knowledge to the extent possible and acting as a major gatekeeper in the selection of the privileged few. The insight into the difficulty of carrying through clearly designed higher education policies consistently, and the predominant mood in favour of at most gradual change, which has been strongly emphasised during about the last ten years, might have led many experts to underestimate the constant instability caused by the unavoidably conflicting functions and also the vulnerability to developments and policies, which were not necessarily meant to deal with structural issues, but turn out to be important for the structure of the higher education system. Thus, efforts to restructure higher education seem to be considered important in many countries in the 1980s, although the approaches are not any longer based on grand visions of a possible optimal model in a modern industrial society. (Teichler, 1988a, 108).

Obviously, however, I did not expect the multitude of structural moves which actually occurred around 1990:

- In countries in which the formal distinction between institutional types was the smallest (in the UK and The Republic of Ireland), political moves could be observed towards further blurring of the distinctions.

- In countries with an especially long duration of university studies and – in most cases – limited or no short-cycle higher education, efforts were made to introduce short course programmes and respective degrees (Denmark, Spain, Finland and Italy).

The decision taken by the EC to consider the completion of three years of higher education as the essential qualification for professional practice, leads France (and possibly Belgium) to reconsider their two-year course programmes (see Jallade 1989/90). It also reinforces the above stated activities towards a reduction of the long duration of university studies.

The political changes in Eastern Europe led to debates about many issues of higher education, among them the establishment of non-university higher education which is partially implemented in Hungary, legally promoted in Czechoslovakia and also discussed in Poland.

It remains to be seen whether the combined outcome of these various strategies leads to a convergence of higher education systems, to a more or less unchanged situation or to a growing variety of patterns of higher education systems in Europe. The various moves towards the establishment of short course programmes could be interpreted as steps towards a general model of two types of higher education degrees.

In addition, we note that such a restructuring takes place in countries in which previously the institutional patterns were relatively 'extreme', i.e. the average length of study was very long and almost any differentiation according to institutions or course programmes was lacking. We might argue that there were indicators of convergence in terms of restructuring previously extreme models, but not in terms of trends towards a single model.

Fifth, we note a renewed interest among scholars in the field of higher education in analysing institutional patterns of higher education systems. The study jointly undertaken by V.L. Meeck, L. Goedegebuure, P. Maassen, O. Kivinen and R. Rinne on 'Policy Change in Higher Education: Intended and Unintended Outcomes' focusses on structural issues. C. Gellert's project of 'Changing Patterns in European Higher Education' aims to identify changing functions of universities which might explain changing patterns. Both projects succeeded in including many known experts in collaborative efforts aiming to seek for more advanced concepts regarding higher education structures and related policies.

I would agree to C. Gellert's (e.g. in this volume) call for renewed attention of changing functions of higher education in the search for explanation of structural trends. For example, the debates on institutional patterns of the higher education in recent years focussed too strongly – from my point of view – on 'internal' aspects: What are the best ways of coping with increased students' numbers under conditions of financial constraints? They did not address sufficiently long-term changing functions of higher education.

It would be desirable to discuss the strengths and weaknesses of institutional patterns of higher education in the light of changing tasks of research, qualification for employment, education for the graduates' civic roles, etc. For example, I argued that we shall most likely move towards a highly qualified society, in which distinctions between ranks and responsibilities of top-rank and intermediate-rank persons will be more blurred than most experts of higher education wished or could imagine in the past (Teichler 1990). If this becomes true, a smaller distance than currently experienced between different types of higher education would be advisable. If, in contrast, clear distinctions between different institutional types or steep institutional hierarchies are advocated: what are the underlying assumptions about the future of the employment system and of the social structure? In any event, scenarios about long-term developments of higher education systems and their societal functions are indispensable if options were to be taken such as a restructuring of the pattern of the higher education system.

Such a plea for analysing changing functions of higher education in the framework of efforts to explain changing patterns of higher education systems, however, should not be misunderstood as being based on the belief that patterns of higher education systems are primarily driven by similar functions of higher education in industrial societies. As argued above, the 'functional' approach only explains partial elements, as the 'idiosyncratic' approach and the 'political' approach do as well. We might, however, assume that changing functions might revive the debates and policies in many countries even though they do not lead to convergent solutions.

References:

Becher, T. and M. Kogan (1991) *Process and Structure in Higher Education.* London: Heinemann (1st edn. 1980).

Burgess, T. (ed) (1972) *The Shape of Higher Education.* London: Cornmarket Press.

Cerych, L. (1980) 'Retreat from ambitious goals?'. *European Journal of Education* Vol 15 No 1, 5–13.

Cerych, L., D. Furth and G. Papadopoulos (1974) 'Overall issues in the development of future structures of post-secondary education' in OECD (ed) *Policies for Higher Education. Paris: OECD, 15–50.*

Clark, B.R. (1977) 'Problems of access in the context of academic structures', in Burn, B.B. (ed) *Access, Systems, Youth and Employment.* New York: International Council for Educational Development, 39–52.

Clark, B.R. (1983) *The Higher Education System: Academic Organisation in Cross-National Perspective.* Berkeley: University of California Press.

Furth, D. (1973) 'Short-Cycle Higher Education: Some Basic Considerations' in OECD, *Short-Cycle Higher Education.* Paris: OECD, 11–42.

Furth, D. (1982) 'New hierarchies in higher education'. *European Journal of Education* Vol 71 No 2, 145–151.

Gellert, C. (1984) 'Institutions- und Strukturforschung über das Hochschulsystem' in D. Goldschmidt, U. Teichler, W.-D. Webler (eds) *Forschungsgegenstand Hochschule.* Frankfurt: Campus, 217–231.

Hermanns, H., U. Teichler and H. Wasser, (eds) (1983) *The Complete University.* Cambridge, Mass.: Schenkmann.

Jallade, J.P. (ed) (1989–90) *Les premières années d'enseignement supérieur dans la perspective de 1993,* 2 Vols. Paris: European Institute of Education and Social Policy.

Neave, G. (1989) 'Foundation or roof? The quantitative, structural and institutional dimensions in the study of higher education'. *European Journal of Education* Vol 24 No 3, 211–222.

Neave, G. (1990) On Programmes, Universities and Jacobins, or 1992 Vision and Reality for European Higher Education. Mimeo.

OECD (1973) *Short-Cycle Higher Education.* Paris: OECD.

OECD (1974) *Policies for Higher Education.* Paris: OECD.

OECD (1983) *Policies for Higher Education in the 1980s.* Paris: OECD.

OECD (1988) *Adults in Higher Education.* Paris.

OECD (1991) *Alternatives to Universities.* Paris: OECD.

Teichler, U. (1988a) *Changing Patterns of the Higher Education System.* London: Jessica Kingsley Publishers.

Teichler, U. (1988b) *Convergence or Growing Variety: The Changing Organisation of Studies in Europe.* Strasbourg: Council of Europe.

Teichler, U. (1990) *Towards a Highly Educated Society.* Paper presented to the Fourth Symposium on Higher Education Research, Jyväskylä University, August 30–31.

Teichler, U., D. Hartung and R. Nuthmann (1980) *Higher Education and the Needs of Society.* Windsor: NFER Publishing Co.

Trow, M. (1974) 'Problems in the transition from elite to mass higher education' in OECD (ed) *Policies for Higher Education.* Paris: OECD, 51–101.

Trow, M. (1979) 'Elite and mass higher education: American models and European realities' in *Research into Higher Education: Processes and Structures.* Stockholm: National Board of Universities and Colleges, 183–219.

Trow, M. (1984) 'The Analysis of Status' in Clark, B.R. (ed), *Perspectives on Higher Education.* Berkeley: University of California Press, 132–164.

UNESCO/CEPES (1981) *Access to Higher Education.* Bucharest: CEPES/UNESCO.

Windolf, P. (1990) *Die Expansion der Universitäten 1870 – 1985: Ein internationaler Vergleich.* Stuttgart: Enke.

CHAPTER 2

Inertia and Resistance to Change of the Humboldtian University

Einhard Rau

Introduction

For a country in which most things seem to work fine, it is astounding that higher education is such a mess. Professors and students alike are chronically discontented. For example, much of the last academic year was spent on 'strike' – meaning that students did not study and teachers did not teach. The main thing that distinguishes a 'strike' from the normal situation is a marginal increase in student demonstrations. Even during the best of non-strike semesters, research output is mediocre, university life is sterile and impersonal, and the quality of teaching is abominable (Kramer, 1989).

Numerous judgments like this on the German higher education system can be found throughout its history and development. That is not surprising. Society and its components go through cycles of prosperity and inflation which open opportunities for appraisal and critique. The university is no exception. Nevertheless, such judgments cast an interesting light on the 'idea' of the German university universally admired until recently. This idea has its roots in Idealism and Neo-Classicism and is closely related to the name of Wilhelm von Humboldt who described the prerequisites of a university to be founded in Berlin. There were forerunners and contemporaries like Kant, Wolf, Fichte, Schelling and Schleiermacher who prepared the ground for the new concept, and there where political and ideological developments which additionally promoted the design of a new idea of the university. But it was Wilhelm von Humboldt who, in 1809, wrote 'On the spirit and organisational framework of intellectual institutions in Berlin' and by that laid the foundations for a concept of a university which since then is connected with his name, the *Humboldtian University*. But doubts must be raised as to whether this university, and those which were created in succession to the foundation in Berlin, ever really implemented the conceptual principles which had been designed by Humboldt.

What then made those ideas famous and the model worth imitating in many parts of the world, and more importantly, how could such ideas form and dominate for more than 150 years an institution which has changed enormously and radically during those years? This is not the place to analyse and interpret in detail Wilhelm von Humboldt's ideas and their philosophical implications. We will only mention the issues which, according to widely accepted interpretations, build the core of the Humboldtian university and are still today often claimed by many as necessary prerequisites of a modern university. These are 'autonomy', 'unity of teaching and research', 'unity of all knowledge', 'education through academic knowledge', and 'scholarly life in solitude and liberty', all of them conditions of an integrated conception of education, scholarship and state (*Kulturstaat*). The latter would tolerate and support those liberties because it realises that they would be beneficial to the welfare of society and its residents.

Like the Humboldtian university, also this kind of state never emerged. On the contrary, real developments went back to the authoritarian, suppressive state. Nevertheless, there was still some room for the ideas Humboldt had developed for education and research. Through 'times of trouble and erosion' the Humboldtian idea of the university was kept alive, and even today still dominates the views and arguments of the majority of academics and their representatives. On the one hand, this is not surprising because the German university as it had developed between 1870 and 1920 had been extremely successful, productive, innovative and famous throughout the world. The principles of autonomy, unity of teaching and research, education through academic knowledge, definitely played a major part in this success. But probably even more important was the impact of industrialisation and the emerging Imperialism on the increasing role of German universities. But productivity and applicability, the main features of industrial research, are not akin to the kind of research which Humboldt had in mind when he designed his plan.

On the other hand, and with respect to the totally different present situation, we cannot orthodoxically adhere to puristic interpretations of Humboldt's ideas. If the concept ever had positive and constructive influences on the German university and its members this, as we will attempt to show, is no longer the case today, at least not for the large majority of students.

Expansion and the Humboldtian University
The reconstruction of the German university after World War II was based on the imputation that the university survived the war and the Nazi State as 'in its core stable', despite the involvement of many members of the institution in Nazism. Thus, the traditional Humboldtian principles were not put into question. Even the enormous expansion of the higher education system which started, as in most Western industrialised countries, during the 1960s, left the conceptions and roles of the German university untouched.

Admittedly, demands for democratisation and participation in decision making dominated discussions of higher education policy. Student unrest laid the ground for changes in the organisation and governance of the universities. Social inequality, restrictions and privileges became equally important issues. Finally, problems of economic growth, competition and technological improvement and the consequential need for qualified manpower had to be taken into account in university reform discussions.

But overall, the Humboldtian ideas were kept alive. Most scholarly contributions to the reform discussions supported those traditional conceptions, either from a professorial, more conservative position (Schelsky, 1963), or from a more radical student perspective (SDS, 1972). That is to say, the whole political spectrum of the groups participating in the reform process, besides all controversies, different solutions and specific actions, did not question the basic principles of the Humboldtian university.

Nevertheless, some modifications took place as a necessary reaction to the continuously expanding number of students and applicants. Institutions such as teacher-training colleges, schools of arts and some other specialised schools, which had been part of post-secondary education but had never been accepted as equals by the universities, became an integrated – if not necessarily equal – part of the higher education system with comparable goals, obligations, prerequisites to teach and study, but different equipment and resources.

This slightly differentiated system of higher education – with the Humboldtian university as its dominating core – was completed through the upgrading of former vocational schools (*Fachschulen*) to professional colleges (*Fachhochschulen*), which resembled the British polytechnics. In a number of respects (admission requirements, amount of teaching obligations, length of studies), they differed again from the above mentioned non-university institutions of higher education, in particular in their greater curricular and research orientation towards needs of industry and the labour market (Gellert, 1989).

The farthest reaching reform concept intended the organisation of an integral comprehensive system of higher education. These *Gesamthochschulen* would offer different kinds of tertiary education and training to students with varying entry qualifications, would be adaptive to changing outside requirements and flexible with regard to study programmes and the content of studies. This new institution would not resemble the ivory towers of the Humboldtian university any longer.

However, the further development of the German system of higher education is an interesting proof of the strength and the endurance of the Humboldtian ideals. First, the teacher-training colleges, most of the specialised schools and the schools of arts became – at least formally – parts of existing universities, enjoying equal rights, or became university-type institutions in their own right. This development, especially in those cases in which former non-university type institutions became parts of existing universities, did not go by without stout opposition and resistance from many university academics. Even those institutions which became universities in their own right faced – and often today still face – a lot of prejudices.

Furthermore, if the intention of the proponents of the integrated comprehensive university had been to create diversity in unity, they have failed. The result of the real development since the 1970s has in many respects been a unified chaos. The concentration of different motives, missions and functions under one umbrella of coherent ideas and homogeneous structures failed, led to functional burdens and remarkable dysfunctions in major parts of the higher education system.

The development of the *Fachhochschulen*, finally, went in a separate direction. In the first years of their existence they had hard times, serving often as a transfer institution which provided access to the university for applicants who did not have the *Abitur*. But over the years they have been able to strengthen their own identity and are at present an established and accepted part of the system.

To sum up these developments, it can be stated that intentions have failed to erect a differentiated but unified one-tier structure for higher education which could have influenced or even changed the Humboldtian university. Also less radical concepts of co-operation, with the parallel existence of different types of study under one organisational umbrella, were hardly successful. Short-term courses and programmes which had been offered in the few existing comprehensive universities, were desiccated, and teaching staff in these programmes began to work towards the upgrading of these programmes and their own positions. Again, the Humboldtian university had survived attempts to turn it into a modern institution of mass education, training and research.

After some years of relative public indifference toward higher education during the mid- and late 1970s, winds of reform started to blow again in the early 1980s, this time from the opposite direction. Referring to the economic recession, and the competition with Japan and America, an intensive critique was leveled at the rigid structures, the excessively long studies, and the overall inefficiencies of the German institutions of higher education. A number of proposals claimed the necessity to revive measures to educate an elite of students and provide opportunities for an elite of researchers. Some of these plans have been realised. Institutes for advanced studies have been founded, business and industry engaged themselves in the funding of a number of chairs at different universities, the co-operation between universities and industry has been strengthened, formalised and institutionalised, a number of discipline oriented post-graduate colleges (*Graduiertenkollegs*) have been erected and competition became (for a rather short period of time) a key word in German higher education.

The revision of the Higher Education Basic Law (HRG) of 1985 can be read in many ways as the juridical formalisation of these developments. Claiming to increase university autonomy, to increase competition within and between institutions of higher education, to increase efficiency in teaching and research, the law, in fact, strengthened the professors' position seemingly at the cost of students and their education or training respectively. As one observer put it:

> The fact, however, that the HRG recommendations contain hardly any references to the professorial obligation to engage in the elaboration of transparent curricula or to assume responsibility in committee work, that they do not mention the students' legitimate expectations for better counselling and guidance, seems to indicate that the professors' vested interests played a dominant role in the formula-tion of the reform proposals. (Gellert, 1984)

Remembering the turmoils of reform discussions in the late 1960s, it seems strange that only minor protests had been raised against the conservative set back in higher education politics. Students and faculty kept relatively quiet, looking for – and often finding – niches where they could (sometimes even comfortably) 'survive' the difficult times which, as the experts had predicted, would be over in the foreseeable future. The climax of student numbers had been predicted for the late 1980s and a sudden and enduring decline of these numbers would bring – according to the experts' opinion – quick relief for those long-overburdened universities and their personnel. But as many times before, the predictions did not describe reality.

Student numbers continued to grow (see Table 1). They grew within an institution which is still bound by the basic ideas of Wilhelm von Humboldt. That, in the first place, means that unity of teaching and research is still the guiding principle, and that the applicability and vocational orientation of studies in most disciplines often have the taste of unscientific and second-class endeavours. On the other hand, the universities nowadays are crowded with differently qualified students who follow a huge variety of interests.

Only a small part of them, those who are interested in a career in research or those who are in a position simply to enjoy a liberal education, can be adequately served through traditional 'Humboldtian' forms of study. Probably the bigger part of the student population of today cannot be adequately served in that way. They need and want a vocational orientation, often look for social, political or ecological meaning in their studies and are often rather bored by the kind of teaching which is delivered at university.

Table 1: Students and freshmen in German higher education 1975-1988

Year	Students overall	Universities	%	Freshmen overall	Universities	%
1975	792.100	640.900	80.9	155.900	111.800	71.7
1978	893.700	715.500	80.1	161.400	116.900	72.4
1980	986.300	777.700	78.9	183.200	126.300	68.9
1982	1136.900	879.400	77.4	211.900	145.000	68.4
1984	1242.200	944.800	76.1	207.000	140.100	67.7
1986	1290.500	972.500	75.4	196.700	131.200	66.7
1988	1384.000	1036.200	74.9	227.400	154.500	67.9

Source: Bundesminister für Bildung und Wissenschaft, 1989, and own calculations.

Different from the strike movements of the late 1960s and early 1970s which focused upon the general improvement of state and society, equality and peace around the world, the strikes of the late 1980s had a different target. This time, students demanded useful and applicable education from qualified and committed professors. They realised that the Humboldtian ideal of 'education through academic knowledge', and its transformation into the routines of teaching and research, no longer served their interests and future plans. There were external factors too which contributed to these developments, such as economic recession, growing competition, high unemployment rates (for graduates too) and reduced opportunities even in professions like law and medicine (not to mention teaching) which formerly had been fairly safe prospects for a decent future. All this led to insecurity within large parts of the student population which felt that it was not trained adequately, not educated according to the necessities of modern society. It blamed the institution and its teachers and educators for those deficiencies.

It is not intended here to argue generally against the Humboldtian university. There is no doubt that positive features have to be secured for those who really 'need' them and who do not abuse them. But there is a lot of evidence that some of the features are no longer suitable in times of large student numbers. The figures below provide evidence for that.

Table 2 shows that the number as well as the proportion of students at *Fachhochschulen* (and freshmen, respectively) has continuously grown over the last 15 years. Similar trends can be detected in the number of examinations as they are presented in Table 3.

This expansion of the non-university sector, in principle, is no argument against the Humboldtian university, because the *Fachhochschulen* are not a part of the university. But those numbers, to some extent, signify a move away from the Humboldtian tradition of higher education towards differentiation in the higher education system of the Federal Republic of Germany. Programmes are discussed and designed to support this development and to further improve the quality (resources and equipment) of the *Fachhochschulen*, which successfully meet demands and expectations from industry and business. The specific, practically oriented interests of business and industry certainly play a role in the largely positive assessment of the *Fachhochschulen* in the Federal Republic, including the positive self-image and self-esteem of their faculty and students.

Table 2: German students and freshmen at Fachhochschulen (FHS) 1975–1988

Year	Students		Freshmen	
	FHS	% (of all HE)*	FHS	% (of all HE)*
1975	138.000	17.4	41.800	26.8
1978	164.200	18.4	41.900	26.0
1980	192.600	19.5	54.200	29.6
1982	240.000	21.1	64.300	30.3
1984	278.000	21.1	64.400	31.1
1986	298.000	23.1	63.200	32.1
1988	327.000	23.6	70.600	31.0

Source: Bundesminister für Bildung und Wissensschaft, 1989.
* cf. Table 1.

Table 3: Examinations of German students, overall, at universities and at Fachhochschulen (FHS) 1975–1988

Year	overall	universities	%	FHS	%
1975	10.700	80.100	72.4	30.600	27.6
1977	115.800	83.900	72.5	31.900	27.5
1980	118.864	86.502	72.8	33.473	27.2
1982	126.235	88.884	70.4	38.440	29.6
1984	136.503	91.854	67.3	43.399	32.7
1986	144.517	95.660	66.2	48.857	33.8
1988	153.051	101.035	66.0	52.016	34.0

Source: Bundesminister für Bildung und Wissenschaft, 1989, Statistisches Bundesamt, 1988, and own calculations.

These colleges, thus further stabilise their standing and their mission inside the higher education system. They are flexible and innovative, prepared to react successfully to changes on the supply-side of the job market. As an explicitly different institution of higher education, the *Fachhochschulen* can play a constructive role in redesigning the Humboldtian university which suffers from a number of dysfunctional developments (Gellert, 1991). A heterogeneous student population inside a homogeneously designed institution is one component of dysfunction. Heterogeneity can be identified with respect to social background, age and educational qualifications of students (Bargel et al, 1989). It is interesting to note that 23 per cent of freshmen at universities in the winter term of 1989–90 had completed a vocational training before starting their university studies. The respective proportion for freshmen at *Fachhochschulen* has been 65 per cent. On the other hand, a growing number of freshmen at *Fachhochschulen* had taken the *Abitur* (which also opens the door to university); already 50 per cent in 1987 (Nigmann, 1989). The fact that important motives for the choice of *Fachhochschulen* are the 'practical orientation', the 'shorter duration of studies' and 'better learning conditions' (Lewin/Schacher, 1989) is perhaps another hint at dysfunctions in the traditional university. In this respect the development of the proportions of students and study beginners in different fields of study over the last 15 years is probably also worth mentioning (see Table 4).

Table 4: Students and freshmen (Germans and foreigners) at universities by fields of study (in % of all students and freshmen)

	1975		1980		1985		1988	
	Stud.	Fresh.	Stud.	Fresh.	Stud.	Fresh.	Stud.	Fresh.
Fine Arts	5.1	6.6	5.1	5.1	5.0	4.8	4.9	4.1
Agriculture Forestry Dietet.	2.1	2.5	2.6	3.1	2.4	2.8	2.2	2.1
Medicine*	8/1	4.8	10.0	7.9	9.9	6.7	9.5	6.6
Engineering	12.2	12.4	11.3	11.4	12.1	13.6	12.4	13.3
Maths Science	19.6	21.2	18.3	18.8	18.5	20.7	19.0	20.2
Law, Scoial Sciences Economics	21.0	20.2	22.4	24.0	24.1	25.0	25.6	28.9
Languages Humanities	32.0	32.3	30.5	29.5	27.9	26.2	26.2	24.6

Source: Der Bundesminister für Bildung und Wissenschaft, 1989.
(*) Veterinary science included

The fact that 60 per cent of all freshmen start their studies between two and three years after they finish *Gymnasium*, is interesting, too. Reasons for such a delay are military service (or a social service for those who resist the draft), vocational training, undecidedness regarding the field of studies, the necessary waiting time to admission in *numerus clausus* fields, and lack of motivation to study at all (Lewin/Schacher, 1990).

These components, some of which seem to be signs of motivational insecurity, contribute to the relatively high age of graduates in Germany, a matter intensely discussed in higher education politics. Even if the arguments against this development and proposals for the improvement of the situation are often wrong and rarely very constructive (especially with respect to the internationally comparative perspective), it has to be accepted that the average age of university graduates is too high. A major reason for this high age is the duration of studies. Again, 'objective' reasons (economic, job and curriculum related) can be found to explain the ever-growing periods of university studies, and it is wrong to blame only the 'ill prepared', 'uninterested', 'lazy' and 'hedonistic' students of today for this development. Besides such reasons and motives, it must be seen that these long times of study for a large number of students are difficult to cope with and are therefore dysfunctional for the Humboldtian university which depends on research-oriented students, interested in academic knowledge, and not so much on those who see their studies as a means to get a vocational training. But 60 per cent of all freshmen put the latter goal first (Lewin/Schacher, 1990). On the other hand, only 20 per cent of a representative sample of students described the relevance of science and research as 'central' to their studies. 22 per cent described it as high, but 39 per cent and 19 per cent respectively as of 'mean value' and 'irrelevant' (Bargel/Gawatz, 1987). The same source states that only 6 per cent of all students are definitely looking for a future career inside the university and not more than 20 per cent have decided to strive for a doctoral degree.

All these developments and facts seem to indicate that the Humboldtian ideas of a university cannot serve any longer as the only guiding principles for all higher education. The modernisation of the university has to take into account the heterogeneity not only of its students but of its membership in general. It should take care of the followers of the Humboldtian ideal who are still around, as well as the pragmatic student who wants a qualified education to get a decent job.

Prospects and Perspectives

A look across the borders of Germany shows that other systems of higher education are also on the move, by trying to adapt to the consequences of expansion and change in higher education (Neave, 1985–1990). In comparison to the Humboldtian university (which is used throughout this paper as a synonym for the traditional German university), much more reform happened in other systems, most remarkably in the Netherlands (Maassen/van Vught, 1989), Great Britain (Becher/Kogan, 1988), France (Lamoure-Rontopoulou/Lamoure, 1988), and Finland (Hüfner, 1989).

Against this background it seems that the Humboldtian university has been able once more to immunise itself against the winds of change. It seems to be immune against the 'market virus' and all the 'diseases' it brings to the university. While competition, differentiation, accountability, and similar issues have been discussed in Germany too, it seems that the higher education lobby has been able to avoid the necessary consequences of this discussion for the institutions (Frackmann, 1990).

Naturally it is difficult (if not impossible) for a university to be fit for competition in times of rising student numbers and shrinking university budgets. It is easy to blame universities for unsatisfying results in training, education and research, at times of inadequate funding. But compared to the situation in other European countries the German universities are relatively well off, and perhaps because of that, are not prepared to respond to changed circumstances.

Furthermore, the comparison of the duration of studies in different national systems of higher education (Teichler/Steube, 1989) and the fact that the length of studies in Germany is rather excessive throws some light on the teaching function of the Humboldtian university. Research has been conducted on the reasons for the extensive study time, plans are discussed, recommendations are proposed and pilot-projects for the shortening of the duration of studies are implemented (Frackmann, 1990; Gellert, 1988). Most people and groups interested and involved in higher education and the majority of institutions affected by these developments agree that something has to be done. But will it really be possible to adapt teaching and training to the changing conditions of higher education? But as in the USA, so in Germany the teaching function of the university became (not least in connection with the duration of studies) an issue in higher education. The magazine *Der Spiegel* sponsored a study on the conditions of studying at universities with particular emphasis on university teaching and teachers. The results where very controversial, but they stimulated discussions on the possibilities for the improvement of teaching at universities. Individuals, commissions, councils, associations are now taking up the issue. But, in general, there is reason to remain sceptical with regard to a genuine change. What should be done? Should something be done? It can be claimed that the Humboldtian university has, throughout its history, been a successful institution. It is quite possible that it will survive the recent turmoils of technological and economic change with similar stability, and that it will in general remain the same as before.

References

Bargel, T. et al (1989) *Studienerfahrungen und studentische Orientierungen.* Bonn: Bundesminister für Bildung und Wissenschaft (Reihe Bildung-Wissenschaft-Aktuell 4/89).

Bargel, T. and R. Gawatz (1987) *Leistungsstand und Förderung im Studium.* Bonn: Bundesminister für Bildung und Wissenschaft, (Reihe Bildung-Wissenschaft-Aktuell 10/87).

Becher, T. and M. Kogan (1988) *Reform of British Higher Education.* London: Education Reform Group.

Clark, B.R. (1983) *The Higher Education System: Academic Organisation in Cross-National Perspective.* Berkeley: University of California Press.

Der Bundesminister für Bildung und Wissenschaft (1989) *Grund- und Strukturdaten 1989/90.* Bonn: Bundesminister für Bildung und Wissenschaft.

Frackmann, E. (1990) 'Resistance to Change or No Need for Change? The Survival of German higher education in the 1990s' in *European Journal of Education* Vol 25 No 2, 187–202.

Gellert, C. (1984) 'Politics and Higher Education in the Federal Republic of Germany' in *European Journal of Education* Vol 19 No 2, 217–232.

Gellert, C. (1988) *Vergleich des Studiums an englischen und deutschen Universitäten.* Frankfurt: Lang.

Gellert, C. (1989) *Alternatives to Universities in Higher Education – Country Study Federal Republic of Germany.* Paris: OECD.

Gellert, C. (1991) 'Andersartig, aber gleichwertig – Anmerkungen zur Funktionsbestimmung der Fachhochschulen' in *Beiträge zur Hochschulforschung,* 1–25.

Hüfner, K. (1989) *Hochschulplanung im internationalen Vergleich: Beispiel Finnland.* Forschungsprojekt "Ökonomische Theorie der Hochschule" Diskussionspapiere Nr 15/89. Freie Universität Berlin: Zentralinstitut für sozialwissenschaftliche Forschung.

Kramer, D. (1989) 'Commentary' in The Wall Street Journal.

Lamoure Rontopoulou, J. and J. Lamoure (1988) 'French University Education: a brief overview 1984–1987' in *European Journal of Education* Vol 23 Nos 1 and 2, 37–45.

Lewin, K. and M. Schacher (1989) *Anhaltender Trend zu höheren Studienanfängerzahlen – Verhaltensweisen, Motive, Erwartungen deutscher Studienanfänger im Wintersemester 1988/89.* Hannover: HIS Hochschul-Informations-System GmbH, (HIS Kurzinformationen A6/89).

Lewin, K. and M. Schacher (1990) *Anhaltend hohe Studierneigung: Ursachen und Hintergründe – Deutsche Studienanfänger im Wintersemester 1989/90.* Hannover: Hochschul-Information-System (HIS Kurzinformationen A4/90).

Maassen, P. and F. van Vught (Eds) (1989) Dutch Higher Education in Transition. Policy Issues in Higher Education in the Netherlands. Culembourg: Lemma.

Neave, G. (1985) 'Higher Education in a Period of Consolidation: 1975–1985' in *European Journal of Education*, Vol 20 No 2 and 3, 109–124.

Neave, G. (1986) 'On Shifting Sands: changing priorities and perspectives in European Higher Education from 1984 to 1986' in *European Journal of Education*, Vol 21 No 1, 7–24.

Neave, G. (1988) 'On the cultivation of quality, efficiency and enterprise: an overview of recent trends in higher education in Western Europe, 1986–1988' in European Journal of Education, Vol 23 No 1, 7–23.

Neave, G. (1990) 'On Preparing the Markets: trends in higher education in Western Europe, 1988–1990' in *European Journal of Education* Vol 25 No 2, 105–122.

Nigmann, R.R. (1989) *Abiturienten an Fachhochschulen.* Hannover: HochschulInformations-System (HIS Kurzinformationen A5/89).

Schelsky, H. (1963) *Einsamkeit und Freiheit. Idee und Gestalt der deutschen Universität und ihrer Reformen. Reinbek: Rowohlt.*

Sozialistischer Deutscher Studentenbund (1972) Hochschuldenkschrift. Frankfurt: Verlag Neue Kritik.

Statistisches Bundesamt (1988) *Bildung und Kultur.* Fachserie 11, Reihe 4.2, Prüfungen an Hochschulen. Stuttgart.

'Studieren heute. Welche Uni ist die Beste?'. *Spiegel Spezial-Nr* (1990) 1/1990. Hamburg: Spiegel-Verlag.

Teichler, U. and W. Steube (1989) *Studiendauer und Lebensalter. Beiträge zur Diskussion in 7 ausgewählten Ländern.* Bonn: Bundesminister für Bildung und Wissenschaft (Bildung – Wissenschaft – international No 1/89).

U.S. News & World Report (1990). 'America's Best Colleges', October 15.

CHAPTER 3

The End of the Dual System?
The Blurring of Boundaries in the British Tertiary Education System

Maurice Kogan

Introduction

It is a commonplace that until the 1980s the UK system of higher education was at one end of the spectrum of academic freedom and generosity of public funding, if only to the benefit of a relatively small proportion of the eligible age groups, and that, as a result of the policies of a heroic Conservative government that has endured for eleven years, it now represents the extreme of both central government *dirigisme* and requirements to conform to market pressures.

These radical upsets provide students of institutions with an unparalleled opportunity to consider whether there is indeed a higher education essentialism, an irreducible core of values and relationships emanating from the tasks which tertiary systems should perform, which will be relatively enduring and impervious to the dictates of government, or whether higher education values can be taken *à la carte*, and the resulting structures created or reformed according not to the logic of the enterprise itself, but to the policy rationales of governments that sponsor them. It also offers a case study in changing institutional statuses.

The evidence of history is not uncontestably in favour of essentialism; higher education includes systems as various as the Humboldtian and Oxbridge ideals of the scholar as sovereign, the training for command and subordination of the military academics of Sandhurst and West Point, and the *grandes écoles* which, taken together with the less selective French university system, are an example of high professional expertise riding high over general and humanistic education, in contradiction to the other Western systems.

In the UK we can see traditional values enduring but under the stress created by many more demanding exogenous pressures. The more pressing demands, produced by greatly increased student numbers, and even more fundamental changes in funding procedures and amounts, are yet to come. How far the traditional assumptions will endure the real prospective changes will constitute a major agenda item for analysts. Already, however, there are clear signs of a reordering of the hierarchy of institutions.

Major Structural Features of the UK System Before the 1980s

The major structural characteristics of the system, as developed between 1945 and the early 1970s – with very little change until the major policy upheavals of the 1980s – can be briefly summarised.

The UK system followed the path of most West European countries in the 25 years following World War II. It widened access to higher education from that for a tiny elite of 3 per cent of school leavers in 1939 and 1945 entering university and a smaller proportion entering non-degree teacher training courses to 14 per cent in degree level courses in the early 1970s. The expansion was achieved by doubling the proportions entering university and by creating what was to become an even larger non-university system led by polytechnics. The intention was that they should pursue objectives and cater for client groups different from those of the universities whilst ultimately achieving their own comparable esteem. In the event, some of them were to become increasingly indistinguishable from some of the universities, at least as far as their ability to award first degrees was concerned.

Throughout this period of expansion the UK system sustained some features exclusive to it, and which derived in part from the general policies of the British Welfare State, and the 'soft' or opportunity version of it. So, staffing proportions remained very generous until the cuts of the 1980s, and were compatible with educational assumptions about the importance of providing personal tutorial care and small group contact. Student aid was generous. Students received free tuition and enough money on which to live, subject to parental contribution according to income although this increasingly became insufficiently maintained against inflation. One knowledgeable critic (Carswell, 1985) has pointed out that the authors of the Robbins Report (1963), which promoted and legitimised expansion to meet the demands of all candidates qualified to enter higher education, failed to anticipate the load on public finance of thus supporting increasing numbers of students.

A further set of assumptions concerned the governance of higher education. That was in fact quite strongly differentiated according to the part of the system being governed. Thus, the teacher training institutions – before they were absorbed into mainly non-university general institutions – were still under the control of their local authorities or governors largely drawn from the denominations which founded voluntary colleges. The polytechnics and other non-university institutions were also controlled in widely different degrees by their local authorities. These controls were becoming increasingly less obtrusive towards the end of the period.

The most important feature of the government of higher education was, however, the great freedom alongside great financial dependency, of the universities. The University Grants Committee, appointed by government, but recruited largely from academics, allocated working resources (capital needs were dealt with separately) to universities for a quinquennium in advance of their use. The UGC made the allocations within policy prescriptions which began by being very broad and indicative, except in some areas which particularly caught the attention of policy-makers, such as the distribution of medical schools or the overproduction of graduates in Russian studies. By the end of the 1960s, however, the allocations were made within frameworks that indicated the balances to be struck between graduate and non-graduate, science and non-science subjects for which funding would be made. In all of higher education planning, student demand was taken to be the imperative; as long as the demand for places could be sustained higher education could rest assured of funding with no real attempt to insist on objectives although feeble and ultimately failing attempts to insinuate degrees of manpower planning were attempted.

The theory of higher education governance was clear, though shaded and attenuated as one went lower in and beyond the university sector. Higher education was taken to be an undisputed good. What was good academically, was good socially and economically, for it would either directly add to the stock of useful knowledge or was part of the critical and expressive facilities that an advanced society needed and which served to provide the educational experience for the UK's governing elite. It followed from this serendipitous convergence between academic objectives and social and economic aims that higher education, particularly its more prestigious parts, should be allowed to govern itself, that funds would follow student numbers and also allow for a sizeable proportion of time and other resources for free research. By the early 1970s, demands were being made that alongside free research higher education and its funders should more eagerly turn to mission-oriented enquiry (Rothschild, 1971), but for many academics that could remain an optional extra. A dual system continued to allow the universities core funding from the UGC which gave them funds for both research and teaching. Perhaps a third of their recurrent grants were imputed to research. They could also apply for funds for fundamental research to the research councils or for mission oriented research and development to industry, commerce, the public sector and government departments.

Major Changes in Structure
The move from this happy state, almost unique to the UK and countries brought up in its academic traditions and parts of some USA state systems, to the drastic changes of the 1980s did not come as a complete surprise. In the 1970s, the universities, for example, lost about 10 per cent of their UGC regulated income, and this with no declared policy change about their objectives of their relationship with the state. As the oil crisis of the early 1970s began to reduce optimism about economic growth, the government became increasingly concerned about the ability of the system to maintain its recruitment momentum. The UGC quinquennial system and the genial assumptions underlying it were effectively abandoned and universities began, for the first time, to suffer the same uncertainties about their income as did the rest of humanity.

At the same time, the scene was set in other ways for increased convergence between the two sectors. Following the government's acceptance of expansion according to qualified student demand proposed in the Robbins Report, the polytechnics and other non-university institutions were increasingly given freedom from their local governing systems at the same time as both they and the universities fell under the closer control of the centre and its intermediate bodies. Many of these changes became explicit policy in the 1980s, but the 1970s with their economic and oil induced shocks, and the recession of belief in Welfare State policies, anticipated many of the developments that were to come.

The main changes which emerged in the 1980s will be canvassed in more detail in the paragraphs which follow.

Differentiation and Convergence: Reordering the Status System
UK higher education has hovered between eliteness and universality in that its age participation rate has never gone much beyond 15 per cent.[1] Although there was a steep status system, partly resulting from the ability of the ancient universities to acquire and nourish much of the best talent, and partly from the policies which governed the binary system which withheld autonomy and research resources from over half of the higher education system, it remained remarkably homogeneous in the activities pursued by

---

1   This APR is not as low as it seems. It excludes some levels of work which in some systems would be deemed part of higher education.

most academics, and the assumptions about standards. Almost all degrees, at all levels, were awarded on the basis of assessments monitored by external examiners, so that in theory a degree from Oxbridge was equivalent to one awarded as the result of a course at a polytechnic. Admission requirements even to the least esteemed institutions were tough; all candidates must possess at least two Advanced level General Certificate of Examination passes. An early study (Trow and Halsey, 1971) showed that nearly two-thirds of university staff believed that their main aim was to undertake research – some three times the proportion of their US equivalents. That proportion is almost certainly higher now; and many academics in the non-university sector engaged in research, albeit under more strenuous teaching commitments and resource constraints than their colleagues in universities.

The homogeneity of the system can be exaggerated and, no doubt, the assumptions that standards were roughly comparable would not always have stood up to close scrutiny. Taken as a whole, however, the ability range of students and activities of the teachers in British higher education would not be far different from the range of any leading public research university in the USA.

Elements of hierarchy and stratification were largely implicit except for the major divide of the binary system. But the informal stratification was made explicit and hardened by actions taken following retrenchment in the 1980s. In 1981, the government decided to take away a further 9 per cent of recurrent funding from the universities as part of a reorientation of public expenditure. Although this was declared to imply no ideological intent, but merely a desire to save money, it was a momentous decision because it was the first explicit cut which would require a reduction in scale of operation, a reduction in staffing ratios and standards or the number of students. The UGC, on whom government had dumped the decision, decided to cut numbers, and the universities lost about 20,000 places at the very time when student demand was likely to rise.

But the loss of places was soon recovered, albeit at lower unit costs and standards, and from our point of view these cuts were more significant as the first step in explicit restratification than for the loss of access. The UGC, for the first time in its history, was required to preside over selective reductions, as opposed to selective expansions. It had to make comparative judgments of worth, and in so doing seriously damaged some universities but, more important, created an explicit status order (Kogan and Kogan, 1963). That structuring was reinforced in 1986 and 1989 when, at the behest of government but with the support of some of the leading natural scientists, it made judgments on research capabilities of all departments. These were published and formed the basis for increasingly wider differentiation of university funding. At the same time, another powerful intermediary body, the Advisory Board for Research Councils (ABRC), pressed its five research council members to concentrate research fundings in centres of excellence and particularly in centres which could undertake interdisciplinary work and work that, whilst grounded in good basic research, was also 'strategic' in its objectives.

Whilst departments in the quite small and elite university system were thus being banded into, in effect, five grades for their research, the polytechnics and other public sector bodies became, as did the universities, subject to stronger planning control from the centre with the creation of first the National Advisory Body for Public Sector Higher Education, and after the 1988 Education Reform Act, the Polytechnics and Colleges Funding Council. But they were also given a considerable lift in status by the conferment in 1988 or legal incorporation which removed them from the control of local education authorities, and gave them status not far different from that of the universities. Thus, the universities' autonomy had been weakened, its standards held up to public scrutiny and its status ladder reformed by external forces, whilst the less privileged public system came alongside in status. In the height of the selectivity surge the ABRC had gone as far to suggest that some university departments would become mainly teaching units. These changes were the result of pressure from government which conveyed the impression of low standards and waste of resources and made 'reform' a condition of various resource settlements. At the same time some polytechnics might be able to chance their arm at more research. The UK system might as a result finish up with five university levels and three or four public sector levels with some overlap in the middle. Within universities, selectivity was also imposed by the requirement, from 1989, that they increasingly reward the abler members of staff, and those in shortage subjects, with higher salaries.

It is the government's intention progressively to reduce the UFC's funding of research and to transfer the funds to the research councils which are open to applications from both sectors. This will further weaken the universities' protected position as the main *locus* of research. Eventually, however, if some universities lost enough of their research funding, and some polytechnics took on enough research, the number of gradations would be reduced and the institutions near the boundary of the two systems would become indistinguishable.

Finally, there are unmistakable moves towards merging the two central intermediary bodies, both of which are to transfer from London to a shared building in Bristol. Most observers give them no more than five years of continued separate existence.

Changes in the Relationship Between Teaching and Research

For a long while, it has been assumed that there was an unbreakable link between teaching in higher education and research. But the assumption had never been refined and very likely derived pragmatically from the fact that those institutions which attracted the best students were also those which trained and served as a base for the researchers. Universities received the core funds from the then University Grants Committee on the basis of the number of students they expected to recruit. The grants were sufficient to allow for staffing at a level adequate to provide time for each teacher to do research – perhaps one-third of funds were predicated on that assumption. The UK honours degree – for which the great majority of students were admitted – culminated in work in the final year that was often close to the research interests of the teacher offering the course. There was an implicit assumption that the first degree course would lead to the production of apprentice researchers, as it did and could for the minority going on to make research their career, although the assumption was always fatuous for the majority; two-thirds of UK graduates have taken courses not directly relevant to their ultimate career of choice. It would be fair to say that the link between teaching and research was of only indirect benefit to the majority of students. They may well have been glad that they were being taught by researchers at the frontiers of knowledge, whilst perceiving no direct benefits from that fact.

Granted, too, the close tutorial attention and personal work provided for in UK institutions, the first degree proved a good base for research careers via Masters and the doctoral courses. There was no division between teachers or researchers – lectors and docents – as in some other systems. Some such convention might now emerge informally from the attempts of some heads of departments to ensure that those teachers who do not contribute to the university's research ratings will be required to take on a heavier teaching and administration load.

But the link is weakening under more fundamental shifts in higher education. The non-university institutions now provide the bulk of first degree courses and a growing number of postgraduate courses, too (Kogan and Henkel, forthcoming). The majority of their staff were not recruited as researchers, this being the criterion almost universally applied by universities, although some do undertake research. There is 'academic drift' in that many Polytechnic staff aspire to the university mode. When asked what the perceived benefits of research were, by far the biggest response (in the research carried out by Touche Ross for a Polytechnics and Colleges Funding Course (PCFC) report on research) was 'improves undergraduate education', although the sector received £30m for research against £800m for universities; the figure spent in 1988–90, £80m, was at the top end of previous estimates and had increased dramatically on previous years. The PCFC Committee 'did not receive a single piece of evidence that was not positive about the benefits of research in the sector' (THES, 21 September 1990).

In a sense the polytechnics have called the universities' bluff, for it is difficult to maintain both that all UK degrees are of equal value and that research is inseparable from teaching, whilst the majority of first degrees are being produced by institutions staffed largely by non-researchers. The widening repertoire of courses has also weakened the teaching-research link. Some areas of professional training or application, including medicine and education, have never assumed that research would be a dominant preoccupation of most of their teachers. Many such areas have developed applied research or scholarship, but an increasing proportion of higher education teaching will not be related to fundamental research findings or saturated by the research ethos. Finally, the differentiation is being enforced by the policy movements towards selective funding. Some universities will lose some of their funding because of assumed research quality. If departments then seek to use their resources selectively, the non-researchers will become confirmed as such.

The intra-institutional moves away from the research-teaching link is reinforced, as we have seen, by government policies. But if in some countries, for example Norway, government has sought to encourage mission-oriented research by placing the bulk of its financing in institutions independent of universities, for the most part that has not been the tendency in Britain.

As we have seen, the UK government has instead pursued two related policies which are intended to strengthen universities' research capacity to respond to government priorities through encouraging 'strategic' research, that is work that is both based on fundamental enquiry but also related to economic and social gain, and to bring about greater concentration of work in centres of excellence. The concentration is being largely achieved through an increasing differentiation of funds to universities in accordance with the quality grading given their research through reviews conducted in 1985 and 1989. The research councils, too, are putting more of their money into large-scale, interdisciplinary initiatives which tend to channel funds to the largest and most esteemed institutions; some 60 per cent of Science and Engineering Research Council research grants find their way to a third of the universities.

The Re-Emergence of Positivism

In the 1960s, considerable faith was placed in the power of social science to illuminate social, economic and educational problems and provide solutions to them. The positivistic approach to policy formation was a long tradition in British public life; for example, Royal Commissions had, from quite early in the 19th century, depended upon the collection of 'objective' data upon which policy proposals could be based. In the 1960s, the place of the social sciences seemed likely to be strongly institutionalised and supported. The Social Science Research Council received its Charter in 1965 and although at first mainly concerned to build up the theoretical foundations of the social sciences soon took upon itself the task at the same time of supporting social enquiry more directly directed towards social problems. Government departments from the early 1960s began to develop a capacity for the commissioning of research useful to policy. In 1971, an official report (Rothschild, 1971) explicitly promulgated the device of the customer-contractor relationship in which government set the objectives for research while researchers received funds to carry it out and reach conclusions.

At the same time, however, two inbuilt safeguards remained in place to ensure that social science remained independent. First, the Social Science Research Council and private foundations were able and willing to produce studies that ran against official trends and which joined the international community of scholars in producing critical social science. The strong tenurial position of academics in universities and other institutions meant that the flow of independent scholarship and enquiry became stronger at the very time that government was setting about commissioning research for its own purposes. Secondly, even those commissioned by government to undertake research did not necessarily, and were not inevitably required to, produce work which diminished the independence and integrity of the social science contribution. Often those commissioning research in government looked to social scientists to formulate the problems as well as the solutions. The work produced reflected a wide range of epistemologies and assumptions about the relationships between knowledge and authority (Kogan and Henkel, 1983).

In the 1980s, however, although enough of the tenurial strength still remained within British higher education to ensure an adequate flow of independent research and scholarship in all fields, the sponsorship system has, as we have already noted, attempted to foster work which is 'strategic' in its direction. Whilst supporting the notion of fundamental and independent enquiry, government also seeks to ensure that its own agenda is addressed. The extent to which those who sponsor social sciences through the Economic and Social Science Research Council have become subservient to government has never been examined. It seems unlikely, however, that those parts of the system still controlled by academics are likely to sponsor crudely positivistic work. The elegant, the theoretical and the independent are still the most highly prized.

The changes are, indeed, of a different kind. Whilst independence still is prized, its funding has been reduced. Alongside independent academic research, there has been a veritable cloudburst of evaluation and social enquiry undertaken by private consultants. They operate at all levels of government. They have gained considerable purchase over central government, where their work is prized for its technical adroitness and for the ability of consultants to work within the objectives, either prescribed or surmised, of the civil servants sponsoring the research (Henkel, 1991). Their work is used by local and health authorities and by such institutions as universities, too. Their work is positivistic inasmuch as it takes as its mandate the objectives of those commissioning the research and its aim is not independent publication to be subject to academic scrutiny but making an immediate impact upon policy making and implementation.

Higher Education and the Labour Market

In the UK, the classic assumption has been that there is a happy convergence between what higher education provides and what the labour market needs. Employees do not expect the majority of graduate entrants to employment to have learned specific knowledge skills. For example, accountancy recruits 10 per cent of all graduates from the whole range of subjects.

A recent study (Boys et al, 1988) of the teaching of six subjects at undergraduate level in nine institutions identified a spectrum of skills that academics were concerned to include in their courses. They included generic study skills, intellectual skills, experimental and technical skills, general and specific work skills. The importance of the labour market was present throughout the range. There was an increasing interest in identifying and promoting those skills which were transferable. There was a general awareness of the need for the literate scientist, the numerate arts student, the socially aware engineer, for computer literacy and for communication and social skills.

Within course offerings there was a range of applications designed to prepare students for work in specific areas. There were then courses which included general work preparation through the provision of skills designed to help the student obtain good employment in which the teaching did not take a vocational orientation. Thus, economists contended that vocational benefits came primarily from the acquisition of core tools of economics analysis. A fourth pattern showed an emphasis on knowledge and the acquisition of cognitive skills, with no particular reference to employment. Here teachers might eschew explicit work-related aims and consider that obtaining a degree was sufficient preparation for employment and that the study of the discipline conferred skills transferable and attractive to employers. But even where this view was held, consciousness of employment needs was represented through a growth of group and oral work, the use of IT and the greater attention to substantive themes which were concerned with current economic problems.

This kind of evidence relates to the way in which the academy has moved to meet the needs of employment. Government has not been content, however, with allowing the hidden hand of student and staff preferences to do the work of fitting people for employment. It has launched an Enterprise Initiative (MSC, 1987) through which higher education institutions were offered substantial sums of money 'to enable higher education institutions to (...) embed activities that promote enterprise into the work of the institutions (...)'. The objectives were that 'every person seeking a higher education qualification should be able to develop competences and aptitudes relevant to enterprise'. At the same time, the government (DES, 1987), while stating that 'meeting the needs of the economy is not the sole purpose of higher education' said that 'this aim (...) must be vigorously pursued (...)'. 'The government and its central funding agencies will do all they can to encourage and reward approaches by higher education institutions which bring them closer to the world of business.'

It is, perhaps, government who are most pressing, and higher education teachers who, in different degrees, are most anxious about the needs of the employment market. Employers are certainly worried about the lack of particular skills. But authoritative statements by employers (Boys et al, 1988) do not regard a more economic focus for higher education as meaning an adjustment of courses towards a narrow vocationalism.

They emphasise the need to maintain humane values and to be strong in all disciplines. They look for versatility to changing work demands which means an understanding of how things work along with specialised knowledge of the subject and the development of personal skills and communication, problem solving, team work and leadership. [They are] far from recognising that the aims of education should be set by business (...) or that courses should be generally adjusted in the direction of their narrow vocationalism (CIHE, 1987).

In examining the changing relationships between higher education and the labour market, the weakening of the binary divide is evident. Institutions which feel most vulnerable, whether universities, polytechnics or colleges, are likely to be the most conscious of the need to introduce into the preparation of students requirements of the labour market.

The Expansion of Opportunity

From 1945, UK higher education expanded. The policy was framed by the Robbins Report (1963) dictum that 'courses of higher education should be made available for all those qualified by ability and attainment to pursue them and who wished to do so'. Robbins made equal opportunity of access a dominant theme alongside the contribution that higher education could make to the economy. But the expansion of the Age Participation Rate (APR) from roughly 3 per cent to 14 per cent between 1945 and 1988 did little to ensure that the beneficiaries were drawn from the full range of social, regional, ethnic and gender groups. The number of university entrants with fathers in social classes A and B actually rose from 44 per cent to 51 per cent between 1970 and 1975 (DES Statistics, 1981). In 1985, 60 per cent of all higher education applicants came from households whose heads were in social classes 1 and 2 (this was twice the proportion of all 18-year-olds) (Redpath and Harvey, 1987). One encouraging breakthrough, however, evident in many other countries too, was that there were more women students (25 per cent in 1960 to over 50 per cent in 1988) (Fulton, 1988).

The gross issue of the amount of access has increasingly been complicated by qualitative issues. We are none too clear about the changes in educational modes and content and the resulting match with employment for different groups that might result. Access is also divided in terms of the distinctions between preferred and less preferred institutions. Admission to one or the other vitally affects the rewards that will follow. Devices for increasing access, particularly in the public sector, include the promotion of experience-based learning intended to partly supplant academic discipline based work, credit accumulation and transfer between institutions, and access courses. Most institutions have been optimistic about future demand for higher education, although subject differences are sharply marked (Fulton and Elwood, 1989). But admissions policy does not reflect the differences in demand. Departments and institutions still hope to recruit from the virtually fixed pool of 'good' A-level candidates. Many may wish to make space for non-traditional or disadvantaged applicants but there are often no active efforts to recruit them. One policy conclusion from research conducted by Fulton and Elwood is that the ability to complete a course, not the entry grade, should be the basic criterion for admission.

The UK government announced in 1989 that students will be partly financed by loans and that institutions will receive a higher proportion of their income from fees. These proposals are intended to stimulate growth in numbers. There is controversy about the effects that these new policies will have on the access of different groups. The movement towards loans and away from the finding of full fees, as modified by parental income, is a significant move away from the welfare statement model of UK higher education.

In formal terms there is no bar to transfer between different types of higher education qualifications. Most institutions in most courses allow for it. It cannot be said, however, that the practice is widespread and, indeed, the autonomy of institutions and their basic units to create courses according to their own vision will continue to make this a minority possibility. The bulk of the increase has in fact been absorbed by PCFC institutions but it remains true that the majority of the most able students apply to and finish up in universities. Many institutions have considerable numbers of undergraduates from EC countries. In some subjects, a majority of graduate students come from abroad.

Effects of European Integration

Institutions are, as noted above, receiving increasing numbers of EC students on courses. This possibility is enhanced by the fact that they have a legal right to pay the same fees as UK students. Institutions participate in projects initiated by the European Community (ERASMUS, COMETT and the like). For the most part, however, changes are in prospect rather than in action.

Non-Academic Factors

There is no doubt that attempts are being made to recast the content of higher education according to external values. We have already noted the extent to which undergraduate education is responsive to the labour market. As we have noted, there are the Training Agency's programmes intended to persuade institutions to teach enterprise skills. The recent adoption of managerialist policies in higher education as through the introduction of performance measurement, the results of which vitally affect university funding, may to some extent be offset by central attempts to ensure that institutions evaluate teaching and the curriculum. It remains open for further analysis, however, to discover the effects of new managerial and government arrangements on the academic outcomes of higher education. This would include a study of the effects of setting explicit objectives and subjecting academic work to performance evaluation on the balance of power between managers and academics. In such a study the important criteria would be those of the teaching and research outcomes of individual academics and their students. The learning experience of students is rarely linked with issues of the managerial and governmental context within which it takes place.

Other objectives have also been reinforced. Increased funding for continuing education implies a greater commitment to wider access for those from hitherto under-represented groups. The UK, as have many other countries, has made major strides in the recruitment of female students, but has made hardly any impact on differentiations associated with socio-economic group, regional origin, or ethnic status. Nor has it done much to recover the opportunities lost by the majority of Britons who had left school at 14, 15 or 16. Wider access has become a shared objective across the systems, partly in order to sustain trade through the ups and downs of demography, and partly under the pressure of Ministers growing anxious in the late 1980s about the shortfalls in skilled manpower.

Changes in the System

The 1988 Education Reform Act introduced new arrangements for governance and financing of higher education. In the past, institutions were financed on the welfare state model in which what they provided was thought to be an undisputed good and therefore deserving of grants that would make up the deficiency between anything they owned or could earn and their full expenditure. At the same time, higher education autonomy was strong in the universities and on its way in public sector institutions.

Institutions in both sectors are now financed under the provisions of the 1988 Education Reform Act to provide programmes approved by the two new funding councils. The funding councils will reflect the objectives of government because they consist of members drawn less from the academic world and more from that of employment. The Chairs are filled by industrialists. Institutions must produce institutional plans for the approval of central funding agencies. At the same time as prescription from the centre has grown, higher education institutions, as in other countries, have been subjected to two forms of market. The first is the genuine priced market in which they must sell their products to those who need them. The second is an artificial market created by government in which institutions bid for student places at prices which they hope government will pay (Becher and Kogan, 1991).

These attempts radically to modify academic behaviour move us away from essentialism in higher education. Instead of its social arrangements being determined by the nature of the tasks being performed, principally independent enquiry and the training of independent minds, these objectives are now strongly combined with social objectives determined by the governing systems. The extent to which the basic values of higher education will bend under these pressures is again a matter for further study. It is clear, however, that whilst the most esteemed institutions will remain relatively unscathed, the status ordering of the other institutions will change while the binary system is already caving in.

References

Becher, T. and M. Kogan (1991) *Process and Structure in Higher Education*. 2nd ed. London: Routledge.

Boys, C. et al, (1988) *Higher Education and the Preparation for Work*. London: Jessica Kingsley Publishers.

Carswell, J. (1985) *Government and the University in Britain*. Cambridge University Press.

Council for Industry in Higher Education (1987) *Towards a Partnership: Higher Education – Government – Industry*. CIHE.

Department of Education and Science (1981) *Statistics of Education*.

Department of Education and Science (1987) White Paper, *Higher Education: Meeting the Challenge*. Cm 114. London: HMSO.

Department of Education and Science (1991) White Paper, *Higher Education: A New Framework*. Cm 1541. London: HMSO.

Fulton, O. (1988) 'Elite Survivals? Entry "Standards" and Procedures for Higher Education Admissions'. *Studies in Higher Education* Vol 13 No 1.

Fulton, O. and L. Elwood (1989) *Admissions to Higher Education: Policy and Practice*. London: Training Agency.

Halsey, A.H. and M. Trow (1971) *The British Academics*. London: Faber & Faber.

Henkel, M. (1991) *Government, Evaluation and Change*. London: Jessica Kingsley Publishers.

Kogan, M. and M. Henkel (1983) *Government and Research*. London: Heinemann.

Kogan, M. and M. Henkel (forthcoming) 'Research Training and Graduate Education: The British Macro-Structure' in Clark, R.B. (ed) *The Research Foundations of Graduate Education: Germany, Britain, France, United States and Japan*. Berkeley: University of California Press.

Kogan M. and D. Kogan (1983) *The Attack on Higher Education*. London: Kogan Page.

Manpower Services Commission (1987) *Enterprise in Higher Education, Guidance for Applicant*. London: MSC.

Redpath R. and B. Harvey (1987) *Young People's Intentions to enter Higher Education*. Commissioned Report from the Office of Population Censuses and Surveys. London: HMSO.

Robbins Report (1963) *Report of the Committee Appointed by the Prime Minister under the Chairmanship of Lord Robbins, 1961–1963, Higher Education*. Cmnd 2154. London: HMSO.

Rothschild Report (1971) *The Organisation and Management of Government R and D.* Cmnd 4814. London: HMSO.

THES (1990) 'Survey Backs Policy Research'. Report in *Times Higher Education Supplement.* 21 September 1990.

CHAPTER 4

Tertiary Diversification in France and the Conditions of Access[1]

Jean-Pierre Jallade, Jean Lamoure and Jeanne Lamoure Rontopoulou

In 1989, 39 per cent of a generation took the *baccalauréat*, as against only 25 per cent less than ten years earlier. This is the result of a long period of extension of access to secondary education and lengthening of schooling, a development with two culminating points: the extension of obligatory schooling to the age of 16 introduced by the 1959 secondary education reform, with the rate of school attendance in sixth form (11-year-olds) going from 43 per cent in 1960 to 95 per cent in 1972, and the extension of duration of schooling after 16 that developed during the 1980s, with pressure this time coming to bear at high school level.

In this context of heavy demand for extended study and of the search by people for the highest-level diploma possible, the baccalauréat has been steadily less regarded as the final stage of schooling than as a requisite entrance ticket to post-secondary education. The foreseeable strengthening of these trends allows us to estimate that the figure of two million students will be passed in a not very remote future.

Education after the baccalaureate in France takes the form, probably more than in other European countries, of a diversified system made up of highly structured streams each with definite functions and well-defined institutional, educational and organisational characteristics. Thus, the first years of post-baccalaureate education contribute to a complex whole, more or less in continuity with the streams of secondary education: in both secondary education and higher education it is possible to distinguish a general sector, a technical sector and a vocational sector.

The diversification of the system is the outcome of history. The *Grandes Ecoles*, originally called '*Ecoles Spéciales*', along with the preparatory classes for access to them, were created in the 18th and particularly throughout the 19th century, to prepare the scientific, and later administrative and commercial, personnel that government and society needed. The universities, after the interruption during the revolutionary period, emerged at the end of the 19th century to train secondary school teachers, researchers and members of the liberal professions, and ultimately to form the centre for the development and propagation of the national culture.

In modern times, therefore, the existence of the *Grandes Ecoles* predated that of the universities. This distribution of tasks enabled the *Grandes Ecoles* very early to weave privileged links with both government and professional circles, given the object of the

---

1   This article is based on a study done for the European Institute of Education and Social Policy (Jallade 1990). It has been translated by Iain Fraser, Florence.

training they gave and the posts occupied by their *alumni*, while the universities remained subordinate to the central administration, cut off from the business world and located below the *Grandes Ecoles* on the scale of academic and social hierarchy.

Post-baccalaureate education is not just diverse, but comes under a wide range of supervisory bodies: the Ministry of Education for the greater proportion of students, but also the Ministries of Agriculture and Health. The number of students registered for private education has grown heavily since the late 1970s, particularly in the STSs (Special Technical Sections) that provide training for tertiary-sector occupations.

The duality of the post-baccalaureate educational system is based on the method of selecting students on entry. Traditionally, an open-access sector and a closed-access sector are distinguished. The first covers the universities, particularly for general disciplines, and the second the preparatory classes for the *Grandes Ecoles* (CPGE) and the *Grandes Ecoles* themselves, the IUTs (Instituts Universitaires de Technologie, a two-year vocational training), the STSs and the para-medical and social vocational training courses. With increasingly tight selection for university first-degree courses, the closed sector at present represents over 60 per cent of the total numbers of those in first post-baccalaureate courses.

This duality in the system underlying the existence of complex relations among the streams emerges also from the use individuals make of them according to their educational strategies and again in the educational policy of the authorities: the differentiation in selection methods on entry is in fact taken as both cause and justification of the social value of the certificate. In this context, the difficulties inherent in mass education are concentrated in one sector only (the DEUG, a diploma given after two years of general university education), thereby causing an imbalance in the system as a whole.

Since the 1960s, the universities have changed radically in content, developing vocational courses in particular to meet the fall in job offers: this process began in the IUTs, and extended more recently to traditional university courses, no doubt because of the difficulty of 'moving from an academic logic of disciplines to a logic of practical life'.

The Structures of Higher Education

University First-Degree Courses

The first university course in general disciplines (*premier cycle*)[2], leading to the DEUG, at present accounts for some 40 per cent of the total university population and 50 per cent of those studying these disciplines. Creation of the *premier cycle* dates back to 1966, when the university courses were restructured into study 'cycles' (first, second and third cycle) in place of the system of certificates preceded by the propaedeutic year (introduced in 1948) that existed previously. The 1966 reform was brought in at the time of and because of the explosive growth in university numbers: the number of students doubled in five years, going from 215,000 in 1960 to 414,000 in 1965. The creation of three successive study cycles aimed at making the system more flexible by allowing a qualification for leaving at the end of each cycle. Despite the intentions of the reform to make university studies shorter and therefore more 'fluid', the first-cycle diploma remained exclusively academic in content.

2　　Law, Economics, Letters/Human Sciences, Sciences, Multidisciplinary.

Eight years later, the 1984 reform made renewal of the first cycle one of the pivots of the transformation of the university institutions. The organisation of DEUG education is aimed at diversifying and vocationalising courses, while incorporating in them a period of orientation for students. In contrast to the tradition of reforms imposed uniformly on all institutions by the central Education Ministry, the DEUG renewal enacted in 1984 was on a contractual basis between the universities that were themselves to set the objectives to be secured, particularly in terms of the internal performance of the first cycles, the necessary changes in organisation of courses and specifying the ways to accomplish them, and the ministerial authorities who, after negotiation, allot the necessary resources.

The vocationalisation of courses, conceived of as a progressive process throughout university studies, is another major pivot of the 1984 reform; but above all this was the first time that a short, explicitly vocational stream was introduced into the first university cycle. The DEUST (diploma in university scientific and technical studies) had the objective of '... enabling the students to acquire the necessary knowledge and methods either to take up employment immediately or else continue or later resume higher education'. This stream, because of the lack of funds coming from the authorities, still remains at an experimental stage (1500 students in 1987 and some 500 degrees awarded in 1986), oriented towards meeting local employment needs and cutting down the numbers of those leaving the first cycle without a certificate or qualification.

Despite the successive reforms, the problem of the effectiveness of the first university cycle remains, with the duality in higher education meaning that difficulties bound up with growth in the student population impinge almost exclusively on the open sector, the first university cycle (National University Assessment Committee, 1987). At the same time, this constitutes the area where the contradictory objectives of the various actors meet: students, for whom the DEUG often represents a 'last chance' solution; teachers, who endeavour to restrict access to it; government, seeking to elevate the population's general skill level by integrating the universities with overall social policy.

Preparatory Classes for the Grandes Ecoles

The principles for creating and developing the CPGE are closely bound up with the existence of the entrance competitions for the *Grandes Ecoles*. The embryo of this institution can be found as from the mid-18th century: the *pension* Berthaud and a number of other colleges or private *'pensions'* prepared pupils for the entrance competition to the Royal School of Engineering at Mézières (founded in 1749). At present, over 300 secondary education institutions have one or more preparatory classes. The theoretical duration of schooling there is one or two years depending on the competition to be sat for; two years for scientific, technical or literary 'prep', one year for the preparatory classes for the national veterinary colleges or commercial colleges (HEC, ESSEC, etc).

The Higher Technical Colleges (STS)

These provide courses for the Higher Technical Certificate (BTS), introduced in 1959; in accordance with the decree creating them, they result in part from new foundations and in part from transformations of previously existing Technical Certificates (BT) and the certificates of the National Vocational Colleges (ENP). The creation of the Higher Technical Sections (STS) is thus the outcome of the natural growth of technical education under the supervision of the Education Ministry and bound up with the reorganisation of secondary education.[3] It was also the product of the reconsideration carried on in the Education Ministry along with professional circles regarding the need to develop long technical courses to meet the growing needs of industry for middle-grade personnel (Guillon, 1972).

The number of students in this stream has grown rapidly and certificates taken have diversified, but the actual structure of teaching has remained unchanged since it was set up: the Higher Technical Sections are post-baccalaureate education lasting two years in courses organised in Technical High Schools or private institutions.

The University Institutes of Technology (IUT)

Their creation met two political and economic imperatives: to enable universities to cope with the heavy growth in demand for higher education generated by the rapid rise in the number of school-leavers with baccalaureates, and to meet needs for highly-trained technicians as estimated by economic forecasters.

Creation of the IUTs was hard to justify given the existence of the STSs; it had been planned that these would be progressively eliminated because of their over-specialisation by comparison with the flexibility required by technological advance. In actual fact, both streams developed concurrently, with no jointly planned growth (Cerych/Sabatier, 1986; Lamoure, 1981). Despite retention of the STSs, registrations in IUTs increased rapidly. The structure and organisation of studies at the IUTs have however remained unchanged on the whole since their creation; like the STSs they train higher technicians for two years after the baccalaureate, but by contrast with them are part of the university system, in which, however, they constitute exceptional types of UER.

Paramedical and Social Training

Courses leading to paramedical or social occupations are among the oldest, and their growth has been bound up with the regulation of these professions. After World War I (in 1922) the profession of nursing became bound up with the possession of a State Certificate, and the same is true of the profession of social workers. From the end of the 1940s, these State diplomas became compulsory for the paramedical professions. Since that time, training has taken on features essentially equivalent to those at present, in terms of both length of study and conditions of admission to the colleges. Since these courses were created, recruitment has been twofold: candidates for nursing colleges had to have an Elementary Certificate, but holders of the Higher Certificate or the first part of the baccalaureate were exempt from the admission tests.

Higher Agricultural Technicians

The Higher Agricultural Technician's Certificate (BTSA) may be regarded as the most recent certificate: the first courses were introduced in 1969. This lateness by comparison with other training courses is explained by the relatively recent recognition of Ministry of Agriculture supervision of agricultural education: agricultural high schools came into being only in the very early 1960s, and courses were reorganised as from 1968 with creation of a short course for the Professional Agricultural Certificate (BEPA, the counterpart of the BEP) and a long course, the Agricultural Technicians Certificate (BTA), and the baccalaureate in Agricultural and Technical Sciences (the D baccalaureate). The BTSA thus offered holders of the BTA and D baccalaureate a possibility of further study, as did the BTS for Education Ministry technical education.

---

3   Creation of the Technical Schools and technical baccalaureates as part of the Berthoin reform.

Summarising, all of these vocational training courses (IUT, BTS and BTSA, paramedical and social diplomas) have since their creation had common features that continue to distinguish them from the academic courses, DEUG and CPGE:

- the recruitment level is very much the same: though the baccalaureate is not always required, the requirement is completion of secondary studies, so that these courses are aimed at an already educationally selected population;
- entry conditions are always selective, whether by competition (paramedical or social colleges) or selection according to qualifications (IUT, STS);
- while the length of courses is not identical (two or three years), the objective is the same: to train higher technicians, at the level of middle management, intermediate between technician and engineer, between auxiliaries and doctors;
- the organisation of study is characterised by alternation between courses, guided work and field experience, a specific feature of vocationally-oriented courses.

These points in common should not conceal the essential fact: short higher technical courses have since their creation constituted a group fragmented both by diversity of supervisory bodies and absence of any joint regulation of their development. While the diversity of supervisory bodies is explicable by the history of the institutions, the absence of regulation reveals that each of these courses corresponds not only to specific social and vocational functions but also to distinct public segments educated in specific streams. This distinction in fact cuts across all post-baccalaureate education, from the most selective (CPGE) to the open sector of higher education, the DEUG.

Flows of Students into Higher Education

The growth in flows of students entering short higher education is directly bound up with that of the pool of baccalaureate takers, like the growth in numbers of every university stream. These characteristics in particular determine aspects of guidance towards post-baccalaureate education and to some extent their internal operating conditions.

Differentiated Growth in Number of Baccalaureate Holders

The growth in numbers in post-secondary education results from a combination of three factors: 1. growing entry by young people into secondary education and increasing length of study; 2. increase in numbers of baccalaureate holders; 3. the admission policy for each post-secondary stream.

As we previously mentioned, the trend noted since 1960 is towards lengthening the duration of studies; in other words, young people are staying in the school system longer than their elders, more of them are reaching the baccalaureate and they more often continue their studies beyond it. Thus, from 1982 to 1987, the rate of attendance at the age of 18 has gone from 19 per cent to over 66 per cent, at 19 from 31 per cent to 50 per cent and at 20 from 21 per cent to 31 per cent.

However, this overall development masks profound disparities: geographical, between the less scholastic north and the south, and by sex, with girls attending school more than boys; but above all social: reaching the baccalaureate varies by a factor of three depending on parents' occupation (Esquieu, 1989). While between 1960 and 1980 the growth in number of baccalaureate holders was spectacular and has even accelerated since 1985, there have also been radical changes in the nature of the baccalaureates conferred, with heavy growth in some types and relative stagnation in others.

Summarising, since 1975, almost all general baccalaureate series have experienced relative stability or moderate growth in numbers, except for the B (economics and social) series which has been the only one to go through heavy growth. This has influenced the growth in numbers of general baccalaureate takers and helped to shift the balance between scientific and literary series. In turn, the technological baccalaureates now account for over one-third of all baccalaureate takers. This growth is due essentially to rapid expansion in series G (economics and administration). This increase and change in flows of baccalaureate takers has however had different effects on post-baccalaureate streams depending on the specific mode of regulation for each of them.

Post-Baccalaureate Openings Bound Up With Secondary Education Streams

The pressure of demand for higher education, a combined effect of the increase in number of baccalaureate takers and of individual searches for the highest possible diploma, is not reflected mechanically and uniformly on all post-baccalaureate streams. It is essentially the modes of entry to the latter that explain the differences: for the open sector, the traditional university disciplines, the baccalaureate is a sufficient entrance ticket, while for closed streams – IUT, STS, CPGE, paramedical and social courses – candidate selection on entry is according to criteria of excellence, choice and elimination of holders of particular types of baccalaureates. The consequences of this selection are all the more important because the closed sector is taking an increasing share of the numbers of those in higher education.

The choices made by baccalaureate holders should therefore be considered not only in terms of the size of flows from the various series into each higher education stream but also considering the spread of possible or at any rate realistic choices[4] towards the closed sector of post-baccalaureate courses, in particular the CPGE and IUT. The school course preceding the baccalaureate, mainly the choices made in secondary education, not only gives different probabilities of continuing higher studies but also largely determines the possible choices. The achievement of registration in one of the post-baccalaureate streams thus does not mean the end of this influence, which remains manifest throughout an educational career.

Selection and Performance

Terms of Entry to Higher Education

While possession of the baccalaureate is the necessary and sufficient condition for entering the DEUG, things are somewhat different in streams in the closed sectors. For these the baccalaureate (often) remains necessary but constitutes only one factor in a c.v. with requirements varying from one stream to another.

The democratisation of access to higher education has been favoured by the increase in the proportion of a generation taking the baccalaureate, but cannot be assessed from this demographic angle only: the guidance and selection mechanisms throughout schooling from the 'dividing primary school' (Baudelot/Establet, 1975) onwards, make the likelihood of reaching the baccalaureate very unequal for the various social categories (Lamoure, 1989; Breillot, 1981).

---

4   There is a gap between theory and practice in registration; in theory, choices are much more
        open than they are in practice for some students.

On top of the social inequalities are those of gender. Since the late 1960s, more girls have gone for the baccalaureate, and taken it, in line with greater success in previous schooling: in 1987 they represented over 57 per cent of admissions to the general baccalaureate and over 54 per cent to the BTN (technical baccalaureate). But these better scholastic performances are in part cancelled out through choices in secondary education and then higher education. In the majority, girls are channelled into the literary series of the A baccalaureate (representing 82% of those admitted in 1987) or the tertiary specialities of the BTN and the G (administrative) and F8 (technical) baccalaureates, whereas they account for only one-third of C (scientific) baccalaureates. The range of post-baccalaureate study choices is correspondingly restricted (Lamoure, 1983).

The inequality of higher education choices according to baccalaureate series and the socially and sexually marked composition of each series are all effects of social reproduction. They allow the hypothesis to be made that educational and institutional mechanisms leading to scholastic marginalisation of certain population categories have effects beyond the baccalaureate both in access to the various higher education streams and during an educational career.

Internal Performance of Streams

While probability of entry to the various post-baccalaureate streams can be estimated by the value of the educational qualifications, with the most elitist guaranteeing entry to the most selective streams, it is not that each of them offers the same chances of success to all. The differentiated probabilities of success in post-baccalaureate education have to do not only with their specific detail of operation but also with the educational characteristics of students; they can be assessed in terms of both internal performance and external performance.

Generally, the performance rate for first-cycles preparing for the DEUG is below 50 per cent three years after the students enter university, but generally over 70 per cent in other streams in the closed sector, though with considerable differences according to the qualification aimed at. Selection on entry to closed-sector streams to some extent makes up for delayed selection for DEUG, more specifically in the first year. Following it, a quarter of students who entered university the year before give it up.

It is however hard to quantify more exactly the influence of selectivity on entry to closed sector streams on end-of-course success; all that can be done is to stress the different ways selection operates. In closed streams, we have seen that it is largely done in terms of the baccalaureate series, to the relative benefit of general and scientific baccalaureates.

External Performance of Streams

Assessed in terms of conditions of access to the job market and/or of continued study, external performance differs considerably according to the main objective of each stream, essentially between those where the aim is continued study in a university second cycle and those with the main objective of preparing students for an occupation.

Any consideration as to openings for graduates from higher education must thus be qualified above all in relation to other level graduates, and here the conclusion is unappealable: for a student, every improvement in level of training has considerable repercussions on speed of securing a job, stability and pay. Assessed over the long term, it is even possible to state that 'for a dozen or so years, employment of students has resisted the employment crisis', even if developments can be different between one post-baccalaureate course and another (Charlot/Pottier, 1989).

Course Volume

In general terms, technological and scientific streams have a greater course volume than literary or social streams. According to stream, the volume varies by a factor of three for the same length of course. Course volume is generally higher in vocationalised streams, corresponding both to the technological training that has to be added to general education and to the actual form of the latter. STS and IUT students in industrial specialisations have the biggest burdens. This specific feature of courses in technological streams can be attributed both to the range of subjects taught and the greater share of applied work.

Altogether, IUT and STS streams offer a course volume ranging from 1800 to 2000 hours spread over two years, or 58 to 64 course weeks. STSA has about the same volume (over 1700 hours on average), thus confirming its similarity to the two foregoing streams, in particular STS.

The professional courses in the paramedical and social sectors have a lower total hourly volume, spread over three years: this is made up for in part by much longer traineeships, sometimes representing the same volume as the theoretical courses. It is therefore hard to compare these courses in detail: at most it can be said that all the vocationalised streams are characterised by a course-hour volume well above that of general university teaching streams.

Future Developments

Developments in existing institutional structures, pedagogical methods and contents, as well as collective and individual actors, are largely dependent both on pressure of educational demand, whether emanating from families or part of education promotion programmes, or of demand for qualifications by various economic sectors. The assumption of two million students by the year 2000 calls for redefinition of the tasks of the various streams of post-baccalaureate education, their methods of recruitment and modes of internal operation, as well as their inter-relationships.[5]

While the low performance rate of the DEUG is one of the stumbling blocks in the situation, there are others bound up with earlier options taken by holders of the various baccalaureates and the specific regulatory modes of each stream, and also with the geographical distribution of training on offer.[6] More than the production of scenarios (from the 'catastrophic' to the acceptable and desirable, as the fashion requires), it is the possible alternative to these various problems that should enable the future development of post-baccalaureate teaching to be forecast.

In view of their marked independence, it seems hard to include the colleges coming under the Ministry of Health or the courses of preparation for the BTSA in this perspective. The latter are planned to double intake capacity by the year 2000, which will certainly entail the setting up of a fine-tuning process with similar STSs or DUTs, or with second-cycle diplomas (notably certain applied biology MSTs, a Masters in science and technology) that come within the same professional sector. This is a (simple) matter of simultaneous national and regional co-ordination which, given the close parallelism between courses of the Ministry of Agriculture and the Ministry of Education, would not seem to raise particular difficulties.

---

5   'Two million students by the year 2000, why, how?'; colloquium of the conference of university
      principals, May 1987, Paris V.

6   Plus an unknown factor, namely the share and role of the private sector, on which there is no
      information available.

The situation is somewhat different for colleges under the Ministry of Health, which because of the weight of the private sector (whether profit-making or otherwise), and the close links with vocational organisations, particularly in specialised paramedical colleges, would seem able really to develop only under pressure from a 'Europe of qualifications' that would bring in competition. If this were effective, it would certainly compel redefinition not only of the content of training but also of the present implementing conditions of the *numerus clausus* on entry into these streams.

Changes in Demand

A consideration of the recent past reveals how demand for entry to higher education is closely linked to developments in secondary schooling and access to the baccalaureate, both in turn depending on demographic phenomena, on social demand for education and on voluntarist educational policies applied. Thus, the 'deficit generations' at college between 1985 and 1990 will to some extent slow down the advance of registrations recorded since 1985 in high schools. But demographic fluctuations have direct effects at the level of compulsory schooling, and are mediated beyond it by growing social demand for education, which nothing suggests will flag: it directly affects numbers in the first years of higher education. We may recall that the proportion of those taking a baccalaureate has advanced rapidly, from 28.6 per cent in 1984 to 39 per cent in 1989.

The education policies of the 1980s have been an incentive to the extension of schooling until the baccalaureate and beyond. One of the main objectives of these policies – which have conditioned the development of both high schools and post-baccalaureate courses – is for 74 per cent of a generation to reach level IV of education (Esquieu, 1988). Looking at the results of surveys done on young people and their families and at models of job growth through to the year 2000, achievement of this objective is where the expectations of all schools by all social actors come together.[7] Thus for 63 per cent of families surveyed, extension of studies beyond compulsory schooling appeared 'normal' beyond the age of 18, and among young people surveyed, 70 per cent regarded the baccalaureate as an 'essential stage': ten years ago, the figure was only 57 per cent.

This 'reversal of industrial demography' can manifestly come about only through a rise in the educational level of the majority of pupils, reflected in the estimates of the High Committee on Education and the Economy (HCEE) for developments in levels on leaving education.

On the basis of these forecasts, the Education Ministry assumes faster improvement in performance of the education system at secondary level and reduction in regional educational differences. Achieving this prospect, which would entail 1,700,000 pupils in high schools by the year 2000 as against less than 1,300,000 at present, would thus largely compensate for the decline in numbers because of previously mentioned demographic changes: the effect on numbers of baccalaureate takers would be large, with the estimated 470,000 baccalaureate takers in 2000 representing 1.8 times the number for 1986.

---

7   Les niveaux de formation l'an 2000: les besoins des utilisateurs, des éléments de réponse pour l'éducation nationale; HCEE BIPE, June 1987.

Consequences at Baccalaureate Level

Prospects at this level are much more complex to define than in the relatively stand-ardised framework of secondary education, particularly as regards links between expansion of the various baccalaureate streams and the specific regulatory modes for each stream in higher education.

In the short term (1991–92) the developmental trend in post-baccalaureate streams should show:

- a moderate increase (from 1.5% to 3%) in university and IUT numbers, unless there is considerable expansion in the latter's intake capacity or else a one-year extension of their courses as hoped by their directors;
- stabilisation of CPGE numbers (annual increase around 2%), after the heavy advance in recent years;
- continued growth in STS numbers (approximately 10% per year), due largely to expansion in the authorised private sector, with STSAs doubling present numbers;
- probable stability in numbers in paramedical and social streams, unless *numerus clausus* rules are radically changed.

These strictly trend-based forecasts cannot be extended further, nor in particular be used for long-term forecasts, since the size and composition of the pool of baccalaureate holders is due for rapid change.

Given the marked inclination by general baccalaureate takers to continue to higher education, increases in their numbers will be reflected on entry to higher education, without losses. For holders of technical baccalaureates, it may be expected that the heavy growth in continued study noted in recent years will continue. It remains to be seen whether more will be admitted to short-term higher education or will continue to enter universities in the same proportions, as a 'last chance' solution. The remaining unknown is the behaviour of the 'new baccalaureates', those holding a vocational baccalaureate aimed at direct entry to employment, where first cohorts of takers have shown a not inconsiderable tendency to continue to higher study, as their baccalaureate title legally permits them to: at least 18 per cent of the first cohort advanced, half to STS, but others to IUT and even university.[8]

In total, numbers of students in higher education would be around 1,800,000 by the year 2000, up 55 per cent from 1986, but slightly less in universities (1,303,000 students in 2000, up 46%), and still less in CPGE (67,000 students, up 39%). The increase would be faster than average in IUT and particularly STS (up 57% and 128% respectively). While IUT and STS growth was not based on any particular change in form of course (duration of study), the main assumption in this model is creation of a new short, specialised stream enabling a qualification on leaving two years after baccalaureate, to improve the internal performance of university first cycle. The findings of the model give the following breakdown of numbers:

Changes in University First Cycles

The performance improvement postulated in the objective of increasing the number of those taking baccalaureate and post-baccalaureate qualifications does call for satisfac-

---

8   'The vocational baccalaureate 1986–7': Information Note 88.03, DEP/MEN, 1988. A survey done by Le Monde de l'éducation (February 1988) indicates a high rate of continued study (33%) because of the later survey date.

tory solutions to be given to some problems having to do with the conditions for implementing it.

What are the conceivable solutions? One scenario consists in diverting part of the flow of new baccalaureate holders to short-term higher education, IUT and particularly STS. But these streams have adopted entry selection rules that favour general baccalaureate holders over technical ones. It is therefore clear that bringing about diversion of flows of these streams presupposes above all a change in their present mode of regulation: abandonment or at least flexibilisation of entry selection, hard to conceive given their intake capacities, or explicit definition of a quota system by type of baccalaureate and disciplines to be pursued by those concerned: this solution would have every likelihood of ending in failure if imposed, and of little result if left up to the institutions.

Table 1: Growth in numbers by stream

Year	1986	1990	1995	2000	change 1986–2000
University	895,000	1,049,000	1,183,000	1,303,000	+ 45,5%1
short stream	–	164,000	190,000	212,000	–
long stream	–	885,000	993,000	1,091,000	–
Engineers	27,000	31,000	35,000	40,000	+ 48%
(university engineers)	(13,000)	(16,000)	(20,000)	(24,000)	
CPGE	49,000	56,000	62,000	68,000	+ 39%
IUT	63,000	74,000	87,000	99,000	+ 57%
STS	130,000	186,000	251,000	296,000	+128%
Total	1,164,000	1,396,000	1,618,000	1,806,000	+55%

University Outposts

The creation of 'delocalisations' or university outposts – extension of training on offer at local level – is based on the principle of bringing supply closer to demand. It is supposed to enable both absorption of additional flows of students and democratisation of access to higher education, so as to allow broader access to children of less-favoured social groups (Lamoure Rontopoulou, 1990).

University outposts are in general the issue of a university to which they are attached, and provide only first-cycle education. Their creation results from collaboration between the university and local authorities (town councils, chambers of commerce and industry, vocational trade unions) of the town where they are located, and of joint provision of the funds necessary for their operation. The present university outposts go back to the university colleges of the 1960s, which provided first-cycle education, since the universities were at the time facing the same problem of absorbing growing demand for higher education. These university colleges have been progressively transformed – with more or less success – into universities, often thanks to pressure of an electoral nature.

There are at present two types of outpost, the 'official delocalisations' and the 'wildcats'. The former, recognised by the Education Ministry, were set up on the basis of an agreement between the mother university and the Ministry, with the latter supplying the necessary teaching posts and staff. They number some 15, located essentially in the North and the Paris region. The second category brings together all those not recognised by the Ministry and therefore not in receipt of any financing from central administration; they have been created on the basis of an agreement with the mother university and local authorities, which customarily supply premises and non-teaching personnel, with the university allotting teachers and providing in various ways for the organisation of courses and examinations. At present there are some 50 outposts of this second type.

In the present context of increases in numbers of baccalaureate takers, extending the education on offer so as to be able to meet the demand from the least well-off groups seems inevitable. But while, for a university, developing outposts may mean diversification and an increase in its 'centres of excellence' particularly in the context of mass education, the operation of many of the delocalisations in existence tends to suggest that this is not the general rule.

Thus there are certainly positive aspects for a large number of young people represented by the possibility of approaching university education, and the more encouraging examination results recorded in outposts. However, it seems that there are three main burdens on their destiny and that of the students who enter them: the fact that teachers come from outside, the absence of diversification of courses, and the educational and social composition of their public.

The 'two-speed' university is not entirely a fiction: the number of 'wildcat' outposts is steadily increasing, while the political regulatory framework for them is not yet very assured.

Conclusion: The Rules of the Game

The range of higher education has considerably changed over two decades, but innovations have essentially related to the levels in the system least affected by the increase in student population, the second and third cycles. Whatever the assumptions made, higher education must in the next few years cope with a pressure of demand that will be higher than at present and no longer permit shilly-shallying: comprehensive regulation and restructuring of higher education has become inescapable.

Solutions being contemplated to reach that with some minimal concern for social equity meet with great risks of unintended effects, resulting from the absence of fluidity in all components of the system: from the rigidity of secondary schooling streams to guidance systems, the complexity and compartmentalisation of institutional structures, and the frequently contradictory strategies of the actors involved: it does not seem that there is (if there ever was) any 'miracle' solution.

The policies at present being applied through 'concerted development schemes for post-baccalaureate education' – a sort of regional education plans – and through multi-year contracts between central government and each university, seem to be inspired by a pragmatic principle of transferring part of the initiative and the responsibilities to the level of local actors. That might be a possible framework for a structuring of post-baccalaureate education to correspond with local demand for education, while not pre-empting national growth objectives.

Education systems are, however, governed by their own logic, which is an expression of a system's historical development and of socially accepted values: the confrontation between this logic and an environment that is now once and for all European will decide the effectiveness also of French higher education.

References:
Baudelot and Establet (1975) *L'école primaire divise*. Paris: Maspero.

Bourdieu (1985) *Epreuve scolaire et consécration sociale. Actes de la Recherche en Sciences Sociales.*

Breillot, S. (1981) *Evolution des probabilités d'accès au baccalauréat selon la catégorie sociale d'origine, 1962–1976.* Etudes et Documents 81.2 SEIS/MEN.

Cerych, L. and P. Sabatier (1986) *Great Expectations and Mixed Performances. The Implementation of Higher Education Reforms in Europe.* Institut d'Education et de Politique Sociale. Trentham Books.

Charlot, A. and F. Pottier (1989) Dix ans d'insertion des diplomés universitaires. *Formation Emploi* No. 25, January–March.

Esquieu, P. (1988) *Evolution des effectifs scolarisés dans le second degré dans le cadre du plan pour l'avenir de l'éducation nationale: hypothèse PRO 74.* Information Note No 88.11, DEP/MEN.

Esquieu, P. (1989) Les progès de scolarisation, allongement des études et accès croissant au lycée. *Education et Formations* No 19 April–June.

Guillon, R. (1979) *Enseignement et organisation du travail du XIXème siècle à nos jours.* La documentation française.

Jallade, J.P. (1989–1990) *Les premières années d'enseignement supérieur dans la perspective de 1993.* Paris: European Institute of Education and Social Policy.

Lamoure, J. (1981) *Les instituts de Technologie en France.* Institut d'Education, Fondation Européene de la Culture.

Lamoure, J. (1983) *Enseignement universitaire, orientation et scolarisation des étudiantes.* Education et Formations No 2.

Lamoure, J. (1989) *Les mentions au baccalauréat.* Information note DEP/MEN, March.

Lamoure Rontopoulou, J. (1990) 'L'Université 1968–88: une institution en mutation'. *Revue Francaise de Pédagogie*, January.

Legoux, Y. (1972) *Du compagnon au technicien; l'école Diderot et l'évolution des qualifications 1873–1972.* Techniques et vulgarisation. Paris.

National University Assessment Committee (1987) Où va l'Université? Report by the National University Assessment Committee. Paris.

CHAPTER 5

Moving Towards Institutional Differentiation
The Italian Case

Roberto Moscati

Major Structural Features of the Italian Higher Education System

Since the unification of the country in 1860, education has been conceived in Italy as one of the most important tools to unify, socially and culturally, different regions and populations with very specific backgrounds. For this reason, the system of education has been kept mostly public and centralised. The new nation had to face from the very beginning two contradictory problems: on the one hand, the need to keep up with the economic development (i.e. the industrialisation process) in the other European countries, which required a fairly large labour force, with different degrees of skill and professional qualification; on the other hand, because of the very low development of large areas of the country the entire supply of labour force could not be absorbed. People from all social strata (but especially from the growing petty bourgeoisie), using education and professional training in order to avoid unemployment, created a surplus of degree-holders on the labour market.

Since then, the system of education in Italy had to face the alternative of either being too open – in order to meet the demand for education, thus creating highly qualified unemployment – or of being too tight and devoted to elite reproduction (but then preventing social mobility through education). Access to higher education was affected by different government choices at any given time.

A comprehensive reform of the entire system of education was introduced in 1923 with the aims 1. of differentiating channels at secondary level in order to separate professionalising tracks (technical and vocational schools) from pre-university tracks (*lycée*), and 2. of allowing admission to university to all pupils coming from the *lycée* without any sort of entrance examination or *numerus clausus*.

After that reform, the system of education has been maintained without major changes until the early 1960s, when the social demand for higher education became strong enough to induce the Government to open the doors of the university to all students coming from a five-year upper-secondary school of any kind. This unlimited admission to university was supposed to be followed by a reform of upper-secondary school which, however, never occurred.

On a formal level, the increasing demand for higher education has produced a number of changes, more in quantitative terms (i.e. new universities have been opened) than in qualitative terms (reforms of upper-secondary schools and consequently of the university, as in many other countries). On an informal level, nevertheless, the pressure of the demand coming from different secondary schools has introduced some 'spontaneous' changes in the actual working of the university, which will be described later.

From the supply side, there were 41 universities in 29 locations in 1960, whilst at present there are 63 institutions located in 48 different cities. Unfortunately, the distribution of students among different universities (being completely left to individual choice and indirectly to the market) is very unbalanced: about 55 per cent of total enrolment is concentrated in 9 institutions with an average of 66,000 students per university, while the other 54 universities have an average enrolment of 11,000. In the same period, teaching and research personnel has grown from 37,976 to 51,292 units.

From the demand side, the number of university students grew from 268,181 in the academic year 1960–61 to 681,731 in 1970–71 and to 1,047,874 in 1980–81, remaining more or less stable since then (1,154,646 in 1987–88). (Table 1)

The ratio of students enrolled in the first year out of those graduated from the upper-secondary schools went up during the 1960s but then dropped constantly for about 20 years. The same trend, which shows a peak in the 1970s due to growing demand and the open door policy, cannot be found in terms of numbers of university graduates. At the same time, the ratio university graduates/university students has been surprisingly declining (Table 1).

Table 1: General trend of university population in Italy: 1960–1987

Academic years	A	B	C	D	E
1960–61	59,708	268,181	21,886	61.3	8.2
1970–71	194,280	681,731	56,414	85.8	8.3
1980–81	244,071	1,047,831	74,118	74.2	7.1
1986–87	246,942	1,085,900	75,810	64.9	7.0
1987–88	258,837	1,154,646	80,974	67.5	7.0

Note: A – 1st year enrolment; B – overall students population; C – Degrees awarded; D – ratio of first-year enrolled over upper-secondary output ('diploma' holders); E – ratio of degree-holders over total enrolment in the university.

Source: ISTAT elab. CENSIS

If this indicator is multiplied by the average length of university curricula (estimated at 4.8 years), only one-third of first year students (freshmen) appear to be able to complete all requirements and get the degree. In the last decade, first year enrolment in the university (all departments) has been stable around 250,000 students, as the total amount of degrees awarded varied between 70,000 and 75,000 per year. The productivity of the university system is evidently very low, and there is also a problem of self-selection which has to be considered. Since 1960, the number of drop-outs in the university grew constantly and faster than the number of graduates (Table 2).

It is also worth noting that the same trend has been followed by a similar tendency at the upper-secondary level (where drop-out rates went up from 5.8 per cent to 23.3% of the total enrolment in the same period). The picture becomes darker if the rate of those university students who are officially behind with their studies (27.8% in 1986–87) is taken into consideration: a typical characteristic of the Italian university is the individual pacing of university studies.

Looking at the university input-output details, we see that 45 per cent of first year students still come from the *lycée*, whilst the others are from technical and vocational schools. As far as the distribution of enrolment is concerned, in recent years enrolments in economics, political science, and engineering show a substantial increase, while there is a parallel decline of enrolments in medicine, agricultural sciences and humanities. These changes are in part due to the labour market situation, but they do not seem to show a stable trend. The variations of the demand for higher education are not directed by a structured system of counselling and/or by a supply side policy. The only stable indications resulting from the enrolment trends are related 1. to the decline of medicine (the traditional field of studies for the elite due to reasons of social and professional prestige), a declining trend which started long before the introduction of the *numerus clausus*, a measure still affecting only this field of studies; and 2. to the relatively low percentage of enrolments and degrees in engineering and sciences that still represent together no more than 26.0 per cent of the total enrolment and less than 21,000 degrees awarded out of 77,869 in 1987. As a matter of comparison it is worth noting that medicine now produces 17.8 per cent of the degree-holders each year, whilst economics counts for 10.7 per cent, law for 12.3 per cent, humanities (including schools of education) for 20.0 per cent.

Table 2: Drop-outs and degrees awarded in several years: 1960–1985

Academic years	A Drop outs	B Graduates	A/B percentage
1960–61	19,078	20,842	91.5
1970–71	60,614	47,520	127.5
1980–81	157,218	74,118	212.5
1984–85	150,000	72,148	207.9
1985–86	150,000	76,000	197.4

Source: CENSIS, 1988.

In general, the level of education among the labour force shows a steady growth. In 1987, 32.8 per cent of the total labour force (including employed and unemployed) had at most the elementary degree; 37.0 per cent the compulsory school degree (eight years of schooling); 24.0 per cent hold an upper-secondary school diploma and 6.2 per cent an university degree (*laurea*) (Rey, 1988; Censis, 1987; Moscati, 1983).

Relationship between Higher Education and Research

Italian universities exercise a key role in the domain of scientific research. About 20 per cent of the total amount of R&D (Research and Development) funds go to universities, as compared to 13.4 per cent in the United States, 16.8 per cent in the Federal Republic of Germany, 15.8 per cent in France, and 14.0 per cent in the UK (OECD, 1986). In terms of financial support, universities receive 16.4 per cent of the total amount devoted to research both, by public sources (central and regional administration of the State), and by private sources (industries), which means the larger amount of money in the public sector. For years, scientific research has been largely neglected in Italy: until 1980, the percentage of GNP devoted to R&D has been less than 1 per cent (it had been kept at the level of 0.8% for the entire 1970s). During the last years, in contrast, efforts to keep up with other European countries have been significant. In 1987, the ratio has been of 1.45 per cent, which meant an increase in the expenses for research at a rate of 11 per cent per year between 1980 and 1987 (in real terms), whilst the increase of the GNP was 1.6 per cent per year between 1980 and 1985; then the ratio was 2.7 per cent in 1986, and 3.4 per cent in 1987. The official goal is to reach a ratio of 3 per cent, although the possibility of another increase is severely jeopardised by the deficit of the State budget.

Of all public funds given to universities (which are almost totally founded by public money), 24.6 per cent is devoted to scientific research, mostly pure research. Applied research in the public sector is basically carried out by public institutions like CNR (National Centre for Research) and ENEA, which are supposed to co-operate with the university. Traditionally, universities had problems in collaborating with other institutions, and only recently a growing number of joint ventures has been established with CNR and also with public and private corporations (as is well known, there is a very important public and semi-public sector in the Italian economy).

It is important to notice however, that these new ways of establishing links between universities and research institutions have been pursued by individual universities and individual corporations as a way of using the degrees of independence and autonomy formally available, but almost never encouraged by central State administration, nor by the local bureaucracy of a single university. Nowadays, these new examples of cooperation are symbols of a new attitude of the university milieu *vis-à-vis* the external world, and all relationships with industry and other research institutions are changing in practical terms (although we are still waiting for an official recognition of the process). In this light, the role of public research institutions like the CNR is becoming a crucial link between universities and corporations. Still, in Italy the real problem of scientific research remains the lack of trained personnel: the number of researchers has never been impressive (the total amount was 61,000 in 1967 and 118,000 in 1985). The stop of recruitment of staff in the public sectors (due to fiscal problems) leads to a continuous rise of the researchers' average age, and there are only vague possibilities of employing new personnel in the near future at the rate needed, in order to keep up with European standards. Costs of financing the recruitment and training of new researchers make the target of 15,000 new people in five years very unlikely (the most recent report to the government suggests that 50,000 are needed in the same period of time). As for the university, it seems that not enough graduates are produced and very few researchers are hired. (CNR, 1987; Capovani/Paolicchi, 1986).

Major Changes of the Italian Higher Education System in Recent Years
To analyse the situation of higher education in recent years it is worth revising the basic characteristics of the Italian university. Since the unification of the country, universities have been under the direction of the Ministry of Education according to the centralised structure of the system of education, which is similar to the French and German school systems, although with some peculiar differences. Like the French system, the ruling class tried by means of national legislation and national administration to establish detailed policies and procedures for the system of education at different levels. Thus, the university structure took the shape of a pyramid, composed, from the top down of 1. the Minister of Education, with an advisory group of academics called 'Superior Council of Instruction', later renamed 'National University Council' (CUN); 2. the Division of Higher Education within the Ministry, headed by a bureau chief and consisting of ten staff sections; 3. university rectors, serving as chief campus officers, and the administrative directors, serving as chief business officers; 4. deans of the faculties; 5. chairholding professors and institute directors; 6. several levels of non-tenured professors and assistants. This organisational structure linked the central power at the State level directly to any single university scattered all over the country.

The Italian system of universities which was valid at least until the early 1980s was based on a national agency created with the aim of co-ordinating all universities through a large body of laws and rules. This agency was unable to operate effectively in a bureaucratic manner due to the internal fragmentation of control and the weak techniques of integration. The result was a sort of balkanisation as a consequence of a combination of bureaucratic overstructure with guild understructure, which – according to Burton Clark's view – had helped strengthening the hegemony of the chair professors.

This peculiar form of a fragmented bureaucratic and centralised structure lasted – with some minor changes and a lot of debate on the need for change – until 1980. In that year a reform law was introduced. The Presidential Decree dated July 2, 1980 No 382, entitled 'Reorganisation of University Teaching, of related Training as well as Experimentation with new Types of Organisation and Didactics', introduced a number of relevant innovations within the general philosophy of a higher education open to the masses and not limited to the elite:

The first innovation concerns scientific research. A new fund for research has been created for projects at both local and national level, to which all members of the professoriate can apply to. This fund is added to those of the National Centre for Research (CNR) and is supposed to stimulate joint projects among different universities.

Introduction of departments. This collective (horizontal) structure goes against the vertical organisation of power and the individual structure of academic activities (both research and teaching) represented in Italy by the holding of a 'chair'. In addition, the introduction of departments is badly needed for an adequate response to the development of knowledge in different fields and in order to supply expertise to the economy.

As mentioned before, economic change is also a reason for diversification in levels of curricula and degrees. In addition to the traditional unified level leading to the *laurea*, the law introduces a higher level: the 'research doctorate', which is similar to the Ph.D. at American universities. There exist a limited number of places for students who want to pursue an academic career through seminars and independent research, very often carried out by a co-ordinated group of universities.

In the same spirit – it is worth remembering – a new kind of 'schools for special purposes' was created (in 1982). Their task is to train middle level professionals, such as nurses in the medical field, who previously required only secondary level instruction for their work. These courses – lasting two years – were suggested to the government by the proliferation of private schools for any sort of 'new professions', and are thus introducing the possibility of short-cycle professionalised instruction at university level.

The need to adapt the university to the diversification of the professions is also reflected in increased teaching activities of 'experts' form different fields who are not primarily involved in a university career. This is also a basic change of the old conception of the university as an independent, autonomous, self-sufficient structure. Similarly, a trend towards closer connections between universities and the outside world has involved the signing of new research contracts, engaging universities in consultation activities for private and public customers. Finally, there is a new possibility for universities to sell educational opportunities to non-traditional students for re-training purposes and/or life-long education activities.

All these innovations – much more than the main aim of regularising faculty members' careers – represent an overall change in the working of the university in Italy, in an effort to give back some relevance to its role in a changing society.

After ten years, the law passed in 1980 has, however, had only a limited impact on university life, both because of the strong resistance against any sort of change coming from academia, and as a consequence of the compromise between conservative and progressive forces which has been at the origin of the law in parliament.

Direction of the Present Development: Differentiation of the Higher Education System
In recent times a new wave of change has occurred which might introduce some real structural modifications in the higher education system. Three projects of reform have been presented to Parliament, two of which have already been passed, whilst one is now under discussion. For an otherwise conservative system this is a peculiar phenomenon.

The new season of reform projects began in mid-1987 with the programme of the new national government which provided also for the creation of a Ministry of University and Scientific Research, i.e. the transfer of the section of the Ministry of Education devoted to the university, to the Ministry of Scientific Research. This project had to be justified by the government and debated by political forces in relation to a crucial point: the autonomy of the university. Almost at the same time, a parallel discussion started out concerning the reform of university curricula. These three issues eventually became intertwined in a general debate over the direction university reform ought to take. The main aspects of this debate were the following:

The creation of the new Ministry of University and Scientific Research has been hailed as a way to unify all programmes of scientific research supported by public authorities, and to maximise the efficiency and productivity of the country in several fields where international competition is tough and challenging. Among its supporters are those who believe the university has to be more closely connected to the economy and to society in general, and – at the same time – those who believe that teaching activities can benefit from close contact with research. Among its detractors are those who fear that the appeal of research activities (not simply its financial attractiveness) will push university professors to neglect teaching duties. Others suspect that the separation between secondary and tertiary levels of education will also damage the former (especially with respect to teacher training), and that an excessive openness toward the economy will increase university involvement in applied research at the expense of pure academic research.

The independence of and the right of self-government for all universities is expressly laid down in the Italian constitution but does not exist in practice. All details of organisation are imposed uniformly by the central authority, not only by means of law and regulations, but also via circulars and replies to requests through which the Ministry makes known its own interpretations of the laws in force.

In recent debates, supporters of the autonomy of the total university system *vis-à-vis* the patronage (and control) of the Ministry of Education have clashed with those who are more concerned with the autonomy of the individual university. The former position aims at reducing differences (and avoiding new differentiations) among universities which are already uneven for many, mainly historical, reasons; the latter is more concerned with connecting the university to the real world. The first position is supported by those political forces which are more inclined to believe that public services should and could be improved, while remaining public and providing *ad hoc* services in order to reduce differences among the representatives of demand. The other position believes in competition and the free market, in order to improve services (including higher education).

The reform of university curricula again represents an area in which two different positions confront each other in a comprehensive struggle between conservative and progressive forces.

The conservative position is represented by the attitude taken by all the commissions for curricula reform created by the former Ministry of Education, and carried out by the deans of different 'faculties' (departments). The general approach to reform and modernise university studies has been characterised by an increase in the length of studies (almost all moving from four to five years), and by an elimination of subjects not strictly belonging to the specific field in question. This led to a cut of the links between similar or related fields, but not to move specialisation in professional terms, since the large majority of professors is against a professionalised university.

The progressive position is represented by those supporting a growing flexibility of the curricula, basically through 1. the introduction of short-cycles and in general a differentiation of possible university tracks, allowing – among other things – for the participation of adults in projects of recurrent education, and 2. the right of individual universities to emphasise a specific field of studies and to give it a specific structure.

Short-cycles are basically opposed – at a political level – on the ground that they will become a second-rate kind of studies, penalising those who will attend them. Inside the university the same position comes from the professors who fear they will end up teaching in second-class institutions. All these positions pay little attention to the situation of the university in foreign countries, and to the needs of professionals which can be seen by looking at the labour market.

Problems and Contradictions
Under these circumstances, the real alternative (and the growing debate) is between those who want to keep the short cycles inside the university (to reinforce the possibility for students to pursue their studies after the first degree), and those who prefer to let the short cycles develop outside the university in order to be closer to the needs of the economy and – at the same time – to protect the teaching and the research quality of the university from labour market pressures.

Professional Courses at Post-Degree Level and the Introduction of the Short Cycle
A similar alternative affects the growing need for professional courses at post-degree (*laurea*) level. The accelerated development of professional courses at university level (mainly involving people holding the traditional degree: *laurea*, i.e. 'master's') affects an increasing number of professional figures. Still, the large majority of these initiatives is related to managerial training. The origins of these courses for managers' training go back to the 1950s, and have been an example of the remedial role played by a private initiative in a situation where the public system of higher education did not consider the creation of Schools of Business Administration. Only in the 1980s, due to the restructuring and modernisation of the economy, did Schools of Business Administration begin to emerge.

Since these courses are not recognised by the State, and consequently do not provide degrees with legal value, only a few universities now have a special section for business administration, mostly departments of engineering and departments of economics in private universities. The large majority of these courses instead are offered by private *ad hoc* institutes, which rise up rapidly and from different sources. The need to establish some common standards of quality is now felt as crucial to control the phenomenon. Thus, the public university system still refuses to soften the traditional resistance to applied knowledge. This is more an opposition coming from the academic milieu than from the government, which, in contrast, subsidises programmes of Masters in Business Administration with special aids for the development of the Southern regions. The general picture that appears is that of a dual system that will progressively be reinforced at this level.

Meanwhile the law on curricula has been passed and the discussions are now related to its implementation. The basic points of the law are the following: 1. short cycles are introduced inside the university and that will allow students to transfer to long tracks (and to change from the latter to the former too); 2. universities have the duty to train elementary school teachers (in new specific courses with new curricula) and secondary school teachers (through a special post-degree one year course of specialisation); 3. new teaching duties are introduced, including student counselling, tutorials and special courses for professionals; 4. researchers are allowed to replace professors in formal teaching activities and to become responsible for courses; 5. professors can be attached to a department and affiliated to a scientific area, instead of being connected with a specific course and a 'chair'.

Furthermore, in the same law the National University Council (CUN) has been modified, including now among its members students, administration members and rectors, in order to combine representation of scientific disciplines with delegations from general university staff (for the first time also giving some room to local interests in accordance with the new autonomy of the individual university structures). The actual role of the CUN will be crucial in determining in practical terms the degrees of freedom and the independence of universities *vis-à-vis* the Ministry and its traditional bureaucratic control. At the moment the CUN simply operates as a consulting agency for the Ministry, but it will become a crucial body operating as a buffer between the government and the university system provided the latter will ever enjoy real independence from central political power.

Public-Private Dilemma: Research Activities

A similar dilemma between public and private sectors affects the development of research activities *vis-à-vis* the system of higher education. As noticed above, a traditional division has kept pure research inside and applied research outside the university. The latter has been carried out by research institutes and centres supported by public money (CNR, ENEA, INFIN and others). The main private and public industrial corporations (FIAT, Olivetti, IRI, ENI) have slightly enlarged their participation in research activities in recent years, also thanks to substantial incentives coming from the government. The problem has an important impact at individual level, affecting – as in other countries – the role and activities of academics. In recent years, more and more research opportunities for university professors have come up at various levels. Many of these opportunities come now from outside the university milieu, as the need for expertise and knowledge application grows in several economic and cultural domains. The result, because of lack of time, is a decline of teaching quality and a growth of students' protest. In this respect, problems are similar in Italy to those in other countries. They are reinforced by the law which formally forbids younger members of the professoriate (the researchers) to teach on a regular basis.

Geographical problems

The combination of teaching and research activities also has a geographical implication (Table 3). On the one hand, a growing demand for individual expertise in different fields of knowledge develops in the major cities and keeps professors and researchers involved where the 'market' is most rewarding. Thus, a growing number of university professors spend a large part of their time far from their universities. On the other hand, the social and economic demand on universities for expertise and research consultancy is mostly visible in the economic core of the country (basically in the same places where the demand for individual competence rises). As a consequence, some specific departments in large universities are very efficient and of top quality (engineering in Milan and Turin, physics in Rome), while very few high quality departments can be found in universities in other parts of the country. From this point of view, it is worth noticing that the university has not contributed substantially to the development of the poor areas of the country, with the exception of awarding a number of degrees.

Table 3: Basic indicators of the university system academic year 1989–1990

Indicators	absolute values		percentages	
	Centre-North	South	Centre-North	South
Population 20–24(values in 000)	2,910	1,878	60.8	39.2
Structures Universities	37	20	64.9	35.1
Faculties	237	128	64.9	35.1
Personnel Full professors	9,058	3,590	71.6	28.4
Associate professors	10,593	4,854	68.6	31.4
Researchers	8,881	4,469	66.5	33.5
Technical Administrators	27,103	20,008	57.5	42.5
Students Total (000)	871	420	67.4	32.6
Freshmen (000)	196	91	68.2	31.8
Enrolment variation (1985–1990)	35,525	11,221	24.4	12.2
On schedule	613	284	68.3	31.7
Behind schedule	258	136	65.5	34.5
Degree owners	58,657	29,057	66.9	33.1
Third level degree (places 1987–88)	2,151	762	73.8	26.2
PhDs awarded	1,196	300	79.9	20.1

Source: ISTAT and the Ministry of the University

Since an informal ranking of universities has been established as a consequence of the concentration of certain quality components (teachers, researchers, and facilities) in central parts of the country (mostly the Northern regions), students from the South have also been pushed to prefer these universities located in far away areas. In general, students who move to a better university are successful students (those who are aware of the difference among the universities, and are looking for a qualified training even if it will be at high cost in terms of various inconveniences. The result is that the quality of universities in the South, and in peripheral areas in general, declines sharply, while the universities in central regions get overcrowded and also lose their traditional level of quality (Table 4, Table 5).

Table 4: Indicators of university composition by geographical area (1989–1990)

Areas	A	B	C	D	E	F
North-West	17.5	17.3	34.9	3.2	45.9	73.0
North-East	18.4	16.1	25.3	2.3	37.0	83.7
Centre	27.4	22.5	31.8	2.6	51.3	120.2
South	14.3	18.7	37.5	3.0	51.8	155.7
Southern Islands (Sicily and Sardinia)	18.6	18.4	31.7	2.8	47.5	113.7

A – Students enrolled on schedule by 100 inhabitants of 20–24 years of age
B – Students resident in the area enrolled on schedule by 100 inhabitants (age 20–24)
C – Students on schedule in local universities by professor
D – Degree-holders in local universities by professors
E – Researcher by 100 professors
F – Technical and Administrative personnel by 100 professors and researchers

Table 5: Ratio between students on schedule and students residing in the area (year 1989–1990)

	Centre-North	South	Total
Students on schedule	603,049	286,294	889,343
Residents (among them)	466,305	253,877	720,182
Ration between residents and students on schedule	77.3	88.7	81.0

Source: ISTAT and the Ministry of the University.

The last question brings up the alternative between a type of reform which allows the individual university the right to go to the market, and sell its expertise in competition with other institutions, thus forcing it to improve its quality; and one which, on the other hand, aims to produce a system of higher education which is public and open to the external world, and which tries to combine the rules of the market with those of public service.

A number of elements characterising the Italian situation make this last option more useful and (in theory) more feasible than the first one. More than anything else the traditional way of conceiving the university as a place of pure research and diffusion of culture, free from any specific interest of private groups (both, politically and economically) is still very much alive in academia and in large sections of society, too. The fact that this rule is constantly violated at individual level does not undermine the value of the abstract principle.

But a lot has to happen with regard to the political will of the major political forces and the entrepreneurial attitude of the university milieu, in order to run a single university, and the system as a whole with a managerial outlook. The growing influence of the European integration exercises an ever increasing pressure on the economy and the business world. The same cannot be said for the university milieu, which is not flexible enough to reorganise itself along the new rules of post-industrial society and its need for a general upgrading of the levels of education, since corporative privileges strongly resist any sort of real change. Thus, the process of keeping up with other leading countries, basically the European partners in the EC, will be longer and more complicated than the public expects, and will depend very much on which kind of coalition (socially and politically) will support the policy of European integration.

Development of a private sector

The same kind of political scenario will also influence the pace of the development of a private (and semi-private) sector, parallel to the existing public one at post-degree level of higher education. The need for a more flexible system of higher education may well lead to a dual system, represented by a public sector (the university), answering to social needs of equity and social opportunities, and by a private (and/or semi-public) one that is more market oriented. At present, this solution seems the only feasible way to modernise the system of higher education in Italy.

Final Observations

Historically, the isolation of the university has been more visible in Europe than in other parts of the Western world, like – for example – the USA. This attitude has been changing in the last decade, and some of the reforms experimented in the 1960s went precisely in this direction (one might mention the Norwegian Regional Colleges as a case in point).

In this respect, Italy is perhaps an exception, since no serious attempt has been made to go the same way. If we look at the Italian situation in a comparative perspective, we have to admit that the university is a conservative milieu which has been able to refuse the mass drive toward higher education, not even trying to experiment with some of the flexible models put at work in other countries. In fact, 1. no attempt has been made to create a comprehensive system of higher education, since the structure of upper-secondary schools with various tracks and different quality of education was kept alive, and the emphasis on selectivity at university is still characterised by a structure for judging more than for teaching; 2. no attempt has been made, either, to make education regionally relevant, and the gap between culturally rich and poor areas in the country has widened constantly; 3. nor has there been any attempt to develop any kind of short-cycle education; or 4. to vocationalise higher education (as has happened in many other countries) (Levin, 1978; Cerych/Sabatier, 1986).

The general impression one can derive from multiple examples is that *academia* in Italy has been trying for decades to make the system work as if it was still intended for an elite, through an informal (although very effective) process of screening those students not culturally equipped for an elite institution. Political forces have pursued different ideological models, but did not address the social drive toward mass higher education, i.e. did not introduce real reforms or provide the university with the necessary structures and personnel. Economic forces found the limited level of productivity of the university system acceptable, in which one can detect islands of efficiency and of high quality in a sea of poor performances. So far this differentiation of quality – which can be observed in almost all fields – has kept the system of higher education in a sort of balanced situation.

Two crucial questions are worthy to be presented for the near future: for how long will this precarious equilibrium go on? And who pays (and will pay) the heavy price for the situation?

A progressive deterioration of the labour market (for medical doctors, in particular), and of the operational quality in the few 'happy islands' (like the departments of engineering and architecture in Milan and Turin), pushes toward severe and politically unpopular measures like the introduction of the *numerus clausus*.

Students living in less developed regions (mostly in the South), are more and more penalised because of the decline of peripheral universities. The rapidly growing polarisation between central and peripheral universities affects the quality of teaching and research activities both for internal and external reasons.

At the same time, the delay of the public system of higher education in answering to the new demands of skill and expertise has created new possibilities for the private sector. Private initiatives of different level and quality have risen everywhere in order to fill the gap, especially between the upper-secondary level and the university degree (laurea), or after the university degree. Both kinds of initiatives are conceived in order to provide new opportunities of vocational training at tertiary level. Leaving aside any consideration on the different quality of the offered training, it is crucial to ensure that these institutions represent the answer to the need for a more flexible system of higher education, and – at the same time – demonstrate the growing direct relationship between the economy and the system of higher education.

Summarising, it seems that the Italian system of higher education is trying to keep up with its traditional partners in the international community. In this effort, the ways that can be chosen are very much affected by the struggle of different vested interests. It remains to be seen which coalition of interests and forces will have the power to direct the future trend of higher education.

References

Barbagli, M. (1982) *Education for Unemployment: Politics, Labour Markets and the School System – Italy, 1959–1973*. New York: Columbia University Press.

Bruno, S. et al (1983) *Le politiche dell'istruzione superiore negli anni '80: L'Italia in un contesto internazionale*. Roma: (unpublished report).

Bruno, S. et al (1989) *Università e istruzione superiore come risorse strategiche*. Milano: F. Angeli.

Capovani, M. and P. Paolicchi (1986) *Università ed enti di ricerca* in "Università Progetto", Nos 13–14, giugno–luglio, 21–26.

CENSIS (1988) *XXII Rapporto sulla situazione sociale del paese*. Roma.

Cerych, L. and P. Sabatier (1986) *Great Expectations and Mixed Performances*. Trentham: Trentham Books.

Clark, B.R. (1977) *Academic Power in Italy: Bureaucracy and Oligarchy in a National University System*. Chicago: The University of Chicago Press.

Consiglio Nazionale delle Ricerche-CNR (1987) *Relazione generale sullo stato della ricerca scientifica e tecnologica in Italia per l'anno 1986*. Roma.

Levin, M.H. (1978) 'The Dilemma of Comprehensive Secondary School Reforms in Western Europe' in *Comparative Education Review*, Vol 22 No 3, 434–451.

Luzzatto, G. (1988) 'The Debate on the University and the Reform Proposals in Italy' in *European Journal of Education*, Vol 23 No 3, 237–248.

Moscati, R. (1983) *Università: fine o trasformazione del mito?* Bologna: Il Mulino.

Moscati, R. (1985) 'Reflections on Higher Educationd the Polity in Italy', in *European Journal of Education*, Vol 20 No 2–3, 127–139.

OECD (1986) *Science and Technology Indicators*, No 2. Paris.

Paci, M. 'Education in Capitalist Labor Market', in Karabel, J. and A. Halsey (eds) *Power and Ideology Education*. New York: Oxford University Press, 340–355.

Rey, G.M. (1988) 'Italia 1960–'86. L'università cambia' in *Universitas* No 28 April–June, 37–47.

CHAPTER 6

The Spanish University in Transition

Emilio Lamo de Espinosa

Introduction: Education and Political Transition Processes

There is without doubt a striking contrast between, on the one side, stability of higher education practices and institutions and, on the other, the accelerating speed of social and political change. Some years ago, Clark Kerr examined how many medieval institutions were still alive and functioning in Europe. He found about 90. Among them the Catholic Church, the British and Iceland Parliaments, some councils in Switzerland and, not surprisingly, about 70 universities. (Kerr, 1982, 152.) His conclusion is still worth remembering: no other European institution, not even the modern State or the market, is older, nor has any other institution shown a better capacity to adapt to fluctuating times.

One would expect that, over time, education will be forced to adapt to new constitutional principles (either in relation to its administrative management and bureaucratic dependency or in relation to new rights to education) and also to a new economic environment demanding higher levels of scholarisation, a better skilled labour force or more support for research.

History has shown that this applied to Spain whose political transition included a deep modernisation and renewal of the educational system at all levels. But, as the apparent stability of universities suggests, education can also be analysed as an independent variable in political change. As a matter of fact, Spain's experience is a proof that education can take the lead in pushing processes of modernisation and political change. From that perspective, political and even economic institutions are the ones lagging behind. The stability of education may thus be misleading; while the black box of the system remains unchanged, its inputs and outputs do change, concealing deep processes of modernisation, while seriously contributing to the creation of the need for political change. The role of education as an independent variable in political transition is linked to its contribution to changes in political culture, i.e. to its capacity to educate politically relevant numbers of the population (Lamo di Espinosa, 1990). This paper will show how education in Spain contributed to political transition and then concentrate on the consequences of the new democratic order for higher education.

The Spanish Universities During the Last Years of Franco's Dictatorship

A short Look at the History of the Spanish Universities

The history of the Spanish university starts, as is well known, with the creation of the University of Salamanca in 1218, together with Bologna and Oxford one of the oldest institutions of higher learning in Europe. The University of Valladolid was created in the 14th, and in the 15th and 16th centuries seven other universities were established. Thus, at the beginning of the 19th century a system of ten Universities, covering practically all regions of Spain, fulfilled the needs of a still semi-rural society.

All through the 19th century the university was the object of a never-ending debate over various proposals for reform. However, the French-Napoleonic model was consistently implemented with a rigid centralised control from the Ministry of Public Education in Madrid. Proposals for liberalisation and institutional autonomy flourished now and then, though they were not fully developed until the Second Republic (1931–1939) – undoubtedly the most brilliant period of the Spanish university.

The Civil War and Franco's dictatorship destroyed the old, minority-oriented, liberal Spanish university. Many professors had to emigrate or were purged and replaced by others loyal to the new regime. From 1939 to 1944, 56 per cent of the places of *catedraticos* (professors with tenured status) were filled with new loyal incumbents. (Maravall, 1978, 58). The fascist oriented *Ley de Ordenacion de la Universidad* (1943) brought the institution under the strict control of an authoritarian regime and the ideological filter of the extremely conservative Catholic Church. As Franco said, Spain would not have Catholic universities since all of them were going to be Catholic (Franco, 1943, 434).

The Liberalisation of Francoism and the Student Movement

However, the mild liberalisation that Franco's government started with the Economic Stabilisation Plan of 1957 was also reflected in the university with far-reaching consequences. Directly, because ideological controls were tempered and new 'disloyal' professors could reach a chair, not infrequently under the patronage of loyal Francoist professors; indirectly, because the Economic Stabilisation Plan and European economic growth – a consequence of the Treaty of Rome of 1957 and the creation of the EEC – induced a decade of strong economic growth in Spain.

The increase in per capita income, demographic growth, urbanisation and the incorporation of women into higher education generated an unexpected growth of the Spanish university during the 1960s, particularly in traditional studies like law, medicine and humanities. At the same time, acute lack of trained managers and technicians started to be felt by businessmen and politicians.

There was in general a qualitative and quantitative insufficiency of human resources in terms of university graduates and skilled blue- and white-collar workers. Thus, the *General Law of Education* (1970), the work of a team of liberal technocrats, tried to reform the traditional university model, as well as the structure of secondary education. As a consequence new universities were created, among them the Madrid and Barcelona Autonomous Universities, which soon took the lead in the modernisation of higher education in Spain.

Even though the 1970 General Law of Education was well conceived and doubtless provided enough instruments for the reform of the whole educational system, its direct practical effects were limited. Either it was not seriously applied or it was developed in a skewed and slanted fashion.

But above all, the fierce opposition of the entire academic community – students and teaching staff alike – to Franco's dictatorship brought them also into opposition to the university reform, a conflict reinforced by the Western student atmosphere of the years 1968–1970. Strikes and demonstrations in Madrid and Barcelona, and later in other universities, were answered by frequent closing of the universities. Demands for institutional autonomy were followed by police intrusions of faculty buildings. Campuses remained under police control for months. From 1965 to 1975 the Spanish university maintained a constant struggle against Francoism, symbolised by the General Law of Education.

The University Student Revolt Against Francoism

As expected, the liberalisation of the political climate at universities contributed directly to the creation of an internal atmosphere of intellectual freedom. A new generation of professors, recently returned from European or American universities, started to develop a new political culture based on free speech, consensus, democracy and equality. The student movement of the years 1963–1975 was certainly permeated by political parties, mainly the Communist Party and the Christian Democrats. Nevertheless, ideas of free speech and university autonomy were also central to them.

In spite of the growth of the number of university students, by 1970 the university was still an elite institution. In the absence of private universities, the political and economic elite were forced to send their sons and daughters to the public universities. There they underwent a cultural transformation. Many of them entered the university as Catholics and Conservatives, only to leave five years later as atheists, mildly anti-clericals and clearly leftists or at least as convinced democrats. Thus, the elite of the Spanish university students moved in just five years (1963–1968) from the Counter-Reformation to the counter-culture, from Trento to Berkeley. As a result of this process they re-established the dialogue with the losers of the Civil War. It was mainly through them that a communication channel between the ruling class and the political underground was gradually established.

The Impact of Higher Education on Spain's Political Transition

The social effects of the student 'revolts', together with the political discussions about the new law and the optimistic economic climate, had far-reaching consequences on the political transition of Spain, consequences rarely if ever emphasised.[1] We will analyse two of these consequences in detail:

1. the continuous growth of the student body had important quantitative and qualitative consequences mixing people from varied social backgrounds and producing a sense of unity and a sense of strong internal cohesion and solidarity.

2. this generation nurtured the seeds of a new political culture that spread through Spanish society pushed by the spread of education creating a generation gap. Young and old people became separated not only by age and cultural barriers, symbolised at the time by a new cultural style (including music, sexual freedom, etc), but also by deep political cleavages.

In addition, we can say that the better educated people became the avant-garde of Spanish democratisation, not only by creating a new political culture, but also by providing the leaders of the transitional process and, more specifically, of the new democratic institutions.

---

1   The literature about Spain's political transition is already overwhelming. A good summary can be found in Tezanos (1989). None of the more than twenty articles deal with the effects of education on the transition. A relevant exception to this trend are the works of Jose Maria Maravall, later Minister of Education in the socialist Government from 1982 to 1989, (1978, 1981). Especially his 1981 publication contains a very interesting analysis of the students' political revolt against francoism and its effects on the socialisation of the new generation.

Rising expectations combined with an favourable economic climate and demographic changes produced an impressive growth in the number of secondary and university students during the 1970s. The number of students in secondary education rose by 43 per cent from 1961 to 1968 and had doubled by 1975. Much more impressive and fast was the growth in university students: 77,000 in 1960, they doubled seven years later, doubled again eight years later and once more another seven years later. Even now there is a growth is of about 50,000 more students each year. (See Table 1).

Table 1: Number of students in higher education

Year	Number of Students in Higher Education
1932	37,079
1940	37,539
1950	54,605
1955	61,359
1960	77,123
1967	152,957
1975	383,000
1982	692,152
1986	903,166
1989	1,000,000

Source: Consejo de Universidades, 1989.

*: Provisional estimate

Thus, when in 1985 the OECD reviewed the Spanish policy of education it stated the following:

> ... today, virtually all children attend compulsory school, 85 per cent of the 5-year age group are in pre-school establishments, the retention rate in secondary education is very high and still increasing, and the universities are no longer providing education for an elite but for a substantial percentage of young people in the immediate post-secondary school age-group (...) This expansion has been more spectacular than in any other OECD country, which says a great deal in view of the expansionist surge that has occurred almost everywhere (OECD, 1986, 12).

This impressive growth had qualitative consequences. Obviously, overcrowded classrooms all over the educational system created huge strains over resources and produced an acute shortage of professors. Thus, the system was unable to offer this widely demanded public service. Education became a crucial arena of political opposition to Francoism. The teachers' and students' demands for better and more democratic education were backed by the population, which understood that equal rights to access to education was a crucial step towards more social equality and the future advancement of their children. Since then, this general support of student demands has remained a feature of Spain's political culture.

But more importantly, for the first time in the history of Spain, huge numbers of young people from different social backgrounds, but all of them still of middle-high or high social status, were put together, reaching a sense of unity. Political events like the Vietnam war, the 1968 Paris revolution, the military occupation of Prague, the common opposition to Francoism, and the memories of the horrors of the Civil War, all contributed to create this internal unity. For the newly developed youth culture, rock music, hippy aesthetics, experimentation with sexual freedom and drugs, also provided

strong symbols of identification, as labels indicating their belonging to a new world of
Gemeinschaft-based attitudes.

In turn, the rejection by the 'official' culture of those 'hairy rebels' manifested in the
media contributed unwantedly to the fusion of the young people. A strong sense of
solidarity developed, strengthening intra-generational bonds and weakening inter-gen-
erational heritage. The sense of 'we' against 'them' became a reality, a youth culture
developed, later permeating all aspects of social life. For the first time socialisation with
peers became more important than socialisation with elders.

This new culture and lifestyle spread beyond universities to secondary education
institutions and was also adopted by young blue- and white-collar workers. But, no
doubt, the new culture found the socio-political conditions for its development in the
universities, and without them it would have been a minority experiment. Thus, political
transition in Spain must be conceived too as a change in political culture coupled with
a generational shift. A new generation, with an alternative view of the political order,
reached the age of replacing the old ruling class and decided to change the order itself.

The Constitution of 1978 and the 1983 Law of University Reform

When the new Spanish Constitution was approved in 1978, there was a lot of excitement
and hopes among those interested in education. Despite the fact that article 27 of the
Constitution (regulating education) had, because of the suspiciousness of the Catholic
Church, been one of the most difficult to negotiate, the result was encouraging. It
contained the recognition of the fundamental right to receive education and to teach,
including the freedom of religious teaching and of founding schools and colleges; basic
education became mandatory; finally, the autonomy of universities was granted constitutional status.

Moreover, it was necessary to modify the public administration of education in
accordance with the rights endowed upon the Autonomous Communities. According
to the Constitution, all Autonomous Communities, now had competence over education at all levels. This raised great expectations, mainly in the old Spanish nations of
Catalunya, the Basque Country and Galicia.

A fast and generous feed-back from the new democratic order to the educational
system was expected. Unfortunately these hopes had to wait many years before being
fulfilled. From 1978 to 1982, the successive governments published about ten different
drafts of laws of autonomy for the university, successively defended by four ministers.
Nevertheless, the ministers as well as the proposals were defeated by internal corporate
pressures and external political rejection.

The Problems of the University at the Beginning of the 1980s

As a result, when the socialist government won the elections in 1982, the internal climate
of the academic community was, once again, desperate. The principal deficiencies were
the following:

- general rejection of all old legal norms which generated demands for a new
  legal order in accord with the Constitution and for more autonomy;
- inadequacy of teaching practices, rigidity of curricula, rising unemployment
  rates among university graduates, reinforced by the economic crisis of 1973,
  but, at the same time, a constant rise in the number of incoming students;
- almost total absence and lack of support of research. Demoralisation of
  academics in the face of job insecurity. More than 80 per cent of the faculty
  members did not have tenure;

- acute lack of resources and constant funding problems;
- slow and inefficient management, reinforced by a strongly centralised administration in the hands of the Ministry of Education and Science.

Therefore, immediately after the socialist party won the elections of 1982, the new Ministry of Education started to elaborate a new law. Finally, the Law of University Reform (LRU) was passed by the *Cortes Generales* (Spanish parliament) in the summer of 1983. Considering that the new law has drastically changed the traditional patterns of the Spanish university it is necessary to analyse in some detail its main objectives.

Higher education in the Constitution of 1978 and the LRU

Based on the constitutional rulings of 1978, the LRU attempted an ambitious reform of the structure of the Spanish universities on the following regulating principles:

- Respect for the traditional predominance of public universities. In spite of that – and for the first time under Spanish law – private universities would be allowed and regulated under principles similar to those of the public sector.
- Considering the autonomy of the universities and their legal dependence on the Autonomous Communities, higher education is conceived as a system of independent and competitive units.
- Finally, and in a clear contrast to the teaching tradition of the Spanish university, a reorientation towards research activities. An essential step for this was the departmentalisation of the university in such a way that the departments would organise research in one area of knowledge. Thus, the internal structure of each university consists of faculties and departments, and each professor depends on both and belongs to both for different purposes: teaching or research.

Re-Distribution of Powers

Along these general lines, the Law of University Reform attributed the capacity to create new Universities not only to the *Cortes Generales*, but also to the parliaments of the Autonomous Communities. At the same time, the already existing Universities would progressively be transferred to the different Autonomous Communities. However, up to this moment, only 18 of the 34 public universities depend administratively on their respective Communities. The other 16 still depend on the central Ministry of Education.

Power over the administration of universities is shared by three centres of authority: central government (i.e. the Ministry of Education), the Autonomous Communities and the universities themselves. By virtue of the autonomy principle, the latter receive most of the power, as the following overview shows:

- First of all they are entitled to organise freely their internal regulation. Students participate with 25 to 35 per cent of the votes, a proportion that has been maintained in many committees.
- They are also entitled to select their own personnel. There is complete freedom with respect to non-teaching staff and some control as to the selection of professors.
- With respect to teaching, public universities have complete freedom to organise their curricula if the studies are not geared towards an official degree. If they are, curricula have to respect guidelines approved by the Council of Universities. As a matter of fact, almost all traditional degrees are of an official kind.

- Internal research activity, i.e. departmental affairs are managed with almost absolute freedom by the universities.

- Finally, the budget is approved by the Social Council, a new body created by the LRU, three-fifths of which is made up of representatives of professional associations, trade unions, municipal governments etc of the communities that surround the university, while the rest is composed of members of the university.

The autonomy of the universities, together with that of the Autonomous Communities, highlights the need for co-ordinating the system as a whole, and planning its development. Such responsibilities are attributed to the *Council of Universities*, a body that has progressively acquired greater relevance since it was put into motion in 1985, and where all academic matters that need centralised regulation are debated and approved. The Council is made up of all rectors of public universities, the Ministers of Education of the Autonomous Communities and representatives of the Ministry of Education and Science, plus 15 relevant personalities selected by the Congress, the Senate and the Government from among prestigious personalities, normally with an academic or research background.

Starting with the date of its approval in 1983, the LRU has been developed and implemented to a great extent. Even though there was a certain initial opposition on the grounds that the academic community had not been sufficiently consulted, it is certain that, as the OECD report on education in Spain points out, 'it is highly probable that if it had been subjected to a process of widespread internal discussion in the universities, the LRU would never have been promulgated, or so watered down as to be ineffectual' (OECD, 1986, 53). At the same time, even if it did not rouse a lot of support, it did not generate serious conflicts either, and today it is commonly accepted as a reasonable framework for regulating and modernising the Spanish university.

The Inflow of Students and Curricula Reform

The Rising Number of Incoming Students

As mentioned above, the impressive growth of student numbers throughout the 1960s continued through the 1970s and 1980s and the figures are not expected to decrease until the middle of the next decade or even later. This is mainly due to the specific demographic pattern in Spain. The cohort with the highest number of newborns is that of 1973 and they are now enrolled at university.

But the rise in number of incoming students is also due to the rise in school enrolment for the 19- to 25-year-olds, a rate that has almost reached 30 per cent in 1990. Also, the continual incorporation of women (Fernandez Villanueva, 1989, 161), the increase in the number of university centres and their geographical dispersion, and the aggressive scholarship policy of the socialist government,[2] have together caused a systematic increase in the enrolment rate. Finally, the incorporation of the adult population into higher education should also be noted (about 10% in 1989), almost all enrolled in the *Universidad Nacional de Educación a Distancia* (UNED), the Spanish Open University. Thus, even if in strictly demographic terms growth should stop by 1992, counter-trends may prove to be stronger.

In comparative terms, however, the number of university graduates in the active population is still very small (about 7%), schooling periods are very long (about seven years on average), and student failure is a serious problem (about a 30% drop-out rate) (Alvarez Corbacho, 161ff.).

Distorted Distribution
However, analysis of the distribution of this strong growth, which in the last few years has shown an annual increase of 50,000 more students a year, shows large imbalances (OECD, 1986):

Among universities. Some have passed their saturation point years ago, while others are still quite small. During the last years the range of university population showed a dispersion going from 4000 students in the smallest to 120,000 in the largest university (see Table 2).

Between long and short study programmes. Again during the last years less than 30 per cent of students were registered in short-term study programmes (three years of official duration), while more than 70 per cent were registered in long-term study programmes (five to six years).

Finally, between liberal arts and science or, to be specific, between professional careers and purely formative ones. According to the latest data available, the distribution of students was the following: 13 per cent in technical studies, 14 per cent in health sciences and 73 per cent in social sciences and the humanities.

Table 2: Distribution of enrolments by university size 1985/86

Size of University	Number of Universities	Percentage of Students
Below 10,000	8	8%
10,000–20,000	6	12%
20,000–40,000	8	29%
40,000–70,000	5	27%
Above 70,000	2	24%
Total	*29*	*100%*

Source: ICED, 1986, 31.

Another problem consisted in structural imbalances which resulted from the expansion of the 1960s and the 1970s, when attention was paid only to producing more of the same without worrying about diversifying or updating programmes or planning for future growth. Thus, under-use still exists side by side with over-use of resources, massified universities side with others with a strong growth potential. Even in the former it is not unusual to find great internal imbalances in the use of resources and the distribution of students.

In any case, the result is that many more student places are offered than demanded in studies with little popular appeal and only few places in highly sought-after disciplines. Altogether, there is a concentration of a large number of students in a small number of universities (e.g. one out of every nine in the Universidad Complutense of Madrid) and careers (e.g. one out of every nine in law).

In order to start solving this difficult problem, the Socialist government devised three sets of measures with the following objectives:

[2]   *The following figures show this increase for the first years of the socialist government:*

	1982–83	*1984–85*	*1985–86*	*1987–88*
Students with scholarships	62,200	90,000	113,884	178,483
Pts. spent (in millions)	3,409	8,910	13,690	26,806

- to improve the use of existing resources;
- to make the system grow as a whole, strengthening the non-massified programmes that fulfill social demands, present or future;
- and especially, to reform and diversify degrees and curricula.

Let us analyse these measures.

Table 3: Growth of enrolment by type of programme

	1971–72	1980–81	1985–86
Faculties			
Number	195,237	423,911	577,578
%	51.2	65.3	67.5
Technical Universities			
Number	44,547	46,147	52,513
%	13.5	7.1	6.1
University Schools			
Number	115,990	179,040	225,032
%	35.2	27.6	26.3
Total			
Number	329,149	649,098	855,123
%	100	100	100

Source: ICED, 1986, 30.

Redistribution of Students

Article 26.2 of the LRU states that the Council of Universities, if so requested by the universities, can limit the admission in those centres where a strong imbalance can be foreseen between offer and demand. Before 1984, the universities were forced to accept all students demanding access and belonging to their educational district. Since 1984, the Council of Universities approves the list of centres allowed to limit capacity for freshmen every year, on average about 70 per cent of all. The results of this drastic change in policy have been manifold.

Firstly, it has deeply changed the meaning of the entrance examinations, the so-called *pruebas de selectividad.* Conceived initially in 1975 as a filter for the flow from secondary to higher education, practically all students now pass the exams. Thus, the so-called Selectivity Examination serves today to distribute the places offered by the universities among the students, according to their scores (scores that are the average of the last four school years of secondary education and of the Selectivity Exam). It is therefore used to order the students in a hierarchy according to performance and not really, as its name seems to suggest, as a screening process for access to university (though a small number of students with very low scores may end up without a place in areas like Madrid or Barcelona).

This policy has forced a redistribution of the student flow, improving the use of the available resources. So, there is now a significant slowing down in the growth of large universities and, on the contrary, a far-above-average growth in small universities. A similar pattern is occurring in the distribution among study programmes; a decrease being observed in the demand for popular study programmes such as medicine or law and a growth in study areas such as engineering or some health studies (like odontology or physiotherapy).

Since the better qualified students demand certain centres in preference to others, a pressure towards competition and hierarchisation among universities has appeared for the first time. Little by little, credit goes to certain universities or faculties, while others receive below-average students.

It should, finally, be emphasised that this policy, which initially met a strong opposition from high-school students, has been accepted on the whole by the university community – including certainly the students – and by public opinion.

Degrees and Curricula Reform

The policy of the Socialist government with regard to the creation of new centres has given a clear priority to their concentration in already existing universities, so as to maintain a minimum of quality control and better use of available resources. At the same time, shorter cycle studies have been strengthened and are being accepted little by little as a valid alternative to better-known traditional studies. This is probably one of the most promising changes, since it takes off pressure from the second cycles (and creates room for research), implies a more efficient use of resources, and brings down the drop-out rates.

A general characteristic of the Spanish university was – and still is – the small number of degrees (and therefore of programmes) offered, especially considering that there is no system of non-university higher education, that is, all higher education in Spain is offered by the universities. The total number of different degrees offered is 56, and the most recent degrees in engineering (aeronautics and telecommunications) were introduced in the 1920s. Since then, the list of degrees offered has undergone only minor modifications.

For this reason the Council of Universities, with the support of the Ministry of Education and Science, is promoting an ambitious reform project of degrees and curricula. It is intended to diversify programmes, vertically, by incorporating new degrees, and horizontally, so that, in some subjects, students would enroll in a programme of two or three years in order to obtain the degree of *Diplomado*, before moving on (if this is the case) to a second cycle of two years to obtain the degree of *Licenciado*. This is expected to allow for an easy alternation between periods of training and education and periods of work.

It is also planned to diversify the study programmes among different universities. The Council of Universities is now defining a central curricular nucleus for each official degree (conceived in a similar way as some EC directives) that under no circumstances will cover more than 30–35 per cent of the total schooling hours. The rest of the curricula will be open to be decided on by the universities or by the students themselves (a minimum of 10% is left for them to fill in). This would constitute a complete break with the centralised and uniform educational tradition.

It must be stressed that, though the Council of Universities launched this curricula reform in 1986, it is still the object of much debate and certainly, opposition, not only from inside the university (professors are afraid that 'their' subject matter will disappear from future curricula, and students are afraid that standards will be lowered too much), but mainly from the Professional Associations. Thus, it is still a matter of debate whether the reform will ever succeed. On the other hand, the reform of the Ph.D. along the lines of the American model, which started already in 1985, is now fully operational, and normally with good results.

Faculty: Selection, Rewards and Research

An Ambitious Project

As can be imagined, the fast growth of the student body generated many problems in the faculties. Indeed, academics were faced with three predicaments in particular:

- a precarious employment situation for the so-called *profesores no-numerarios*, PNN, non-tenured professors (more than 80% of the total).
- proliferation of different categories, salary levels and types of dedication.
- finally, a mechanism of access to tenure with a strong ritualistic component that disregarded research activities.

The LRU tried to radically modify these three negative situations:

First of all, in order to get clear of the past, specific aptitude tests (the *pruebas de idoneidad*) were held in order to permit easy access to tenure to all the professors that had been teaching in the university on a regular basis for more than ten years. However, even after these *pruebas de idoneidad* not even 50 per cent of all university professors had tenure.

Secondly, the categories of professors with tenure were reduced to only three types: *Catedrático, Profesor Titular de Universidad* and *Professor Titular de Escuela Universitaria*, with either a full-time or part-time dedication. Further, it was clearly established that the teaching assistant (the *ayudantes*) could collaborate on a sporadic basis in teaching activities. Together with these, new categories were created: Associate Professor (to incorporate qualified professionals into the teaching staff), Visiting Professors and Emeritus Professors (this to alleviate the lowering of retirement age of the *Catedráticos* from 70 to 65 years of age, a measure that was, and still is, highly controversial.

Finally, the system of access to tenure was deeply modified. The examinations are now managed by the universities – not by the Ministry – who designate two of the five members of the Board of Examiners; the other three are randomly selected from a list of professors of the same area of knowledge, but working at another university. The procedures have been simplified to just two: an evaluation of the academic *curriculum vitae* of the professor and his/her exposition of a major research project already finished.

Endogamy in the Selection Processes

The results of the policy for professors are ambivalent. To start with, the new mechanism of faculty selection, even though it is recognised as a clear improvement, has reinforced strong endogamic tendencies, up to now present only in the hiring of non-tenured professors. Studies carried out by the Council of Universities show that approximately 80 per cent of the professors selected already work at the same university that had the opening. Even though this endogamy has the positive side effect of retaining professors in the small provincial universities, which are not any longer considered as mere transit places towards Madrid or Barcelona, the disadvantages are self-evident.

Everything seems to indicate that this gross deviance from what was expected and desired is a joint product of two causes. On one hand, universities have irresponsibly delegated to their departments the capacity of selecting their two representatives on the Board of Examiners. The result is that the younger professors, who frequently control the departments through internal pacts, end up designating their future evaluators. The other and major cause behind this generalised pattern of endogamy is the lack of Ph.D.s willing to follow a career as university professors, combined with the constant growth of the universities. This lack of adjustment between offer and demand leads to a generalised pact of the type: 'I won't try to enter in your University, don't try in mine'. Almost everybody knows that, sooner or later, they will have a place in 'their own' university. As a matter of fact, in almost 70 per cent of the openings only one candidate applies.

Inadequate Rewards

The lack of control of the *Catedráticos* over the recruitment of new professors, substituted by the control of the University and, as seen before, by that of the department, also has ambivalent effects, since the latter seem to have maybe less, and certainly not more, interest in quality, and frequently selection follows narrow particularistic criteria.

This loss of power of the *Catedráticos*, together with the lowering of retirement age to 65 and with comparatively low salaries (the economic development that started in 1985 has opened a large gap between public and private salaries), has produced a draining of good professors away from of the universities, especially those located in large cities. One must add that the salary of a university professor was practically constant all along his/her career, independently of the quality of work and even of the number of years of work.

Though the LRU allowed the universities to pay their professors according to quality criteria, strong corporatist levelling tendencies have blocked the use of such provisions; even today not even one university has made use of such freedom to fix salaries. As a consequence, the Ministry of Education has recently introduced new economic rewards to compensate for teaching on the one side and for research on the other. No doubt this change moves in the right direction, introducing economic rewards for the best and more dedicated professors and opening the range of salaries; however the amounts involved are not very impressive and one may doubt the effects of such a measure in the short run.

The lack of professors constitutes, without doubt, one of the most serious problems for the immediate future of the Spanish university. Its continual growth demands a continual recruitment of new professors at a level not reached at present. The reform of Ph.D. studies makes it more difficult to obtain the degree, but at the same time a growth of 50,000 to 60,000 students per year makes it necessary to attract between 2,500 to 3,000 new professors a year just to maintain the present student/professor ratios. This is exactly the number of Ph.D.s finished every year (a number that has almost doubled since 1980), but obviously not all want to enrol as university professors. This lack of qualified professors has distorted another of the new categories introduced by the LRU, that of *Profesor Asociado*. Conceived as a way to incorporate good professionals into teaching activities, it is now being used by the universities (with the tacit consent of the Ministry) to maintain as university professors people lacking their Ph.D.s.

Conclusions

The Law of University Reform has been generally accepted and is today considered as a satisfactory and reasonable model for the organisation of this much-discussed sector of the Spanish educational system. Following the provisions of the Constitution of 1978, it has undoubtedly contributed to the introduction of respect for the law in a formerly unruly sector. A relevant level of autonomy has been granted to non-central bodies in a historically centralised system, and institutions have been brought nearer to their users: students and the general public. There has been an improvement in the quality of teaching as well as research, and a rationalisation of the use of available resources has taken place. The initiative, until a few years ago in the hands of the Ministry of Education and Science, has been passed on to the academic community. On the other hand, public opinion is taking an active interest, demanding greater quality. The Spanish business community, in particular, has come closer to this reality through the Social Councils, at a time when professors and students are abandoning old anti-business feelings.

However, within this generally positive panorama, considerable problems do, in fact, exist. The growth of the student body has been enormous. For 1,000,000 students, approximately 50 universities are necessary, not only the 38 existing ones. Teaching is mostly a routine matter, in terms of pedagogical methods, as well as in terms of curricula, and the question is what impact curricula reform will have if there is not going to be an improvement in available funding. Moreover, there have been obvious mistakes in faculty policy, mainly in salary matters and in the incapacity, until now, to control the endogamy of selective processes. Management of resources, including the very availability of reliable statistics, is also seriously lacking.

In spite of the many remaining problems, one should be optimistic about the future of the Spanish universities, since maybe the best side result of the LRU is the appearance of a new generation of rectors, vice-rectors, deans etc. who are deeply concerned, young, active and possess a more entrepreneurial spirit. This, combined with the growing competition between universities (competition for funds, professors and students), soon to be strengthened by the establishment of new private universities, is creating a very active environment for the nurturing of new ideas and initiatives. If we remember the state of the Spanish university only 20 years ago, we realise that we are moving fast towards a normalisation in European terms, and that the conclusion about the future of the Spanish universities can only be positive.

References

Alvarez Corbacho (1984) 'Rendinmientos y Equidad Social del Gasto Publico Universitario: al Caso de la Universidad Gallega' in Consejo de Universidades, *La Financiación de la Enseñananza Superior.* Madrid: Ministry of Education.

Carabaña, J. (1988) 'Comprehensive Educational Reforms in Spain: Past and Present'. *European Journal of Education* Vol 23, No 1, 213.

CIDE (1985) *The Spanish Educational System. Report of Spain.* Madrid: CIDE.

Consejo de Universidades (1989) *La Financiación de la Enseñanza superior, Ministerio de Educacion.* Madrid.

Consejo de Universidades (1989) *Estadisticas Universitarias.* Madrid: MEC.

Fernandez Villanueva, C. (1989) 'La Mujer en la Universidad Española' in *Revista de Educación* 290, 161.

Franco, F. (1943) *Palabras del Caudillo.* Madrid.

Gonzalez Hernandez, A. (1989) 'Recruiting of Spanish University Teaching Staff' *Higher Education Policy* Vol 2, 50.

Kerr, C. (1982) *The Uses of the University.* Cambridge: Harvard University Press.

Lamo de Espinosa, E. (1989) *Youth and Education in Spain's Political Transitión.* Budapest: Higher Council of Scientific Research and the Hungarian Academy of Sciences, Symposia on Political Transitions, May 1990, unpublished manuscript.

Maravall, J.M. (1981) *La Politica de la Transicion; 1975–1990.* Madrid: Taurus.

Maravall, J.M. (1978) *Dictadura y Disentimiento Politico.* Madrid: Alfaguara.

OECD (1986) *Reviews of National Policies for Education. Spain.* Paris: OECD.

Tezanos, J.F. Cotarelo R. and de Blas, A. (Eds) (1989) *La Transición Democratica Española.* Madrid: Ed.Sistema.

Part II

Adaptation and Distinctiveness
Diversification in European Tertiary Training Sytems

CHAPTER 7

The Transformation of Higher Education in Portugal

Eduardo Marçal Grilo

The Higher Education System in Portugal

Compared to other EC countries, the Portuguese economy is relatively backward. However, it is undergoing rapid modernisation and a process of swift internationalisation is changing the face of the country.[1] In this process, the education system has an important role to play. Below, the present situation of higher education in Portugal will be analysed, especially with a view to determining which problems will have to be dealt with in order to adapt the system to changing demands.

Structure and Organisation

According to the Basic Law of the Education system, higher education includes two sub-systems – universities and polytechnics. The universities, which in Portugal have existed since the 13th century, aim to deliver a solid basic scientific and cultural preparation as well as technical and technological training. The polytechnics, which were created in 1977, have as an essential objective the training of technicians for the productive sector. However, the pre-conditions that students have to fulfil for admission to both systems are similar.

The university system awards three different academic degrees: *Licenciatura* for courses of four to six years' duration; *Mestrado* which implies a post-graduate course of one to two years' duration and the presentation and discussion of a thesis; and *Doutoramento* which is awarded following the submission to a jury and the public discussion of an original thesis on a specific scientific domain.

The polytechnic system awards one academic degree and one diploma: *Bacharelato* for courses of three years' duration; and *Diploma de Estudos Superiores Especializados* for courses of two years' duration following the *Bacharelato* (for careers in the public sector this diploma is equivalent to the *Licenciatura* degree).

The two systems are not entirely separate, and it is possible for students to transfer from one system to the other. In practice they are two systems with their own objectives and degrees but with *passerelles* between them which allow transfer both ways in order to increase free choice and to stimulate mobility of students.

Diversification exists in both public and private higher education systems. The private system came into being at the beginning of the 1970s with the establishment of the Catholic University, a private institution with a special statute created by a

---

1   For a more detailed description of this process and an analysis of the development strategy
     needed, see Marçal Grilo and Carmelos Rosa (1988).

decree-law under the *Concordata* signed between the Vatican and Portugal. The private system has been expanded in particular during the last decade, and in some academic disciplines private institutions already absorb a considerable percentage of the total number of students.

In 1989–90, the public sector was composed of 14 universities, 14 polytechnic institutes, 2 university colleges not integrated in universities, 25 polytechnic colleges not integrated in polytechnic institutes, and 3 colleges of *Beaux-Arts*. Parallel to these public institutions, the private sector, which is regulated by a specific decree-law, comprised 6 universities and 35 university or polytechnic colleges. It must be emphasised that in 1987 the number of students in higher education in percentage of the corresponding age group did not exceed 11 per cent, which compared with 25 per cent as the average figure for EC countries.

The total number of students was around 118,100 in 1986–87. It must be be noticed that the private sector, with regard to the number of students, represents 20 per cent of the total, but in some subject areas, such as social sciences and law, it represents around 30 per cent and 49 per cent respectively. Another interesting development is that between 1983–84 and 1989–90 the percentage of students enrolled in public polytechnic institutions has grown from 11.2 per cent to 17 per cent.

In the last decade, expansion of the higher education system took place through the growth of the polytechnic system (which has grown 84% in the last 12 years compared with 33% of growth in the universities in the same period), as well as through the increasing number of places available in the private sector.

Teaching Staff

The lack of qualifications of teaching staff in universities is one of the main problems facing the higher education system in Portugal. Although some effort to improve the situation has been made over the last 20 years, the number of professors and lecturers holding a Ph.D. is nevertheless insufficient for the needs of a large number of departments, particularly those in universities. In fact, the percentage of teaching staff with a Ph.D. is less than 20 per cent. In addition, teaching staff with Ph.D. qualifications is largely concentrated (86%) on the four 'classical' universities of Coimbra (15%), Porto (20%), Lisbon (22%) and Technical University of Lisbon (18%), as well as in the New University of Lisbon (11%) (see Table 1).

Table 1: Teaching staff in public universities with Ph.D. degrees

Universities	Number of Ph.D.'s
Açores	23
Algarve	11
Aveiro	60
Beira interior	18
Coimbra	269
Evora	24
Lisboa	404
Madeira [1]	
Minho	78
Nova Lisboa	207
Porto	371
Tecnica de Lisboa	327
Tras Montes Alto Douro	15
Total	*1,807*

[1] Established by Royal Decree of 13 September 1988

In the private sector, in 1988–89 teaching staff amounted to almost 2500, of whom 12 per cent had a Ph.D. degree (for the qualifications of teaching staff employed in private institutions see Table 2). The number of professors and lecturers in public universities is growing rapidly: 6.1 per cent between 1985–1986 and 1986–1987 and 4.9 per cent between 1986–1987 and 1987–1988. However, a large number of teaching staff in the private sector is also included on the 'pay roll' of the public sector, which does not allow us to add both figures in order to achieve the total teaching staff in the higher education system. Nevertheless, it is clear that with the expansion of the polytechnic system a large increase in number of teaching staff has taken place (39.1% for professors and 32.2% for lecturers).

Entry Conditions and Numerus Clausus

Entry conditions in the Portuguese higher education system have been changed almost every 2 years over the last 15 years. Before 1974, admission to university was regulated through an examination that each student had to sit directly in each faculty. Between 1974 and 1977 admission was unlimited, which gave rise to a rapid growth in the number of students and to a decrease in the quality of the teaching. In 1977 the Government defined by decree a *numerus clausus* system based on an examination and a national contest through which the student could apply for a certain number of courses and institutions.

Table 2: Qualifications of teaching staff in private institutions by discipline 1988–89

Discipline	Dout	Mest	Lic	Other	Total
Law	43	40	228	–	311
Management	56	20	463	–	539
Computer Science	9	5	51	1	66
Applied Mathematics	19	5	108	–	132
Economics	26	3	130	–	159
History	17	6	79	–	102
Modern Language/Literature	6	3	37	–	46
Architecture	2	–	92	–	94
International Relations	4	2	12	–	18
Psychology	11	–	65	3	79
Secretarial training	7	3	78	18	106
Languages and Tourism	–	3	40	19	62
Translation/Interpretation	1	4	32	16	53
Social Communications	4	1	17	4	26
Public Relations	1	1	22	1	25
Social Security	3	–	25	–	28
Social Work	5	1	49	22	77
Drama/Verbal expression	–	2	30	53	85
Teacher Training	28	4	125	50	207
Philosophy	17	–	64	–	81
Theology	23	–	108	–	131
Engineering	13	–	21	–	34
Total	295	103	1876	187	2481

Dout = *Doutoramento*; Mest = *Mestrado*; Lic = *Licenciatura*

In 1988, after a long political debate, the Government approved new selection criteria based on a national and compulsory general examination, aiming to evaluate the global cultural level of the student as well as proficiency in the Portuguese language. The results of this specific examination are determined by the universities and the polytechnic institutes and by a national contest through which the students may apply to a maximum of six course/institution combinations. In the national contest, the marks obtained in upper secondary as well as in the general examination and in the specific examinations are taken into account. The proportional weight of each of the marks within the formula through which the final average mark is obtained has been established by law. Within those limits, different percentage weights may be adopted by the universities.

As regards the number of vacancies available in the public sector, in 1989–90 the university system offered 15,610 and the polytechnics 6207, which means that the total number of vacancies was 21,817. The ratio between the number of vacancies available in each discipline and the number of students who have chosen it as first option in the application form presented in the first phase of the national contest is shown in Table 3.

The number of students applying for law and social sciences is around five and four times, respectively, the number of vacancies available, while only in the sectors of exact and natural sciences does supply exceed demand. This mismatch between supply and demand in the public sector is one of the main reasons why the private sector has flourished in the last decade. The unsatisfied demand is transferred to the private sector, where the number of vacancies available this year has already exceeded the number of vacancies in the public sector.

The Main Constraints of the System
The major constraints continuing to characterise Portuguese higher education at the beginning of this decade are basically the following:

- a low proportion of the corresponding age-group entering higher education (11%);
- a very high ratio of *licenciatura*-course students following short courses at a time when all labour demand data in Portugal point to the priority need to train technical students to upper-secondary education level or vocational courses and, at the higher level, to offer intense practical and vocationally-oriented training;
- the difficulties facing the most disadvantaged social strata in gaining access to higher education, especially in those regions most remote from the major urban centres;
- still inadequate levels of teacher training courses covering every level of education, including pre-primary;
- a failure to establish postgraduate courses in areas of strategic importance for the country's economic and social development;
- deficiencies in the link between research activities and education;
- inadequate links between the higher education system and production activities, particularly in certain agricultural areas which must be seen as priority areas, given the country's food resource situation;

**Table 3: *First options of applicants for entry in public
higher education institutions***

Field of Study	Ratio between the number of vacancies and the number of students who have chosen the course as first option			
	Old univ	New univ	Poly	Total
Languages/ Literature	2.25	1.11	-	1.95
Teacher Training	1.00	2.33	2.00	2.02
Primary School Teacher Training	4.15	3.70	3.87	
Other education	1.00	1.72	1.04	1.33
Beaux Arts	2.94	1.94	0.87	2.68
Law	5.14	-	-	5.14
Social Sciences	6.30	3.59	2.25	4.33
Natural Sciences	1.00	0.72	1.38	0.94
Engineering	1.57	0.92	0.97	1.17
Medicine	2.50	3.15	-	2.57
Agriculture	2.45	2.76	0.92	1.77
Other courses	2.39	0.33	3.78	2.20
Total	3.07	1.94	1.60	2.35

Old univ = Universities of Coimbra, Lisboa, Porto, Technica de Lisboa, Belas Artes and ISCTE
New univ = Universities of Açores, Algarve, Aveiro, Madeira, Minho, Nova de Lisboae and UTMAD.
Poly = Polytechnics

- difficulties in revitalising higher education, given budgetary constraints in current and personnel expenditures as well as official red tape, incompatible with efficient and responsible modern management;
- uneven spread of students over the various courses, pointing to a lack of student information and guidance during secondary education;
- insufficient preparation of students for entry into higher education, especially in basic areas such as the Portuguese language (comprehension and expression), history (what we were and what we are) and mathematics (logical reasoning);
- deficiencies in the operation of the system generally, through lack of facilities and equipment (including libraries and, in particular, access to data banks) appropriate to a modern education system and geared to the main aims of tertiary education;
- excessively slow development of new universities and delay in the launching of higher polytechnic education in line with the initial programme, leading to serious blockage in the *numerus clausus* system, since it is not through the expansion of the 'old' universities, but rather through the 'new' universities and polytechnic education, that the necessary and desirable growth in student course attendance figures must occur;

- very low budgetary allocations, with a particularly high percentage (between 80 and 90%) devoted to staff, even in the case of schools running courses with a sizeable laboratory/experimental contents;
- problems at the level of operation of the central administrative machinery, which lacks the technical capacity to ensure the overall co-ordination of the higher education (sub)-system and the horizontal links between the bodies and entities involved.

On the question of access to higher education, characterised by a *numerus clausus* system since the mid-1970s, it will be necessary to emphasise the need for increased participation in higher education if the level of access achieved by the corresponding age-group is to be compatible with the present EC average. This growth is going to have to occur through the expansion of higher polytechnic education, which will need to move towards a 50% enrolment rate of higher education students in the near future if the country is to provide for the training of higher or intermediate-level technical staff which it needs for its economic development.

As regards university education, it is basically at new university establishments, created during the 1970s, and which are far from accommodating the student numbers for which they were set up, that expansion needs to occur. The four oldest and already well-endowed universities, on the other hand, need to stabilise – or even slightly reduce – their student numbers (in the academic year 1986–87, some 75% of all university students were enrolled at the old universities).

A rapid expansion of higher education in Portugal can in any case, only take place when certain conditions have been fulfilled, the most important of which is large-scale investment in education. Without this investment, the infrastructure needed to cater for a growing number of students cannot be established, nor can the scientific equipment essential to the ongoing modernisation of education be purchased. At the same time, a major effort is required in terms of the budgeting of running costs so as to guarantee that quality teachers are trained or recruited and to meet the various maintenance costs involved – an area in which serious problems have been encountered in recent years.

Recent Developments in Higher Education

The most important modifications that have occurred in the Portuguese higher education system during the last decade can be summarised as follows:

- establishment of new academic courses, modifications of the curriculum of several courses and of the contents of many subjects;
- development of new curriculum arrangements based on the credit system;
- expansion of the system through the creation of new institutions: technician training colleges, teacher training colleges, and universities (public and private);
- development of new research projects, particularly in connection with the productive sectors;
- creation of new research institutes linked with the universities but closely related with the productive sectors;
- awarding of a new administrative and financial autonomy statute to the universities as well as to the polytechnics.

In regard to the modernisation of the system it is important to mention that universities and polytechnic institutes have made a great effort in the last decade aiming to offer new academic disciplines, to modify existing curricula and to introduce innovations in the contents of several disciplines.

New universities and polytechnic institutes have introduced a large number of new academic courses and training activities in the area of agriculture and food production as well as in the industrial technological fields. Some of these courses are directly related to the predominant productive sectors in the geographical region where the universities and polytechnics have been created. As an example it is possible to refer to some courses of the University of Minho and of the Faculty of Science and Technology in the New University of Lisbon, which were created in the last ten years and which did not exist before in the Portuguese university system. These courses are: biology engineering, metallomechanic engineering, production engineering, information and system engineering, textile engineering, environment engineering, sanitary engineering, materials and physics engineering as well as a diversified number of postgraduate courses among which the MBA (Master of Business Administration) is one of the greatest successes.

At the polytechnic institutes, there is also a move aiming to increase the relevance of the system through the launching of new courses, namely in areas complementary to existing productive sectors. These are for example courses in design, marketing, international relations and others.

Although new courses have been created mainly by the new universities and polytechnics, the 'old' universities have paid great attention, as well, to the modification and introduction of new subjects in the actual curricula of existing courses. In this context these universities were enabled to create new training courses in several different domains such as: biotechnology, applied chemistry, technological physics, applied mathematics and informatics, nutrition, biochemistry, food technology, solid state physics, materials engineering, etc.

One of the innovative measures taken in higher education is that universities have introduced a credit system which allows for new curricula arrangements in order to increase the options of students. This system is being used mainly in postgraduate or specialised training courses.

Regarding the expansion of the system, we have made some comments on this subject above, but there are two particular aspects which have to be mentioned. Within the polytechnic institutes there is one type of college which is aimed to train teachers for pre-primary and primary (grades 1–6) levels of the education system. This means that in the large majority of existing polytechnic institutes, there are colleges with different objectives. On one hand, the 'technician-training colleges' and, on the other, the 'teacher-training colleges'.

In the past, this gave rise to some problems in terms of the co-ordination and management of these institutes. The 'teacher-training colleges', whose majority were created on the basis of the transferring of the former *Escolas do Magistério* to a 'teacher-training college', had, from the beginning, a critical mass of teachers and students, while the 'technician-training colleges' had to be developed from scratch. This means that from 1980, when the polytechnic system was created, to approximately the second half of the last decade, this polytechnic system was dominated essentially by the problems of the teacher-training colleges, whilst the development of the technician-training colleges was disregarded. This was an unfortunate development, because from the beginning of the project the technician-training colleges were considered a first priority in the strategy to tackle Portugal's manpower needs.

With the increasing importance attached to the training of technicians and with the financial resources available from international organisations such as the World Bank and EC, the situation is now quite different and polytechnics are actually a very important mechanism for the training of new professional profiles and new types of skilled people badly needed for the development of the country in strategic economic sectors. The second aspect which has to be mentioned in this context is the Plan for the Development of Education (PRODEP) which was negotiated between the European Commission and the Portuguese Government. The Plan with a budget for higher education of 318,629 MECUs is divided into two sub-programmes, one for the improvement of infrastructure and another for the training of trainers. The first has a budget of 266,883 MECUs and the second a budget of 51,746 MECUs. The share of the European Community in the two sub-programmes is respectively 68 per cent and 65 per cent. The main objective of this large investment plan is to increase the number of teaching places in the universities as well as in the polytechnics (35,000 new places before 1993). This is to be achieved through expansion of laboratory spaces, libraries, seminar rooms and lecture theatres with first priority for the scientific fields of engineering (37%), exact and natural sciences (24%) and management and organisation sciences (15%).

In global terms the PRODEP corresponds to a great co-investment effort in the next three years which can have a large impact on the development of the system and on the quality increase of the teaching-learning process in higher education.

The development of research projects particularly in connection with the productive sectors is one of the most relevant innovative aspects of the development of higher education in the last couple of years, in particular following the integration of Portugal in the EC.

The links that have been established by universities with the productive sectors are the result of three main factors. Firstly, the new mentality of academics, in particular of the young generation trained in universities abroad. Secondly, the budget constraints which affect the universities, and finally, the new attitude of some entrepreneurs/businessmen aiming to develop co-operation programmes with university laboratories or with university researchers and professors.

This new approach motivated the development of several co-operation efforts involving not only large public enterprises but also private and multinational enterprises operating in Portugal. However, in 1980, public expenditures on R&D was nevertheless 64 per cent of the total, while the enterprises have spent not more than 27 per cent. Regarding the total expenditure on R&D, Portugal has spent around 0.46 per cent of the GNP in 1988, which compares to 0.33 per cent for Greece and 0.59 per cent for Spain, but is still very far from the figures in Germany, France, the UK and the Netherlands where expenditures in R & D reach 2.69 per cent, 2.25 per cent and 2.22 per cent of the GNP respectively.

Portugal is now giving special priority to the development of research and to the consolidation of co-operation mechanisms between universities, research institutes and enterprises, (public or private). In this context the Portuguese Government and the European Commission have negotiated a large investment programme for the period 1990–93, in the sector of scientific research (*Programa Ciência*) with the fundamental objective of developing the scientific and technological Portuguese System. The programme involves an investment of 304 MECUs divided into four sub-programmes: sub-programme 1 (47%) aims to expand the infrastructures of the sector; sub-programme 2 (25%) is dedicated to advanced training and innovation in priority sectors; sub-programme 3 (25%) aims to give global support to the scientific and technological system; and finally, sub-programme 4 (3%) is dedicated to the management of the programme.

In parallel with the PRODEP, this Science Programme is one of the strategic instruments in developing the country. However, the programme has been severely criticised by some members of the scientific community who consider that this programme does not meet the main problems of the sector. Firstly, because it does not attach first priority to the fundamental sectors of humanities and social sciences. Secondly, because this huge investment in research is, in practice, a programme for the construction of buildings and for the purchase of equipment, while the budget for the running costs remains insufficient to cover the actual needs of laboratories and of research projects in progress, including personnel costs.

Nevertheless, it is clear that the Science programme is an extremely important instrument for the development of R&D activities. The adoption of the programme, however, implies the mobilisation of other financial resources and if this mobilisation does not take place the objectives of the foreseen investment may not be entirely achieved.

The development of new research projects is closely associated with the creation of new research agencies and institutes linking universities and enterprises, private or public. Since the beginning of the 1980s, there is a trend towards the establishment of institutions, associating universities and enterprises, and aiming to the develop scientific research and scientific consulting activities. The activity programme of these institutions, like FUNDETEC, INESC, INEGI or UNINOVA, is very diversified and includes professional training, upgrading or retraining of professionals, scientific research, enterprise and business incubators and external consulting. The evaluation of the activitities of these institutions has been very positive, but an independent evaluation should be carried out in the near future aiming to reinforce the process or to introduce some necessary corrections.

In the last three years, the most important decision taken by parliament, in what concerns the higher education system, was the approval of the statutes of universities and polytechnics, through which administrative and financial autonomy was awarded to these institutions.

These laws represent a very important turning point in the history of the Portuguese higher education system. In fact, after a long period of subordination to central Government, Portuguese universities have, through these laws, obtained a high degree of autonomy regarding the political system. This means that higher education institutions are more independent, but also more responsible for their actions. In the autonomous statutes, the universities have the authority to approve their internal regulation framework, while the central Government keeps the right to analyse the regulations and to confront these with national laws as well as the prerogative to confirm the internal regulation.

Conclusion

As Portugal is a country in transformation, which only recently started to develop its economic potential, it comes as no surprise that the higher education system is undergoing profound changes, too. Nevertheless, it must be noted that the number of students in higher education is still very low in comparison to other EC countries. Demand for places in the public system far exceeds the number of places available, and the surplus demand is increasingly swallowed up by an expanding private system. The other sector which is growing considerably is the polytechnic system. Polytechnical institutes have been characterised by a heavy bias towards teacher training which has hampered their technician training vocation, regarded so important for Portugal's manpower needs. Only very recently, this situation has started to change, partly because of large-scale investments in the training of technicians from the World Bank and the EC.

The constraints of the Portuguese system are to be found in a lack of investment in education and research and a very uneven spread of students and qualified staff over regions and institutions. As regards modifications of the curriculum and innovation in general, the polytechnics have taken the lead, followed by the new universities and, to a lesser extent, the more established universities. The new administrative and financial autonomy acquired by universities and polytechnics, will hopefully give them more room for manoeuvre to deal with the problems currently experienced in Portugal's higher education system. However, they will only be able to do this effectively, when an investment is made, not only in building new universities, institutions or facilities, but also in the day-to-day running costs of Portugal's higher education institutions.

Reference

Marçal Grilo, E. and M. Carmelos Rosa (1988) 'The Contribution of Higher Education to Modernisation in Portugal'. *European Journal of Education* Vol 23 No 3, 203–211.

CHAPTER 8

Main Features of Higher Education in Greece

Christos A. Saitis

Introduction

Tertiary education in Greece consists of two types of institutions: the universities and the Institutions of Technological Education. The latter are three-year-programme institutes, somewhat similar to *Fachhochschulen* in Germany or the polytechnics in the UK. Their role is to provide theoretical and practical training which allows the application of scientific, technological, artistic and other methods, ideas and skills in professional activities.

University-Level Education

The first Greek university institution, the University of Athens, was founded in 1837, soon after the constitution of the new State. Since then, the Greek system of higher education has developed rather slowly (Saitis, 1988, 249–250). Two other institutions, the National Technical University and the School of Fine Arts, although founded almost at the same time as the University of Athens, were granted university status only in 1914 and 1930 respectively. The first Greek university outside the capital, the University of Thessaloniki, was founded in northern Greece in 1925. In the 1950s, the Greek system of university education included three universities and six university-level schools, all of which were located in urban centres.

In the 1960s, social pressure for greater access to higher education, the need for further economic and cultural development, and demands to modernise the structure and organisation of the Greek universities, led to the creation of a series of new universities in the regions. From 1964 to 1984, eight new universities were established, bringing the number of higher education institutions in Greece to a total of seventeen (see Table 1).

Academic Structure

The institutions of higher education are composed of faculties. The faculties are divided into departments which constitute the basic academic unit. The syllabus of a department leads to a uniform degree. Responsibility for formulating teaching and research policy in connection with the subject areas for which degrees are awarded now lies with the departments. The sections are responsible for implementing the basic policy decisions taken by their respective departments. Each department is run by a general council which formulates teaching and research policy and exercises control over all of the department's affairs.

Table 1: Teaching staff and student population in Greek universities

University-Level Institutions	Academic Year 1989–90		
	Students Ratio	Staff	Staff/ Student
University of Athens	59,507	1,491	1:40
Techn University of Athens	9,127	396	1:23
University of Thessaloniki	19,157	1,717	1:29
Athens University of Economics and Business	8,279	63	1:131
Agricultural University of Athens	2,124	84	1:25
School of Fine Arts	466	26	1:18
Panteios University of Social and Political Sciences	6,540	111	1:59
University of Piraeus	10,892	52	1:209
Macedonia University of Economics and Social Sciences	8,425	35	1:241
University of Patras	10,378	435	1:24
University of Ioannina	7,363	322	1:23
University of Thrace	7,281	161	1:45
University of Crete	4,432	231	1:21
Techn University. of Crete	551	13	1:42
University of Aegean	1,157	31	1:37
Ionion University	442	9	1:49
University of Thessaly	267	4	1.67
Total	18,388	5,163	1:36

Source: MNER, Athens, September 1990.

The teaching and research staff (DEP) consists of full professors, associate professors, assistant professors and lecturers. Full professors and associate professors have tenure.

Administrative Structure

The organisational pattern of Greek universities is the same everywhere. Within the framework laid down in the University Reform Law No 1628/1982, the highest governing body is the Senate. It has principal authority in academic and financial matters and consists of the Rector, the two Vice-Rectors, the Deans of the Faculties and representatives of the teaching and special administrative staff as well as the students of the institution.

The Rectorial Council, responsible for the implementation of relevant decisions of the Senate, consists of the Rector, the two Vice-Rectors, one representative of the students and one of the administrative staff as an adviser.

At the level of Faculty and Department, there are the following bodies: the General Assembly of Faculty, the Deanship, the General Assembly of the Department, and the Board of the Department. These bodies consist of members of teaching staff, special administrative staff and students of the Faculty or Department.

The Dean of Faculty is elected by the members of Faculty for a three-year term. The Head of the Department and the Director of the Sector are elected by the members of department and sector, respectively. Finally, the Head of the Secretariat is elected by the Senate, for a three-year term. It should be noted that all the above officers-members of university bodies are appointed by the Minister of Education on the nomination of the Senate.

From the above description we observe that: firstly, the university officers of each level have limited powers – compared to those of some other public organisations – in the sense that the power lies with a decision-making body comprising either the whole staff of the unit or at least representatives of each group. Secondly, the collective bodies of Greek universities do not include members from outside the university, and the power lies in the hands of academics and students. Lastly, the existing structure of university bodies led to a fragmentation of university activities. Particularly, the university organs constitute a 'chain' with final decisions made at the upper level committees, Senate or Rectorial Council. There is no doubt about the democratic nature of the decision-making process within universities. However, the Ministry of Education, Ministry of Finance, Council of the State, etc sometimes raise questions about the efficiency of Greek universities.

Entry Requirements

The system of selection and allocation is operated by the Ministry of National Education and Religion (MNER). It applies to all public institutions of higher education, the universities and the TEIs. Applicants indicate an order of preference for courses and institutions and are then allocated to the highest choice on their list for which they have the appropriate marks. Thus, unlike other selective institutions, such as the universities in the Republic of Ireland or the UK, the institutions themselves have no power of selection, but have to accept those students allocated to them by the ministry.

Organisation of Courses and Costs of Education

Courses in universities last between four and six years, depending on the subject. The Greek academic year is divided into two semesters and the law lays down the minimum number of semesters required for a degree. In most subjects, 8 semesters are required, but in engineering 10 and in medicine and related subjects 12 semesters are necessary. The courses in the TEIs are shorter, lasting six semesters.

According to Article 16 section 4 of the Constitution (1975) education (primary, secondary and tertiary) in Greece is free of charge at all levels. Therefore, students of institutions of higher education do not pay tuition fees. Moreover, textbooks are provided to all students free of charge.

Postgraduate Studies

Taught postgraduate courses are available in Greece. This is a comparatively recent development and not many are yet in operation, although a number have been approved. In fact only five university-level institutions offer this kind of course.

Due to the scarceness of postgraduate studies, many students from Greek universities prefer to go overseas for postgraduate studies as a way of broadening their qualifications and improving their foreign languages. There are, therefore, large numbers of Greeks to be found studying in the European Community as well as in the USA.

Non-University-Level Education

Historical Development

Until 1970, most higher technical schools were in private hands. The exception were three State Higher Schools for sub-engineers in Athens and Thessaloniki. The demands for higher technical and vocational education were chiefly met by various private schools and these three state schools. The ever increasing number of young people in higher education and the growing demands of the labour market for highly trained personnel in the 1960s made it unavoidable for the State to take the necessary steps towards organising the non-university higher technical education on a realistic and systematic basis. The outcome was the law for higher technical education of 1970, which established the legal frame for a modern system of technical training.

Act 652/1970 provided for the creation of State operated Centres of Higher Technical Education (KATE in Greek) with many branches of specialisation, which gradually became the main institutions for non-university tertiary technical training. Seven years later, Law 676/77 constituted the legal frame of secondary and tertiary non-university technical and vocational education. By this law the KATE were abolished and replaced by Centres of Higher Technical and Vocational Education, known as KATEE. The objective of these Centres is 'to provide its students with the necessary theoretical and practical knowledge, so that they may become higher level technical specialists, able to assist in the development of the national economy'. In 1983 Act No 1404 reorganised the Institutions of Higher Technological Education. By this Act the hitherto controversial KATEEs were abolished and replaced by Technological Educational Institutions, known as TEI. Greece currently has 11 TEIs with 127 departments and 50 different specialisations.

Academic and Administrative Structure

The TEIs belong, together with the universities, to the higher level of education. The TEIs are self-governed legal entities subject to public law which receive financial support from the State. Each TEI comprises at least two faculties and each faculty at least two departments. Each department is subdivided into different classes. Each class corresponds to a specific academic and technological level. Freedom of academic teaching is guaranteed within the framework of the curriculum, scientific research and the communication of ideas in the TEI.

Within the framework laid down in Educational Act 1404/1983, the existing administrative structure of TEI is the following: Assembly of TEI, TEI Council President and Vice-President. At the level of Faculty and Department, there are the following bodies and officers: General Assembly of Faculty, Director of Faculty, General Assembly of Department, Head of Department. The governing bodies of the TEI are elected by all members of teaching staff, representatives of the administrative staff and the students.

Organisation of Studies

In the TEIs, teaching is divided into semester courses. In addition to the theoretical courses and workshop exercises, the curriculum also includes a compulsory six-month practical in-service training period. The academic year starts on 1 September and finishes on 5 July the following year.

There are no formal postgraduate studies at the TEIs. However, within the framework of their mandate, they organise specialised programmes in order to enable TEI degree holders to carry out work in a more specialised field of study.

Recent Developments

In the 1980s, as a result of the 1982 Education Act No 1268, a series of changes have taken place. The most important innovations were the following:

The establishment of a National Academy of Letters and Sciences (EAGE), charged with the co-ordination of research, teaching and postgraduate studies for the improvement of teaching staff and selection standards. However, eight years after its establishment, this organisation is not yet active. Also, the new Council for University Research and Postgraduate Studies, which would advise the Minister of Education on all pertinent issues, has not yet been implemented. This means that there is still no assessment of teaching staff and no supervision or co-ordination of research in higher education institutions.

The foundation of a National Council for University-level Education, known as SAP, which makes recommendations to the Government on university matters, such as the establishment or dissolution or reorganisation of faculties. SAP includes representatives of the government, political parties, local government, university-level institutions, scientific and social groups and the two sides of industry. The members of this Council participate on an equal basis and its operation rests upon a democratic dialogue. How well it fulfils its aims, however, depends upon the degree to which the participant bodies respond to the responsibilities with which they are entrusted by the State. This requires a systematic analysis of problems, as well as creative utilisation of scientific and social experience. Given that 1. it meets only four times a year; 2. its members are liable to be changed at any time; 3. the representatives of university teaching staff and students are in a minority; and 4. the representatives of political parties usually present divergent views about the development of university education, it is doubtful whether the National Council will fulfil its aims. The questions which immediately arise are whether or not the SAP limits the self-administration of universities, and whether or not its decisions are implemented by the Government.

With regard to the first question, the answer is affirmative in the sense that SAP directly controls all the vital areas of internal management (e.g. selection of students, determination of research, the size of institutions of higher education, and the allocation of funds) in which a university normally has a measure of self-government (Mountford, 1966, 159). Regarding the relationship of SAP to governmental policy, we may say that while it makes recommendations to the government on university matters, its decisions are not binding by law. Hence, SAP decisions which are opposed to government policy may be a waste of time and money.

The transfer of authority to academic departments, which replaced the European chair-system introduced to Greece in the 1830s. Now, authority is organised in a way similar to American university departments, which are largely independent in structure, function and administration.

The introduction of student participation in the general assemblies of departments on a 2:1 ratio in favour of the teaching staff. In the Senate the ratio is 1:1. It is assumed that democratic university management demands participation, i.e. the right of all members of the university community to have a voice in management through general and compulsory elections within each constituent part. In the case of Greek universities the 'equal' participation of students at the upper level of self-government may be an expression of university democratisation, but it is questionable whether this form of Senate composition serves the interests of the university well. Doubts are based upon three factors. Firstly, the university life of a student is an average of four years only. Secondly, the students' representation changes every academic year while university management demands continuity and responsibility. Finally, students usually mingle political issues with problems of university development (Psacharopoulos, 1988, 122).

The foundation of postgraduate schools in all university institutions. It is important to note that since 1982, a number of legislative measures (e.g. Law 1566/1985, and

Presidential Decrees 380/89 and 234/90) have given postgraduate studies new impetus. However, eight years since their establishment they have not yet been implemented.

The transfer of the two-year teacher training programmes from Pedagogical Academies (which were abolished) to universities, which has meant the extension of the period of study/preparation from two to four years.

All these innovations represent an attempt to restore some importance to the role of the university in Greece. Given that the above-mentioned changes are not sufficient to increase the efficiency of Greek institutions of higher education, a new wave of change has risen and might be able to introduce some real structural changes in the higher education system. Three subjects of reform are now under discussion:

Firstly, the establishment of the *Ministry of Universities and Scientific Research* as a way to unify all programmes of scientific research supported by public authorities, and to maximise efficiency and productivity in several fields where international competition is tough and challenging.

Secondly, the foundation of private universities. Article 16 of the Greek Constitution states that higher education is free and in the responsibility of the State, and that private higher education is prohibited. Despite the constitutional prohibition, this subject is discussed by the Government. Among the supporters of this idea are those who believe that private universities might reduce the exodus of Greek students abroad (Psacharopoulos, 1988, 135). It is argued that many would prefer to study in Greece, instead of going to Italy or the UK. A higher quality of instruction would be possible for private universities, since they could recruit staff on the international market and would not be bound by civil service pay-scales. A policy which encouraged the establishment of private universities would also introduce an element of competition between governmental and private higher educational institutions. Still another effect of such a policy would be substantial savings in foreign exchange, especially if the private universities undertook to provide for graduate studies and high quality research. On the other hand, there are those who fear that the foundation of private universities will lead to violation of the main university principles: self-administration, academic freedom for teaching and research, and wielding of social control (Dionysis, 1989).

Thirdly, legislative measures on postgraduate studies, the role of TEIs, the relationship between the State and institutions of higher education, etc are currently discussed within the Ministry of Education.

We do not know whether the above mentioned subjects will lead to a new educational reform; it is true, however, that the Greek institutions of higher education (as we will see below) are going through a crisis and are in need of modernisation both from the academic and from the administrative point of view.

Considering the Main Features of Greek Higher Education

Looking at the organisation and operation of the Greek institutions of higher education, we may point out the following characteristics: concentration of student population, centralisation of power, arbitrary educational policy, student emigration, inefficient co-operation between the institutions of higher education and industry, and student reluctance to leave the system.

Concentration of Student Population

Despite the rapid development of new regional universities in the last three decades, the student population of these institutions is relatively small and their contribution to higher education rather limited in this respect. There were some 55,000 students attending university in 1965–66. They were all concentrated in the Athens/Piraeus and Thessaloniki urban centres. Since then the student population has more than tripled and it was hoped that the new regional universities would absorb a considerable percentage of the total student population. However, today these universities comprise only 16 per cent of the total student population (see Table 1).

The same can be said about TEIs. In the academic year 1989–90, there were approximately 65,000 students at the TEIs; 50 per cent of them were concentrated in the Athens/Piraeus and Thessaloniki urban centres, where only three TEIs are located.

Table 2: Number of students per TEI

	1980–1981	1984–1985	1989–1990
TEI of Athens	6909	12,426	18,730
TEI of Tessaloniki	3790	7378	9179
TEI of Patras	1627	3882	3472
TEI of Larissa	1855	4347	9568
TEI of Heraklion	1431	3949	6353
TEI of Kozani	1108	2257	2505
TEI of Messolongi	107	1676	2646
TEI of Piraeus	2402	3071	4874
TEI of Kavala	938	2471	1622
TEI of Serres	560	1586	2739
TEI of Chalkida	180	1775	3363
Total	*20,907*	*44,821*	*65,321*

Source: MNER, Athens 1990.

It means that the remaining 50 per cent are divided among the other eight TEIs (see Table 2).

Centralisation of Power

Education in Greece is the responsibility of the State. Article 16 of the Greek Constitution of 1975 declares: 'Art and science, research and teaching, shall be free of impediment and it shall be incumbent on the State to develop and advance them. Academic freedom and freedom in teaching shall be subject to the provisions of the Constitution.' For higher education, in particular, it states that all university-level institutions must be legal entities in public law and totally self-governing. These institutions are financed and supervised by the State and are organised in line with specific laws which deal with their operations. Under the Constitutional order, the University Act of 1982 stipulates that the institutions of higher education covered by public law are completely self-governed; the authority for supervision by the State is vested in the Ministry of National Education and Religion (MNER).[1]

From this statement it is evident that the nature of the relationship between universities and the State depends upon the definition of the two significant words 'self-governed' and 'supervision'. By the term 'self-governed', the Greek legislator intends that the institutions of higher education should enjoy the authority to select their teaching staff and administrative officers, make decisions about their affairs, and

---

1   Law No 1268/1982, article 3.

carry them out under the 'supervision' of the State and in particular of the MNER. In turn, the purpose of the State's 'supervision' is precisely to prevent the corruption to which a completely independent university could be exposed (Jaspers, 1966, 138). Thus, on the one hand, a university is free to decide how its affairs are to be conducted so as to achieve the best possible results. On the other hand, the State as paymaster accountable for national development may insist on setting limits to university growth and demand certain standards of economy, efficiency and fairness in relation to students and staff. But what about the reality?

In theory there is 'absolute' independence for university institutions to manage their affairs as they wish; in practice, however, the sense of self-administration has disappeared because all university decisions need ministerial approval. When, for example, the appointment of a lecturer or a member of the administrative staff or approval to change the name of an academic position needs to go through the bureaucratic process as far as the MNER and other Ministries or public services, it makes little sense to talk about effective self-government. Moreover, there is no clear-cut policy regarding the extent of the control that the State exercises upon the universities through the MNER. In many instances (the number of students is a recent example), the universities have opposed measures taken by the Ministry of Education, accusing it of interference in the administration of university institutions. Finally, the way the existing system of financing operates at present, forces institution to keep to a year to year time-scale of management, thereby hindering the implementation of medium and longer term development plans. Moreover, the strict financial control exercised by the public auditing services reduces their managerial autonomy to almost zero rendering them all the more inefficient (Saitis, 1986, 237–254).

Arbitrary Educational Policy

Another worrying aspect of Greek educational policy is the decision-making process itself. In Greece, as in other countries, educational reform often becomes a salient issue after major political upheavals and periods of crisis or rapid social change.

After the fall of the junta in 1974, change was expected in all sectors and educational reform suddenly became a major issue. We do not propose to deal in detail with specific aspects of the educational reforms which took place after 1974, but we can say that policy proposals for educational reform are usually taken by small groups of educational pundits, scientists or bureaucrats commissioned for the task by the MNER and acting on behalf of central administration and government. Greek legislators thus act on advice which is remote from the national community. Finally, the decision-making process itself lacks adequate national consultation or responsiveness to the views of a wide cross-section of the population, and this suggests that the process is more arbitrary than democratic.

Too Much Student Emigration?

Greeks have traditionally been one of the most mobile of European nations, with a long tradition of going abroad to find work. There are, of course, very large expatriate Greek communities in certain European countries (notably Germany and the UK, as well as in the USA and Australia). Greek graduates are not only mobile in looking for jobs abroad but also in studying abroad. With regard to the latter, we see that recently many thousands of students travel abroad to study at foreign universities. In 1984, for example, more than 41,000 students (or 50 per cent of the total student population) were studying abroad. This student mobility can be attributed mainly to the following reasons:

1. After World War II, a steadily increasing demand for studies in higher education appeared. The main reason for which Greek students study abroad – apart from their initial desire to be educated – is the fact that the Greek State is not able to meet this still growing demand which is backed up by factors that were formed and strengthened during the last decades such as (MNER, 1988, 6–10):

   a) an increase in family income

   b) the abolition of teaching and examination fees, provision of all textbooks free of any charge and a number of other beneficiary measures have added to such a pressure

   c) favourable perspectives for university graduates

   d) a traditional emphasis on the humanities which has not allowed vocational training to develop accordingly

   e) the influence the family has on their children as far as their studies are concerned. In fact Greek families still influence the future of children by selecting occupations for them. Given that parents believe a university degree to be a golden key to life-chances they direct the children to university learning. This belief is partly due to an absence of a government employment policy, leaving parents uninformed about the institutions in which they wish their sons and daughters to study. The result of this situation is that many students who are not assured of success in their entrance examinations for an institution of higher education at home, due to strong competition (see Table 3), travel abroad to study in foreign universities.

However, this professional orientation is not always successful and, furthermore, thousands of students who today are studying in foreign universities will return after graduation to swell the ranks of unemployed professional people.

Table 3: University applicants and successes

	Applicants	Successes	Percentage
1968	33,086	9,191	27.8
1974	54,955	14,262	25.95
1977	72,481	13,223	18.24
1981	75,206	14,746	19.6
1984	129,374	23,598	18.2
1985	149,269	23,666	15.5
1990	124,658	22,890	13.3

Sources: For the year 1968, (Kintis, 1980, 56). For the years 1974 and 1977, (OECD, 1980, 101). For the years 1981, 1984, 1985 and 1990, (MNER, 1990).

2. In the past, there was a preference for the model of the 'economy of demand'. In brief, this choice in policy means that only as many students will be accepted in institutions of higher education as can be absorbed by the market. The result is that a considerable number of young people is left out of higher education in Greece, leading a large number of students to enrol in foreign universities.

3. Another factor that has made Greek students go abroad for their studies has been the bad quality of undergraduate and postgraduate studies in Greece. Most of the scientists who returned to Greece after their studies abroad have been highly successful in all scientific fields. That is how the image of 'the scientist with guaranteed and concrete knowledge from abroad' was created and as a result prestige was given to degrees from foreign universities.

Inefficient Co-operation Between Institutions of Higher Education and Industry

As in most universities all over the world, research is an essential function of the Greek universities. Most research conducted by university personnel takes place within the universities themselves, while some research activities are carried out in several non-university research institutions, most of which have close scientific links with the universities.

It is difficult to delineate the volume of university research in Greece or to describe its exact nature, as there are no complete statistics on research activities or publications of universities; and the participation of the universities in the research carried out in non-university research institutions cannot be accurately determined. Examining however, the role of university research in linking university institutions and industry, we see that in Greece this collaboration is not satisfactory. With a few exceptions (e.g. the Athens Technical University, and the Universities of Thessaloniki, Patras and Crete), most of Greek institutions are clearly in difficult circumstances as regards co-operation with industry in this field (Psacharopoulos, 1988, 123). This fact can be attributed to the following reasons:

1. The lack of laboratories (properly supplied with equipment and experienced research staff) which could be assigned to research programmes by State and private institutions. In Greece there is a shortage of research personnel. There are about 6,000 researchers, 75 per cent of them at universities. Only 10 per cent can be found in research institutions and 5 per cent in industry. Not so much the small number of available researchers is the pressing problem, but even worse, the fact that the qualified researchers are not engaged in the most needed areas of research. In some areas there is a surplus of qualified researchers, as in law and in sociology, while in other areas they are very few, as in micro-electronics. In terms of available equipment and other infrastructure support, the supply is quite adequate but the picture is still bleak. This is due to the fact that it is relatively easy to order and get very expensive equipment but extremely difficult to have a technician put it in operation or keep it running because of the complicated red tape. At universities, there are no positions specifically devoted to research. In 1988, an act was passed which states that special research institutes will be established at the universities; but nothing has been done yet. University professors have three tasks to perform: teaching, administration and research. With the large numbers of students the professors have to teach, and with the numerous administrative activities they have to participate in, there is very little time left for research.

2. The weakness of the present legislation concerning co-operation between institutions of higher education and private enterprises. More specifically, the legislation in force does not deal with the institutions of higher education and technological institutions as a whole, and does not offer substantial incentives to research personnel.

3. The limited financing of scientific and technological research. Private enterprises in Greece finance only 9.4 per cent of the total cost for research. Enterprises are small and traditional, and they cannot afford to carry out systematic research programmes. Given that Greece spends only 0.33 per cent of the gross national product on research and development (while in France it is 2.3% of GNP), we may say that the conditions for collaboration between institutions of higher education and industry are not favourable.

4. The lack of co-ordination and supervision of scientific research. Since neither the National Academy of Letters and Sciences Act (1268/82) nor the Academic Re-

search Institutions Act (1771/88) have yet been implemented, we can say that in Greece no assessment of teaching staff or co-ordination of research in universities takes place. On the contrary, the planning and execution of research lie in the hands of the staff of a unit, whereas the distribution of funds among the various units is decided upon by the respective departments. This freedom of planning and conducting research explains why, up to this day, the Greek institutions of higher education have not succeeded in clearly formulating their needs, on the basis of which the funds provided could be distributed to specific areas of scientific research.

Students' Reluctance

For various reasons, many students take longer than the minimum period of time to complete their studies. In 1989–90, 186,000 students were enrolled at Greek universities. Among them 69,000 can be considered as 'stagnating' students in the sense that they have remained at university much longer than the minimum period of time to complete their studies. With regard to the reasons for this delay, some will take more than the minimum number of courses required to get the necessary credits, some will retake courses either because they fail or because they wish to improve their grades. There are also many advantages in being a student in terms of cheap rates for travel etc, and for men the possibility of postponing military service at least until the age of 29. All these factors may serve to encourage people to continue their studies longer than would be strictly necessary. A student can stay at university regardless of the number of times he fails to pass a course. A student can be a student for life. Thus, attrition rates are almost zero. A student can try as many times as he chooses until he/she passes a course.

Conclusions

From the foregoing analysis, one may conclude that in Greece the institutions of higher education are going through a crisis. In other words, the system of higher education does not operate in a way which can cope with the problems and the needs of modern society.

To remedy this low efficiency of the Greek institutions of higher education a series of changes can be proposed, including the following:

1. A rational educational policy. Political instability and political pressures over the years have created over-flexible education policy-making. This type of 'flexibility' has not only produced a plethora of laws, but it has also led to a series of careless changes. Therefore, to avoid opposition from different university groups after legislative measures have been taken, and to reduce the legislative 'production' of Greek Parliament, all plans for higher education should first be considered by all social groups whom those acts might affect.

2. Devolution of power from the Ministry of Education to universities and TEIs. True self-administration demands that all university affairs (e.g. creation of new positions, appointments of staff, etc) should be carried out by university management. To this end, it is very important for Greek policy-makers to define exactly the authority of academic institutions because authority is the basis for accountability.

3. Further attention has to be given to: decentralisation of the student population from the institutions of higher education in Athens and Thessaloniki to regional universities and TEIs; improvement of student attendance at universities; the im-

plementation of postgraduate departments; and the introduction of modern specialisations.

4. Effective co-operation between institutions of higher education and private enterprises. One way to this end is the introduction of obligatory practice for all undergraduates in the working environment where they will be employed in the future,
as a prerequisite for obtaining their degree. However, further bold and rapid steps
are needed for industry to approach universities. Industry ought to acquaint universities with the problems it faces in its attempts to improve the quality of its
products and services and of maximising its profits. Universities in their turn
ought to direct their attention towards production, study its problems, exploit at
length the huge potential it possesses so as to solve these problems and give original advice and views. In other words, universities ought to be in a position to be
commissioned by State and private enterprises to work out technical, economical
or other research studies on current problems and issues they are preoccupied
with.

5. Efficient university management. The above reforms cannot be implemented without some managerial arrangements such as the introduction of new methods of
work and improvement of the ability of administrative staff. Duties and responsibilities cannot be delegated to academic committees, when they operate under
the traditional organisation, nor can financial law be changed when the university
financial managers lack modern knowledge and experience to manage the financial affairs of their institution.

In Greece, there still exist many problems (e.g. over-centralisation of administrative
power, too much student emigration, etc.) which demand both rational planning and
a successful implementation strategy. Only in this manner can efficiency be promoted
in Greek institutions of higher education, and in the Greek educational system at large.

References

Brychea, A. and K. Gavroglou (1982) *Attempts to Reform Higher Education 1911–1981.* Thessaloniki:
Syghrona Themata.

Jaspers, K. (1960) *The Idea of the University.* London: Peter Owen.

Gordon, P. and D. Lawton (1984) *A Guide to English Educational Terms.* London: Batsford Academic
and Educational.

Kazamias, A. (1980) 'The politics of education – the case of Greece' in Helmes, B. (Ed) *Diversity
and Unity in Education.* London: Allen and Unwin, 135–136.

Kintis, A. (1980) *Higher Education in Greece.* Athens: Gutenberg.

Kladis Dionysis (1989) 'Private or Public Universities' in *Economikos Tachydromos* 12 January 1989
(in Greek).

Mauridis, L. (1979) 'The Greek University System: Organisation and Autonomy' in *Reform and
Development of Tertiary Education in Greece.* Athens: MNER, 23–24.

MNER *Report of Committee for the Greek Students Abroad.* Athens 1988.

Mountford, J. (1966) *British Universities.* London: Oxford University Press.

OECD (1980) Educational Policy and Planning: Paris.

Parry, J.P. (1971) *The Provisions of Education in England and Wales.* London: Allen and Unwin.

Psacharopoulos, G. (1988) 'Efficiency and Equity in Greek Higher Education' in *Minerva* Vol 26
No 2.

Saitis, C.A. (1986) 'A Comparative Study of Some Aspects of the Administrative Systems of English
and Greek Universities' Chapter 5, Doctoral Thesis. University of Hull.

Saitis, C.A. (1988) 'The Relationship between the State and the University in Greece' in *European Journal of Education* Vol 23 No 3, 249–260.

Taliadouros, A. (1983) *Reform in Higher Education 1974–1981*. Athens: Triandafillis (in Greek).

CHAPTER 9

Goal Enlargement and Differentiation
The Evolution of the Binary Higher Education System in Ireland

Patrick Clancy

This paper commences with a brief account of the evolution of the university system in Ireland. The main body of the paper describes the structural change and diversification which occurred in the 1970s. The non-university sector became the main focus for development, reflecting an explicit vocationalism and a heavy emphasis on technology. The universities also evolved to embrace more utilitarian objectives and now much of their teaching and research is legitimated by its contribution to technological development and economic growth. The final section of the paper examines the pattern of participation in higher education, and briefly reviews some class, gender and regional differences in participation.

Evolution of the University System
The oldest institution within the present system of higher education in Ireland dates from 1592. The establishment of Trinity College Dublin followed a number of abortive attempts to found a university during the previous 300 years. However, the institutionalisation of higher learning in Ireland predates the establishment of the modern university. From the 6th century, monastic settlements became centres of learning which attracted not only Irish youth but also students from abroad. This 'golden age of scholarship' lasted for several hundred years during which time many monks and scholars extended their activities overseas and made a noteworthy contribution to European civilisation (McGrath, 1979).

While the pursuit of higher learning was first sponsored by the church, the religious question subsequently became a major impediment to the development of higher education in Ireland. Trinity College Dublin (TCD) was designed to encourage English culture in Ireland and to promote the reformed religion in its statutory form. It provided no opportunities for higher education for the majority Catholic community or for Protestant dissenters, mainly Presbyterians, concentrated in Ulster. Starting in the late 18th century, various attempts were made to provide an acceptable form of higher education for those who had been excluded from TCD. A first approach to the problem was the partial removal of the religious tests governing admission to TCD. An important second step was the setting up, in 1795, of Maynooth College for the education of Catholic clergy, who since the late 16th century were forced to attend Irish colleges in other European countries. Fifty years later, three Queen's Colleges were established at Belfast, Cork and Galway. The Belfast college was successful, but the others did not flourish because they did not meet with the approval of the Catholic hierarchy. Meanwhile a Catholic university was established in 1854 under the rectorship of John Henry Newman. A variety of further initiatives were taken in the late 19th century, including the establishment, in 1879, of the Royal University, which functioned primarily as an examining body. However, it was not until 1908 that the university question was resolved to the satisfaction of the major political and denominational interest groups.

The Irish Universities Act of 1908 provided for the dissolution of the Royal University and the creation of two new universities, the National University in Dublin and Queen's University in Belfast. The Queen's College in Belfast was converted into the new Queen's University, while the Queen's Colleges at Cork and Galway became constituent colleges of the National University. In Dublin, the Catholic University, which since 1883 had become entrusted to the Jesuits and had become known as University College Dublin, and the Catholic University School of Medicine, became the new University College Dublin, the third constituent college of the National University of Ireland. The status of Trinity College Dublin was not altered by this act. Finally two years later, St Patrick's College Maynooth became a recognised college of the National University of Ireland.

Thus, the new independent state inherited an established university structure. It had two universities, Trinity College Dublin (The University of Dublin) and the National University of Ireland. The latter was a federal university with three constituent colleges and one recognised college. This university structure remained essentially unaltered for more than 40 years after independence, apart from its absorption of some pre-existing specialist colleges which provided education in agriculture, engineering, veterinary medicine and pharmacy. In contrast to this well-established university structure, higher education outside the university remained underdeveloped until recent decades. As recently as 1965, less than 19 per cent of total full-time enrolments in higher education were outside the universities. Teacher training colleges represented the most significant element (43%) of the non-university sector, the remainder consisting of a private medical school, some vocational technological colleges and a number of other small specialist colleges.

Structural Reform and Diversification

The 1960s marked a crucial transition in the modernisation of Irish society. The economic and social transformation followed from a number of initiatives taken in the late 1950s. Henceforth, the pursuit of economic growth was established as the dominant project in Irish political life. Economic development was to be pursued through a policy of rapid industrialisation, to be achieved with the help of foreign investment and to be sustained by export-led growth. To facilitate this transformation, the education system was restructured and expanded.

The adaptation of the education system was given direction and impetus by the deliberations of two important government initiated inquiries, *Investment in Education* (1966) and the *Commission on Higher Education* (1967). Although the latter report was directed specifically at higher education, it appears that the analysis contained in the *Investment in Education* report was more instrumental in legitimating the reorientation of the entire education system.

The *Investment in Education* report has been described as one of the foundation documents in Irish education (Coolahan, 1981). While the analysis in the report was wide-ranging and included an extensive considerations of topics such as patterns of inequality and resource utilisation, its major thrust was its commitment to the formation of human capital and to meeting the labour market needs of an expanding economy. In future the success of the educational system would be assessed by its capacity to facilitate the achievement of the state's economic objectives.

In contrast to the highly instrumental orientation revealed in *Investment in Education* the report of the Commission on Higher Education was more circumspect. In responding to its brief 'to inquire into and make recommendations in relation to university, professional, technological and higher education generally', the report presented an in-depth analysis of the system of higher education in Ireland in the early 1960s. While it acknowledged the substantial achievements, it was severely critical of many aspects of the system: it felt that academic standards were endangered within the university because of increasing numbers of students, low entry standards, inadequate staffing and accommodation; it pointed to the weaknesses of postgraduate studies and research; it urged changes in the modes of university governance and academic appointments; it noted that higher education outside the universities had remained comparatively underdeveloped. The Commission's recommendations reflected its view of the universities' proper concern with first principles and basic research as distinct from professional training and applied research.

Its major proposal to meet the need for increased higher education was to establish a network of 'New Colleges'. The New Colleges would operate in three main fields – the humanistic, the scientific and the commercial – and would work up to the standard of a pass degree. While it was envisaged that the courses offered would have 'a stronger vocational bias than would be appropriate to university courses', it was suggested that 'they would be planned to provide a broad and balanced education together with a certain amount of specialisation' (Commission on Higher Education, 127–128). A further proposal, which reflected this demarcation between basic research and pure scholarship from applied research and vocational relevance, was its recommendations to establish a separate National College of Agricultural and Veterinary Sciences (Coolahan 1990). Neither of these proposals was acted upon, thus suggesting that much of the tenor of the report was out of step with government thinking.

Perhaps the most consequential of the Commission's recommendations to be implemented was for the establishment of a planning authority. The Higher Education Authority (HEA) was established on an *ad hoc* basis in 1968 and on a statutory basis in 1972. The Commission had envisaged that the new planning authority would have jurisdiction over higher education as a whole. However, the remit of the HEA is more restricted. While its advisory and planning functions relate to all higher education, its executive functions relate only to those institutions which have been designated by legislation. The non-universities colleges were not so designated and, thus, remained under the direct control of the government department of education.

Before the Commission had reported, a smaller and much less publicised government-appointed committee was at work to advise on the development of technical education. In particular, the Steering Committee on Technical Education (1967) was asked to provide the Department of Education's building unit with a brief for the new Regional Technical Colleges (RTCs) which the government had already decided to establish. The committee reported in 1967, one year after its establishment, and recommended a broad role for the new colleges, suggesting that the main long-term function of the Colleges will be to educate for trade and industry over a broad spectrum of occupations ranging from craft to professional level, notably in engineering and science, but also in commercial, linguistic and other specialities. They will, however, be more immediately concerned with providing courses aimed at filling gaps in the industrial manpower structure, particularly in the technician area (Steering Committee on Technical Education, 11).

Five Regional Technical Colleges were established in 1970 and four more were established between 1971 and 1977. It was originally envisaged that these colleges would cater primarily for senior-cycle second level courses with a technological orientation, in addition to their involvement in apprenticeship training, together with some third-level courses. However, the colleges quickly shed almost all the second-level teaching and began to concentrate on the provision of third-level courses in engineering and construction studies, business studies, applied science and art and design. In addition to their strong vocational emphasis, the course offerings of the RTCs are also distinctive in that they are mainly short-cycle and sub-degree level. The majority of courses are of two-year duration leading to a National Certificate awarded by the National Council for Educational Awards.

There are, in addition, a small number of one year certificate courses, a significant number of three-year courses leading to a National Diploma and a limited number of four-year degree level courses. Concurrently with the development and rapid expansion of the new RTCs, the enrolments in the five colleges of the Dublin Institute of Technology also expanded. In addition, the Limerick College of Art, Commerce and Technology developed rapidly.

A concern for the development of technological education was also the driving force behind the establishment of the National Institutes for Higher Education (NIHE), the other major structural addition to the higher education system. The initial impetus behind the establishment of the NIHE came from the campaign to establish a university at Limerick (the third largest city in the country). This claim was rejected by the Commission on Higher Education which, instead, recommended that a New College be sited there. The Limerick claim for a university was subsequently referred by the Minister for Education for the consideration of the newly established Higher Education Authority. The HEA supported the views of the Commission that 'there is no national need at present for another university college'. However, it did recognise another national need, observing that Ireland was 'to a great extent lacking in a new and increasingly important form of higher education of which the primary purpose is the application of scientific knowledge and method'. Technological education, it argued, had not yet found its proper level; its content needed to be further upgraded and the scope of its operation extended. Furthermore, it suggested that technological and higher technician roles needed to become 'status carrying in their own right' (HEA, 1969, 9).

The authority was impressed by the success of the Polytechnics in Britain and saw this as offering a model for a College of Higher Education which would meet both national and local needs. The new college would combine the 'prestige of degree granting courses with an extensive provision of certificate and diploma courses'. From its inception it was envisaged that the new college (to become known as The National Institute for Higher Education) would offer courses at a higher level than the RTCs. However, like the RTCs, it has also experienced 'academic drift' and now operates primarily at degree level; in addition, it offers some postgraduate courses up to and including doctorates. Indeed, when the second NIHE opened in Dublin in 1980 it did not offer any sub-degree level courses. Of the 4820 students attending the NIHEs in 1988, 34 per cent were pursuing courses in commerce, 32 per cent courses in engineering and a further 10 per cent courses in science, while the remaining 24 per cent were divided between communication and information studies, European studies, art and design and education (HEA, 1987).

It is clear that the establishment of the RTCs and the NIHEs represents the main structural development in higher education over recent decades. An important complement to the development of these colleges was the establishment in 1972 of the National Council for Educational Awards (NCEA). The primary functions of the NCEA are to approve and recognise courses in colleges outside the university system and to confer degrees, diplomas and certificates on students successfully completing these courses. It has been suggested that the granting of degree awarding powers to the NCEA was significant in institutionalising a binary third-level system.

In 1974, the Minister for Education announced his intention of restricting the awarding of degrees to the universities, confining the NCEA to the awarding of certificates and diplomas. His argument was that this would lead to a comprehensive rather than a binary system. However, a change in government occurred before legislation was introduced and the new government restored degree-granting power to the NCEA. Most of the courses validated by the NCEA are offered by the RTCs, the other colleges of technology and, until 1989, the NIHEs. The NCEA also validates the courses offered by the National College of Art & Design (NCAD). This college was formed from a reconstituted National College of Art and was, in 1976, designated as an institution of higher education under the Higher Education Authority.

While the development of technological education represents the major transformation on the non-university sector, the colleges of education, the other major component of this sector, also experienced significant structural reform. In 1974, a new three-year B.Ed. degree programme was inaugurated in each of the six colleges which prepare primary teachers. Three of the largest colleges became recognised colleges of the National University of Ireland, while the three smaller colleges became associated with Trinity College Dublin. The new degree programme replaced a shorter two-year programme. The vast majority of second-level teachers has always earned their degrees and teaching qualifications from the universities. The penultimate steps in the creation of an all-graduate teaching profession were also taken in the 1970s with the establishment of Thomond College which provides degree-level courses for specialist teachers of physical education, woodwork and building construction, metalwork and engineering sciences, business studies and general and rural science. Furthermore the two colleges which prepare home economics teachers were also affiliated to the universities and now offer a degree programme. Finally, many art and design teachers now enter the profession with a degree from the NCAD. However, a degree qualification is not necessary; it is possible to qualify as a second-level teacher with an appropriate National Diploma in Art together with a teaching diploma.

Consolidation of Policy Change

The extent of the restructuring of the higher education system is reflected in the changing pattern of student enrolment. The latest year for which published data are available is 1987–88, and the distribution of students in this year is compared with the pattern which prevailed 10 and 20 years previously. Table 1 reveals a strong pattern of growth over the 20-year period with total enrolments increasing by 173 per cent. However, the main feature of the table is the differential growth by sector. While university enrolment increased by a modest 68 per cent, enrolment in the technological sector increased more than twenty-fold. In 1967–68, enrolment in the technological sector accounted for less than 6 per cent of the total, this had increased to 43 per cent by 1987–88. The changing balance between these two sectors is illustrated more clearly by the flow of new entrants, where the technological sector has now become the largest sector. In 1986, 55 per cent of new entrants to higher education enrolled in the technological sector, while 37 per cent commenced their studies in the university sector (Clancy, 1988). The difference between the percentage of new entrants and that of total enrolments is accounted for by differences in the duration of courses. Most of the colleges in the technological sector specialise in short-cycle courses, thus achieving a greater throughput of students.

Table 1: Enrolment of full time students in higher education, by sector in 1967–68 and 1987–88

Sector	1967–78		1977–78		1987–88	
	N	Percentage	N	Percentage	N	Percentage
Universities	16,881	77.7	23,526	63.6	28.344	47.7
Technological	1202	5.5	8094	21.9	25.647	43.2
Colleges of Education	1543	7.1	3171	8.6	2703	4.5
Other	2111	9.7	2,226	6.0	2,725	4.6
Total	21,723	100	37.01	100	59,419	100

Source: HEA 1990.

The pattern of growth in the colleges of education is more varied. Enrolment doubled in the first half of this period, partly accounted for by the lengthening of the programme of study. In contrast, in the most recent decade enrolment has declined. The curtailment of intake into teacher education colleges is due to a surplus of teachers and a declining age cohort, and has already resulted in the closing of one of the largest colleges of education.

The dramatic structural shift in the distribution of student enrolments testifies to the heavy emphasis on technology and the explicit vocationalism which characterises higher education policy. This policy imperative finds expression in government statements of policy such as *The White Paper on Educational Development* (1980) and *The Programme for Action in Education* (1984–1987). In both documents it is assumed that vocational preparation is the prime purpose of higher education and that the main justification for state expenditure on higher education is its contribution to economic development and economic growth. This utilitarian policy emphasis finds legitimation in the *Investment in Education* report, rather than in the report of the Commission on Higher Education.

The strategy chosen to affect this policy reorientation was to establish new colleges which were given a specific mandate to cater for the labour force needs of an expanding industrial economy. The main alternative strategy, that of a unitary system, might have been less amenable to such a policy reorientation. If a unitary policy was to have been successful, it would have required an explicit acceptance of the desirability of such a policy change by the then dominant and largely independent university sector. In choosing the binary option and in targeting the technological sector for more rapid growth, Irish higher education followed the path which found favour in most other European countries. This is the second in the general sequence of strategies identified by Scott (1985) in his review of changing priorities in higher education. This strategy involves dividing national systems of higher education into distinct categories and assigning to each category a different function. This replaced an earlier strategy which Scott describes as the 'trust the institution/faculty/department approach'. This policy involved allowing the college or constituent unit within it decide what to teach and to how large a constituency it should be offered.

Developments over the past decade reveal the operation of the third of the strategies identified by Scott whereby the rather crude institutional stratification has been replaced by more finer-grain programmatic discrimination. This third strategy shows governments attempting to determine the disciplinary balance in all higher education institutions. Having successfully developed a highly vocationally oriented non-university sector, the government has more recently become less accepting of the autonomy previously enjoyed by university institutions. The operation of a sequence of strategies shows a process of progressive state intervention. Initially public control of the universities consonant with the need for some accountability for public funding was achieved by the establishment of a 'buffer planning authority' which would guarantee institutional autonomy. In contrast, the colleges in the technological sector, with the exception of the NIHEs, were under the more direct control of government. Recent developments reveal that the government is becoming less satisfied with the autonomy which it previously granted to the HEA and is anxious to exercise more direct control of the entire higher education system (Clancy, forthcoming). The more directive government approach has been legitimated by an appeal to vocational and industrial development imperatives and, more recently, by the state's fiscal crisis.

While the main focus for the reorientation of policy was on the non-university sector it was inevitable that the universities would also reflect the changing priorities. One example of the universities' adaptation to vocational imperatives can be found in their willingness to incorporate as recognised colleges, the teacher training colleges which prepare primary teachers and home economics teachers. Similarly, the education of physiotherapists, speechtherapists and more recently that of occupational therapists have all been integrated within the universities.

However, the universities themselves have also changed and this is reflected in the distribution of students by field of study. In a climate which emphasises a technological orientation and vocational relevance, the universities have been most anxious to develop their engineering, science and business studies programmes. In 1988, 29 per cent of all full-time university students were in the faculties of Science and Engineering (HEA 1990). In contrast, in 1950 only 19 per cent of all students were in these faculties. There has also been a huge growth in student enrolments in the commerce and business studies area. For example, in the three constituent colleges of the National University in 1988, 12 per cent of all full-time students were in the faculty of Commerce while 13 per cent of full-time enrolments in TCD were in the faculty of Economic and Social Studies. Twenty-five years earlier less than 5 per cent of all full-time students in these four colleges were studying commerce or business studies. The strengthening of these faculties represents a gradual evolution of the university's vocational emphasis and, in general, occurred without conflict. Objections arose only when it was perceived that continued development in this direction might only be possible at the expense of the humanities and other 'non-vocational' programmes. The Arts faculties in particular have felt themselves under siege and, belatedly, have commenced a rearguard action to justify their relevance (Masterson, 1983; Lee, 1983).

Perhaps the most eloquent testimony to the changing ideological climate concerning the universities' role is the legislation in 1989 establishing two new universities, the University of Limerick and Dublin City University, based on the two National Institutes of Higher Education. This ministerial decision followed the recommendations of an international study group which was established to examine arrangements for technological education outside the universities and to consider the case for a technological university of which the two NIHEs would be constituent colleges. The study group expressed the view that the standards of scholarship at the NIHEs are as high as those of universities and that they had reached a stage of development and achievement where they should be self- accrediting. While noting that the mission statements of the NIHEs hold that their teaching and research are largely determined by what is needed in Ireland, the study group expressed the view that there is no inherent conflict between what is useful and what is scholarly. In advocating the granting of university status, the study group decided against the title 'technological university', because of the likelihood of confusion and because 'its appellation to the universities might appear to diminish the excellent work of the existing universities in the area of technological education and research'. It is clear that the concept of university which prevails at the end of the 1980s is quite different from that which prevailed in the mid-1960s.

Research function

One of the consequences of the radical restructuring of the system which accompanied the growth in enrolment is that Ireland now has a high proportion of students taking sub-degree level courses. In a comparison with nine other European countries it was found that, with the exception of the Netherlands, Ireland had the highest proportion of its students (39%) enrolled on sub-degree level courses with correspondingly fewer taking degree level and postgraduate courses (Clancy, 1989). The relatively high concentration of students on short-cycle courses has a strong appeal for government, understandably concerned with unit costs – two students can follow a two-year certificate programme for the same cost as one student enrolled on a four-year degree programme. However, the relative rate of return to individuals with different levels of certification is an issue which has not been examined.

The trend towards an increasing percentage of students taking sub-degree level programmes outside the university sector has been partly compensated for by a contrary trend in the universities where there has been a noticeable increase in the number of postgraduate students. While the number of primary degrees awarded in the universities increased by 27 per cent between 1977 and 1987, there was an increase of 116 per cent in the number of postgraduate degrees awarded. Although the number of doctorates awarded increased by 82 per cent during the period, the absolute number awarded in 1987 was still low (216) and the ratio of primary degrees awarded to that of doctorates was thirty to one.

The growth in postgraduate programmes, especially at doctorate level, points to the universities' research role. More rapid development in this area has been inhibited in recent years by cut-backs in state funding to the universities. These cut-backs have led to a decline in staff student ratios, reduced financial support for postgraduate students and left inadequate resources for the purchase of scientific equipment (Mulcahy, 1988). Notwithstanding the reductions in the real value of state funding, which form part of the government strategy to stop the country's accelerating spiral into debt, the research potential of higher education institutions has been assigned a crucial role in the context of national economic development. Since industrial development policy has placed a heavy emphasis on high technology and knowledge-based industries, government have sought to forge close links between higher education and the industrial sector. Higher education institutions have responded willingly to these exhortations (Kelly, 1985).

As a result of this policy, there has been a shift in focus in the kind of research which is favoured for state funding. Areas which have attracted increased funding by the state include biotechnology, information technology, and engineering and materials, while there has been a fall in the areas of energy, marine environment and food. In 1984, the National Board for Science and Technology, the agency responsible for the dispersal of most of state funds for research, declared that it had moved towards a selective strategic approach to research funding, 'not just promoting good science for the sake of good science', but developing 'a cost effective, national effort on science and technology, emphasising its application to industrial and economic development' (Mulcahy, 1989). Further initiatives taken include the establishment of 'centres of excellence' to promote strategic areas of research. Thus, it is clear that while the overall climate for research in science and technology is favourable, state support is limited and highly focused within a narrow utilitarian framework. Not surprisingly, university researchers have increasingly sought financial support from other sources, notably the private industrial and commercial sector and from EC research programmes.

The research activity of the universities and other colleges of higher education is complemented by that of a number of specialist research institutes such as The Dublin Institute for Advanced Studies and the Economic and Social Research Institute. Most of these specialist institutes were established in response to a perceived major lacuna in research activity in specific fields and before the strengthening of the universities' research role. While there is no explicit statement of government policy on the relationship between existing research institutes and the universities, it is unlikely that any new separate institutes will be established or that there will be any significant expansion of existing institutes. It seems more likely that evolving research needs will be met either within the existing university system or at least in association with a university. The evolution of the National Micro-electronics Centre, the most recent national centre to be established, may provide a model for the future. It evolved from an existing centre established by University College Cork and is now a semi-autonomous unit attached to the university.

Pattern of Participation

If the restructuring of higher education has been driven by government perceptions of labour market needs, and is thus supply led, the growth in enrolment has been driven by buoyant student demand. The enrolment growth reflects increasing participation rates since the size of the 18-year-old age cohort has changed little over the past two decades. In 1986, the rate of admission to higher education was 25 per cent, having increased from 20 per cent since 1980. Although precise figures are not available for more recent years all of the indications are that the rate of admission has continued to increase and is estimated to have reached at least 28 per cent by Autumn 1990. While the increasing take-up of higher education may partly reflect poor employment prospects for school leavers, thus illustrating the 'discouraged worker' thesis (Raffe/Willms, 1989), the most crucial factor has been the rising participation rates at second level. There has been a dramatic and continuing increase in retention rates at second level. Between 1964–65 and 1986–87 the participation rate in full-time education for 16-year-olds increased from 38 per cent to 84 per cent; for 17-year-olds the increase was from 25 per cent to 60 per cent while for 18-year-olds the increase was from 8 per cent to 40 per cent. Presently about 70 per cent of the age cohort take the Leaving Certificate examination, and while many of these would not wish to or would not have the required level of attainment to pursue higher education, it still leaves a large pool of potential third-level entrants. The increasing demand for places in higher education is likely to continue until the end of this decade. By 1999, however, the age cohort will begin to decline reflecting the steep drop in the birth rate which marked the 1980s.

There is considerable evidence that in spite of recent expansion, the higher education system is not able to meet the growing demand from suitably qualified candidates. This is reflected in the rising level of attainment required to secure a third-level place. One response to this unmet demand has been the increase in the number of students seeking a place in higher education outside the state, especially in the UK. This trend has been further stimulated by high tuition fees charged in Irish universities (in excess of IR£1200 per annum), with only a third of students in receipt of state grants, and by the European Court ruling which defines the terms under which students can avail of higher education in other member countries of the community.

Prior to the latter development Williams (1985) had analysed the operation of market mechanisms accounting for fluctuations in the movement of students between the Republic of Ireland and Northern Ireland. By the mid 1980s the traditional net cross-border movement of students from south had altered. In 1986, there were 208 full-time students from the Republic enrolled in first-year courses in northern colleges compared to 116 northerners in colleges in the Republic. The flow of students more than doubled by 1988 (Cormack et al, 1989), during which time it is unlikely that there was any increase in the number going in the opposite direction. While the two universities in Northern Ireland have proved to be the most important destinations for students going outside the state, there is also a significant outflow of students to universities and polytechnics in England, Wales and Scotland. It is estimated that about 2000 students from the Republic commenced their higher education in the UK in 1988.

The willingness of Irish students to seek higher educational opportunities outside the state is also demonstrated by the level of student applications under the EC Erasmus programme. In 1978, Ireland was involved in 7.3 per cent of all applications and 7.1 per cent of all ICP acceptances under this programme. This rate of involvement was well ahead of other member states taking account of population size, and while Ireland's relative involvement has fallen back in the two most recent years this is due mainly to the low level of grants available. Because each country allocation is tied to a population based financial quota, an above average success rate in terms of participation tends to have an adverse effect on the unit value of student grants.

While the sustained growth in overall enrolments in higher education represents a considerable achievement, the pattern of access reveals the persistence of marked inequalities. In particular, large social class disparities in participation have endured. The first data on socio-economic inequalities in third-level participation rates date from the early 1960s. Although these data are only available for the universities, this is not a serious limitation since at this stage the universities accounted for more than 80 per cent of total higher education enrolments. Table 2 provides some indication of the pattern of change between 1963 and 1986, a period of far- reaching change in Irish higher education. Data for 1963 are taken from *Investment in Education* and compared with data for new entrants to university and with data for all new entrants in 1986. The participation ratios shown in Table 2 show the degree to which each social group is either proportionately represented, under-represented or over-represented in higher education.

The overall picture revealed by this comparison is one of consistency rather than one of change; large discrepancies persist between the social groups in their representation at university. The main change over the 25-year period is the improvement in the position of the Farmers social group which was under-represented in the universities

**Table 2: Participation ratio of socio-economic groups among new
entrants to higher education 1963 and 1986**

	University Entrants Entrants		All Third Level
Socio-Economic Groups	1963	1986	1986
Farmers	0.79	1.13	1.45
Professional/Managerial/ Intermediate Non-manual	3.21	2.27	1.82
Other Non-manual	0.30	0.27	0.50
Skilled Manual	0.40	0.31	0.51
Semi-skilled/Unskilled Manual	0.08	0.19	0.30

Source: Investment in Education.

in 1963 and had by 1986 13 per cent more places at university than would be justified on the basis of its proportionate size in the population.

The rise in the participation rate of the Farmers group is compensated for by a decline in the over-representation of the higher socio-economic groups; their participation ratio at university fell from 3.21 in 1963 to 2.27 in 1986. The other three socio-economic categories which were grossly under-represented in 1963, were still seriously under-represented in 1986. While the position of the semi-skilled and unskilled had improved, the participation ratio of the Other Non-manual and the Skilled Manual groups had actually declined over the period. When we combine these three categories to calculate a single participation ratio index, the reduction in inequality is very modest: the participation ratio increased from .21 to .26. Overall, it is clear that when we confine our analysis to university entrants only, there is relatively little movement in the direction of equalisation in participation rates. However, the picture is somewhat more optimistic when we look at all new entrants to higher education.

Because of the absence of data, it is not possible to monitor changes over the period in the socio-economic background of students in the non-university sector. However, it is clear from the differences between the participation ratio of university entrants and all new entrants (Table 2) that the socio-economic group disparities are less marked in the non-university sector. This conclusion has been supported by recent research which demonstrates that, while all higher education is socially selective, the degree of selectivity is significantly less in the non-university sector. This inter-sector selectivity is complemented by a further intra-sector selectivity within the university sector where recruitment to the more prestigious professional faculties is especially dominated by the middle classes (Clancy, 1988).

Participation in higher education also reveals significant gender differentials, although there has been considerable movement in this area in recent decades. As recently as the mid 1960s, females constituted only 29 per cent of full-time students in higher education. By 1986–87 their representation had increased to 46 per cent of total enrolments and 48 per cent of new entrants. Although increasing at a faster rate than males, it remains an anomaly that females are still in a minority amongst new entrants, since they have significantly higher participation rates in the senior cycle of the post-primary sector. In 1986, there was a per cent differential in favour of females in the final year at second level, compared to a per cent differential in favour of males in admission to higher education.

With increasing gender equality in overall participation rates, most interest has shifted to an analysis of gender differentials by field of study. Change in this area has proved more difficult to achieve with the persistence of large gender differences. While overall, females constitute the majority of entrants into nine out of eleven fields of study they remain a small minority in technology and agriculture, representing less than 15 per cent and 23 per cent of new entrants respectively (Clancy, 1988).

In addition to class and gender differentials, the pattern of access to higher education also reveals significant regional inequality. While the rate of admission to higher education was 25 per cent for the country as a whole, in 1986 the rate varied from 35 per cent in some counties to 20 per cent in other counties. The variation in admission rates revealed a distinct regional pattern with higher rates in western counties: six of the nine counties with the lowest rates were from Leinster, while the three counties from Ulster made up the remaining three. Contrary to the experience in other countries, Dublin, the capital city and the largest urban centre, has the lowest rate of admission to higher education. Part of the explanation for this is located in the second level sector where retention rates are lower than for the rest of the country.

Conclusion

It is clear from the foregoing that the past two decades have witnessed a major transformation of higher education in Ireland. The major expansion and diversification have been accompanied by a process of goal enlargement whereby new objectives have been superimposed on the universities' traditional cultural mission. Since these new imperatives are being pushed with great vigour one of the many dilemmas which faces higher education is whether goal enlargement can be achieved without goal displacement.

References

Clancy, P. (1988) *Participation in Higher Education*. Dublin: Higher Education Authority.

Clancy, P. (1989) 'The Evolution of Policy in Third-Level Education' in D.G. Mulcahy and D. O'Sullivan (eds) *Irish Education Policy: Process and Substance*. Dublin: Institute of Public Administration.

Clancy, P. (forthcoming) 'Numerical Expansion and Contracting Autonomy in Irish Higher Education' in G.R. Neave and F. Van Vught (eds) *Prometheus Bound: The Changing Relationship Between Government and Higher Education in Western Europe*. Oxford: Pergamon Press.

Commission on Higher Education 1960–1967, Report. Dublin: Stationery Office.

Cormack, R., R.L. Miller, R.D. Osborne, and C.A. Curry (1989) *The Higher Education Demand Survey; Factors Influencing Post A Level Destinations*. Belfast: Policy Research Institute.

Coolahan, J. (1981) *Irish Education: History and Structure*.

Dublin: Institute of Public Administration.

Coolahan, J. (1990) 'The Commission on Higher Education, 1967 and Third-Level Policy in Contemporary Ireland'. *Irish Educational Studies* Vol 9.

Higher Education Authority (1969) *A Council of National Awards and College of Higher Education at Limerick*. Dublin: HEA.

Higher Education Authority (1990) *Report Accounts and Student Statistics, 1987–1988*. Dublin: HEA.

Investment in Education, 1986. Dublin: Stationery Office.

Kelly, J.J. (1985) 'Higher Education and Industrial Development in Ireland'. *European Journal of Engineering Education* Vol 10 No 2, 133–142.

Lee, J. (1983) 'University, State and Society in Ireland'. *The Crane Bag Vol 7 No 2, 5–12.

McGrath, F. (1979) *Education in Ancient and Medieval Ireland.* Dublin: Skellig Press.

Masterson, P. (1983) 'The Arts Degree in an Age of Science and Technology'. *The Crane Bag* Vol 7 No 2, 33–40.

Mulcahy, M.F. (1989) 'Research in Irish Universities'. *Higher Education Management* Vol 1 No 1, 58–65.

Programme for Action in Education 1984–1987. Dublin: Stationery Office.

Raffe, D. & J.D. Willms (1989) 'Schooling the Discouraged Worker: Local Labour Market Effects on Educational Participation'. *Sociology* Vol 23 No 4, 557–581.

Steering Committee on Technical Education (1967) *Report.* Dublin: Stationery Office.

Scott, P. (1985) 'Higher Education: The Next Twenty Years'. *International Journal of Institutional Management In Higher Education* Vol 9 No 2, 195–207.

White Paper on Educational Development (1980) Dublin: Stationery Office.

CHAPTER 10

Social and Political Conditions for the Changing Higher Education Structures in the Netherlands

Peter A.M. Maassen, Leo C.J. Goedegebuure, and Don F. Westerheijden

Introduction

It can be argued that two basic characteristics of the Dutch higher education policy in the first three decades after World War II were that higher education should be open to everyone qualified, and that there should be no qualitative differences between comparable higher education institutions and programmes. Terms linked to this policy are 'open access' and 'equality'. It resulted in a publicly financed, rapidly expanding higher education system, increasingly oriented towards vocational training.

The explosion of student numbers in the 1960s and early 1970s was followed by a sharp increase of resources for higher education and a tremendous growth in the number of (tenured) academic staff of the institutions. This quantitative expansion was not accompanied by formal quality control mechanisms: quality was not a criterion in the selection of students, in the funding of higher education, or in personnel matters. Security was emphasised instead of stimulation, equality instead of excellence (Maassen, 1987).

In the 1970s, the Dutch higher education system came up against the limits of growth. The second half of this decade brought, for example, the political end of more or less unconditional government funding of (public) higher education. The problems related to the tremendous quantitative growth of higher education became more and more apparent. In the political and budgetary situation of that time, the government was forced to design and implement restructuring operations to deal with these problems, without being able to develop a policy framework to accompany the 'repair activities'.

A new strategy towards higher education, characterised as 'remote government control', was developed after the restructuring operations. It has received considerable attention outside the Netherlands, mainly because at first sight it seems to be one of the more prominent European examples of a successful attempt to change the relationship between the government and higher education by actually increasing institutional autonomy. The main policy goals to be related to the new strategy are 'quality' and 'differentiation', replacing equality as a policy objective. In addition to quality and differentiation, open access is still an underlying governmental policy goal with respect to higher education, despite the budgetary problems it has created.

In this chapter a number of aspects of the restructuring operations as well as of the new governmental strategy towards higher education will be described and analysed.

In order to set the stage, an overview of the Dutch higher education system will first be presented.

The Dutch Higher Education System: Structure and Trends

The Netherlands, with around 15 million inhabitants, has 13 universities, 86 institutions for higher vocational education (HBO institutions), and an Open University, providing higher distance education.

All higher education institutions in the Netherlands are funded primarily (80–95%) by the government. Additional resources come from teaching, research, and services performed for third parties. All institutions operate within the legal and funding framework established by the government. In the remainder of this section the funding mechanism, student enrolment and the administrative organisation of higher education institutions are described in more detail.

Funding

Dutch higher education receives three 'flows of funds'. The *first flow of funds* is direct funding of institutions by the government. Most governmental funding through this flow is based on normative models for: 1. universities and 2. HBO institutions.[1] The main difference between the two sectors is that the HBO model does not contain a research component, since fundamental research is not considered a task for these vocationally oriented institutions. The principles underlying both models are (DMES, 1988, 44):

- a normative relationship should exist between duties and funds, from which funding rules are defined;
- application of these rules produces a total amount (lump sum) considered necessary for an institution to perform activities funded by the government;
- institutions are free to spend this lump sum as they wish, on condition that the activities agreed upon are carried out in a fitting manner.

The central elements in the models are the number of students and, in the case of the universities, the volume of 'conditionally-funded research', a non-student based allocation of research funds. Although the total volume of conditionally funded research is fixed nationwide for 'many years ahead', allocation among institutions can change as a result of the outcomes of a quality assessment procedure (Bijleveld/ Goedegebuure, 1989).

Table 1: Government expenditure on higher education (in Dfl.mln)

	1983	1984	1985	1986	1987
HBO	1577	1557	1538	1563	1572
Universities	3784	3718	3665	3694	3664
Research institutes	397	420	427	448	477
Academic hospitals	629	580	599	630	596
Total	6386	6274	6229	6335	6309

Source: DMES, 1990, 269

---

1   The open university, because of its special nature, is funded on the basis of a special agreement instead of a normative model.

The *second flow of funds* is provided to universities for fundamental research through an autonomous research organisation (NWO) that receives its resources from the government. The *third flow of funds* is income generated by institutions through contracts for third party activities. In 1986 the ratios for the three flows were: 62 per cent first, 16 per cent second and 22 per cent third flow based on a total of 11,241 full-time equivalent (FTE) staff units (DMES, 1990, 199).

At the moment the funding system is under review. One of the most imported changes suggested is separating teaching and research funding. This would imply equalising governmental teaching expenditures for both universities and HBO institutions, and allocating research funds on a competitive basis through NWO.

Government expenditure on higher education has remained more or less constant, as can be seen from Table 1. Over the period 1983–1987 the balance in funding between HBO institutions, the universities and the independent research institutes has remained virtually unchanged, with the universities receiving around 60 per cent of the resources, HBO institutions 25 per cent, and the research institutes 6 to 7 per cent.

Although funding levels remained more or less constant, the relative magnitude of higher education expenditure overall has decreased slightly, as indicated by Table 2.

Table 2: *Government expenditure on various education sectors as a percentage of the total government expenditure on education*

Year	BAO	index	SP	index	VWO/ AVO	index	LBO/ MBO	index	HBO	index	WO	index
including other expenditures:												
1981	25.14	100	4.71	100	15.68	100	19.50	100	6.91	100	18.52	100
1982	24.79	99	4.36	93	16.04	102	19.10	98	6.99	101	17.93	97
1983	23.72	94	4.40	93	15.70	100	18.88	97	7.43	108	17.56	95
1984	23.13	92	4.69	99	15.92	102	18.67	96	7.51	109	17.45	94
1985	23.83	95	4.70	100	18.46	118	16.06	82	7.35	106	17.47	94
1986	23.41	93	5.08	108	15.44	98	17.68	91	7.38	107	16.67	90
1987	21.05	84	4.78	102	14.19	90	16.74	86	6.33	92	16.06	87
1988*	22.34	89	4.95	105	14.18	90	16.58	85	6.63	96	15.04	81
1989**	22.32	89	4.95	105	14.22	91	16.57	85	6.62	96	15.05	81
1990**	22.31	89	4.95	105	16.57	106	14.23	73	6.63	96	15.06	81
excluding other expenditures:												
1981	27.79	100	5.21	100	17.33	100	21.56	100	7.63	100	20.48	100
1982	27.79	100	4.89	94	17.97	104	21.41	99	7.84	103	20.09	98
1983	27.05	97	5.02	96	17.90	103	21.53	100	8.47	111	20.03	98
1984	26.48	95	5.36	103	18.22	105	21.36	99	8.60	113	19.98	98
1985	27.12	98	5.34	103	21.00	121	18.28	85	8.36	109	19.88	97
1986	27.33	98	5.93	114	18.02	104	20.64	96	8.62	113	19.47	95
1987	26.59	96	6.04	116	17.93	103	21.15	98	8.00	105	20.29	97
1988*	28.02	101	6.21	119	17.78	103	20.80	96	8.32	109	18.86	92
1989**	28.00	101	6.21	119	17.83	103	20.78	96	8.31	109	18.88	92
1990**	27.98	101	6.20	119	20.78	120	17.85	83	8.31	109	18.88	92

Source: Statistical bulletin CBS nrs 9 (1985), 10 (1986), 13 (1987), 17 (1988), 28 (1989) and 21 (1990).

* preliminary figures

** budget figures

Other expenditures: expenditure on administration, additional expenditure of a social nature, expenditure that can not be divided, expenditure on other education.

Various Dutch education sectors: BAO = primary education; SP(ec) = Special education; VWO/AVO = pre-university and general secondary education; LBO/MBO = secondary vocational education; HBO = higher vocational education; WO = university education.

In 1986 and 1987, important changes took place with respect to the government expenditure on study grants (part of the 'additional expenditure of a social nature' in Table 2). As a result one gets a clearer picture of the developments as regards the share of higher education expenditure in total government expenditure on education if one looks at the second part of Table 2 where 'other expenditures' are excluded. Of course, one can only get an insight into higher education expenditure if it is related to student enrolment.

Student Enrolment

In the Netherlands, everyone qualified has the right to enrol as a student at either a university or an HBO-institution, provided the standard entry requirement of a secondary school diploma (see Figure 1) are met. These enrolments are regulated and registered by the Ministry of Education and Science. In 1989, some 171,000 students were enrolled in university education, while some 225,000 students (including part-time) enrolled in the HBO sector (Ministry of Education and Science, 1990). The right of admission to higher education for everyone holding the adequate diploma is a principle objective (open access!) of Dutch higher education policy (in 1987, about 32 per cent of the population in the age-group 18–23 years was enrolled in higher education). There are a limited number of courses for which a *numerus clausus* applies, either based on institution's capacity or on labour market conditions.

Tuition is at the moment (1990), for all university as well as HBO students, Dfl. 1750 a year. In addition, a registration fee has to be paid to the institution. Furthermore, every student is entitled to a basic grant from the government.

Enrolments have increased steadily throughout most of the 1980s in both sectors of the system (Ministry of Education and Science, 1990, 85–124) and have exceeded original estimates. In combination with the existing grant system, this has created substantial budgetary problems for the Ministry of Education and Science, even though government expenditure on higher education has not kept up with rising enrolment levels.

Personnel

The personnel structure of the university sector was reorganised in the first half of the 1980s. One of the starting points of this reorganisation was that personnel policy in this sector should no longer be career oriented, but should instead be position oriented. Since 1984, enrolment figures, disciplinary nature, and a number of other considerations form the basis for the number of academic staff positions in every university department.

As can be seen in Table 3, this had important consequences for the number of traditional, in most occasions tenured, academic staff members, i.e. full professors, senior lecturers and lecturers, in the universities. Compared to the situation in 1983, the number of senior lecturers, for example, has dropped in 1989 (as expressed in FTEs) by more than 60 per cent. The reorganisation has led to a decrease (in FTEs) of the traditional academic staff positions of over 30 per cent. The category 'other academic staff' more than doubled since 1983. More than 90 per cent of the positions in this category are temporary, as are all positions in the new category of 'assistants in training'. Since student numbers did not drop, this development also had consequences for the student-staff ratio in the university sector. While in 1981 this ratio was 13.95, in 1989 it had risen to 18:96.

In the HBO sector the number of positions (in FTEs) for teaching staff increased by around 16 per cent in the period 1985–1987 (Table 4). During this period student

Figure 1: Diagram of the Dutch education system

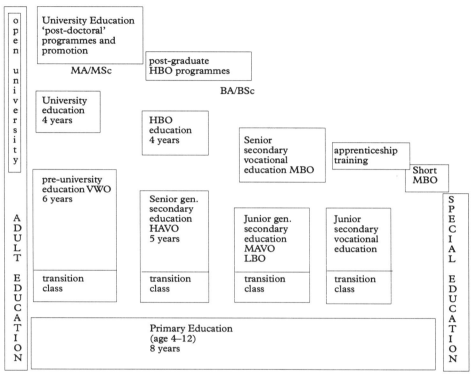

Source: Kouwenaar and Stannard, 1989

Table 3: University staff

	1983	1988	1989
HGL	2761	2446	2391
WHM/UHD	6073	2280	2351
WM/UD	6494	6175	5973
OV.WP	3134	7496	7381
AIO		2674	3814
NWP	20970	21294	20867
Total	39432	42365	42777

Source: DMES, 1990, 269; APOWO, 1990.

HGL= full professor; WHM/UHD= Senior lecturer (or associate professor); WM/UD= lecturer (or assistant professor); OV.WP= other academic staff; AIO= Assistants in Training; NWP= non-academic staff.

Table 4: Teaching staff in HBO

| Persons | FTEs | | | |
	1985	1987	1985	1987
Male	10250	11060	7302	8412
Female	3915	4242	2086	2456
Total	14165	15302	9388	10868

FTE= full-time equivalent
Source: DMES, 1990, 269

numbers increased by around 9 per cent in the HBO sector, leading to a student-staff ratio of about 17:4 in 1987.

Academic Organisation

As a result of existing legislation, there are differences between the academic organisation of universities and that of HBO institutions. The internal structure for universities is prescribed in far more detail than is the case for HBO institutions. With regard to the universities, three tiers can be distinguished, i.e. the central institutional level, the faculty level, and the department level. An overview of university administration is presented in Figure 2.

With respect to HBO institutions, the basic legislative requirement is that every institution must have representative advisory councils for both staff and students. One reason for the lack of detailed regulation is that most HBO institutions are private organisations, although fully funded by the government.

In general, an HBO-institution has an executive board of three persons, with strong powers delegated to it by the so-called 'competent authority', the board of the association or foundation that founded the institution, and that holds the formal statutory powers. In many institutions, strong consultative arrangements exist between top and middle level management.

Policy Change in Dutch Higher Education: From *ad hoc* Restructuring to Dialogue

During the late 1970s and the 1980s, higher education policy in the Netherlands underwent some far-reaching changes. In this respect a distinction has to be made between two types of policies: 'corrective' governmental policy initiatives that prevailed during the first half of the period, and 'option supplying' policies that have evolved since 1985. The first type intended to increase efficiency in the system. The latter type relates to the emergence of a new governmental strategy towards higher education.

Corrective Reforms and Retrenchment

At the end of the 1970s, the circumstances of higher education were not very bright. The main problems concerning the university sector were the student drop-out rate being very high and the average length of study very long compared to the situation in other countries. In addition, many of the academic staff appointed during the sharp rise in student numbers lacked the qualities and motivation needed to cope with the challenges of the coming decade, while institutional management was in general rather powerless, weak and not very professional. As a consequence the universities were inefficiently run.

In comparison with the university sector, the HBO sector received far less political and societal attention. It did not have its own law, its activities were regulated by the

Figure 2: University administration

Tier	Body/Composition	Powers
top	Executive Board (EB) 3 members • Chairman • Rector • Member large universities max. 5 members	• preparation decisions UC • implementation UC decisions • financial control • staff policy • contracts/representation • daily management • annual report
top	University Council (UC) max. 25 members min. 1/3 teaching staff max. 1/3 non t. staff max. 1/3 students large universities max. 30 members	• administr./election rules • internal budget allocation • development plan • guideline teaching/research • student facilities • (new) degree courses • appeals (gvt decisions)
middle	Faculty Board (FB) max. 5 members majority academic staff chairman FB Dean	• organisation/co-ordination teaching and research • preparation FC decisions • implementation FC decisions • supervision/annual report
middle	Faculty Council (FC) max. 15 members min. 1/2 acad. staff max. 1/2 students/non as	• faculty rules • teaching programme • approval research progr. • advice on appointment to EB
middle	Standing Committee majority ac. staff	• advice on research
middle	Degree Course C'tee	• advice on teaching
bottom	Department teaching staff in some cases students and non academic staff • Board of Deans Deans (chairmen of faculty boards)	• teaching and research • proposals for teach. progr. • research programme • granting doctorates • advice to Exec. Board/ Univ. Council/Faculties

Source: DMES, 1988, 50

Secondary Education Act. Next to that the central institutional decision-makers were in general former teachers with little or no administrative experience or skills. The sector as a whole was organised very inefficiently, with too many very small single-subject schools.

Major restructuring was believed to be necessary to make higher education more efficient and more effective. The most important reform and retrenchment operations were a restructuring of university education through the introduction of the *Two Tier Structure,* two retrenchment operations for the university sector called the *Task Reallocation and Concentration operation* and the *Selective Concentration and Expansion operation,* the introduction of a system of *Conditional Funding of research,* and the *Scale-enlargement,*

Task Reallocation and *Concentration operation*. With the exception of the last one, all operations have been directed at the university sector.

In 1981 parliament passed the *Two Tier Act*. The major aim of this act was to restructure university education. The objectives were to increase efficiency, shorten programmes, increase programme diversity and student choice, decrease actual duration of studies, stimulate planning and monitoring of study-load, and integrate university and HBO-education. These were to be achieved through introducing a 'first tier' with a four-year duration, limiting enrolment in the first tier to a maximum of six years, and introducing a 'second tier' in which selected students would take specialised courses and receive research-fellowships (Bijleveld, 1989).

The introduction of the two tier structure was followed by an important retrenchment operation in 1981, called *Taakverdeling en Concentratie* (*Task Reallocation and Concentration*). The purpose of this 'TVC' operation was to reduce the costs of the university sector, stimulate co-operation between disciplinary locations, concentrate research activities and prevent further disintegration. The cuts amounted to a total of Dfl. 258 million. Although this retrenchment operation was only partially successful (Van Vught, 1989), it has left its mark on Dutch academia, especially because it was the first time severe budget cuts were implemented.

In 1986, another retrenchment operation, *Selectieve Krimp and Groei* (*Selective Concentration and Expansion*) was forced on the universities. The 'TVC' operation was primarily efficiency-driven, without explicit reference to quality. The 'SKG' operation, as is indicated by the term 'selective', tried to use quality arguments to implement budget cuts.

With respect to the research activities of universities, the government in 1983 introduced the system of *Voorwaardelijke Financiering* (*Conditional Funding*) seeking to increase accountability, promote quality and improve university research policy. The 'VF' system brought about several changes in research funding. In the first place, the institutional funding model shifted from being enrolment-based to being based on norms and criteria, including scientific quality and societal relevance. In the second place, a system of quality assessment was introduced. Research programmes had to be approved by external bodies, before they could be included in the 'VF' system. The results of quality assessment processes were to be used for reallocating budgets among universities.

The system was supposed to develop on the basis of 'learning by doing': experience gained would be used to further refine and adapt the system, so over a number of years it would evolve towards its final form. One of the main changes so far has been the replacement of quality judgments in advance by quality assessments afterwards. In effect, the introduction of the 'VF' system has been the first attempt to introduce a formal system of quality assessment in Dutch higher education. Although the system is currently under review because it did not fully meet the government's expectations for distinguishing between excellent and good research, it has resulted in external assessment being accepted by the academic community (Bijleveld/Goedegebuure, 1989; Spaapen, et al., 1988).

In 1983, the government initiated an operation, entitled *Schaalvergroting, Taakverdeling en Concentratie* (*Scale-enlargement, Task Reallocation and Concentration*) with the basic objective of strengthening the HBO institutions both in a managerial and an educational sense, so as to become a full part of the higher education system, equal but different to the universities (Goedegebuure, 1989). Or, to use a different phrase, the objective was to 'upgrade' the HBO institutions.

It should be noted that before the 'STC' operation, the HBO sector consisted of approximately 350 small, mono-purpose institutions of which two-thirds had an enrolment level of less than 600 students. By 1987, the number of institutions had dropped to some 85, out of which 51 were large to very large, mostly multi-purpose institutions. At present mergers still continue within the HBO sector. The end result of this operation has been that HBO has become a potentially powerful force next to the universities in the Dutch higher education system.

Although it can be argued that the process also brought unrest and uncertainty to the sector, the results of the merger operations show the potential strength of a government operating at arm's length. Contrary to the retrenchment operations of the early half of the 1980s with a dominant role of the government, the 'STC' operation was structured in such a way that only a limited number of boundary conditions were specified by the government, no fixed goals in terms of number of mergers or institutions were stated, and the actual process was left to the institutions and the umbrella organisation of the sector, the HBO Council, themselves. In effect, the policy adopted strongly resembles some of the basic concepts incorporated in the new government strategy toward higher education as introduced in 1985.

A New Governmental Steering Approach

The corrective retrenchment and restructuring operations described in the previous section have been criticised for being all *ad hoc*, sometimes even contradictory. An overall policy framework was lacking and the major factor motivating them was budgetary constraint. In 1985, a more comprehensive and general policy framework has been introduced in a ministerial policy document called *Hoger Onderwijs: Autonomie en Kwaliteit* (HOAK: *Higher Education: Autonomy and Quality*).

The new steering strategy announced by the Minister of Education and Science in the HOAK document was considered necessary, because many in and around the higher education system were of the opinion that the administrative and legislative framework for higher education could no longer be considered as optimal for meeting the future demands to be placed on the system (DMES, 1985, 9). A ministerial analysis of existing governmental policy instruments for steering the higher education system was the basis for the new strategy. This analysis showed that:

- control is not general enough and is concerned with units that are too small to merit attention;

- partly for this reason, a number of steering instruments do not work well;

- insufficient recognition is given to an institution's own responsibilities, particularly regarding teaching;

- quality control is underdeveloped (DMES, 1988, 23).

The new strategy is based on the assumption that there is a positive causal link between institutional autonomy and quality of higher education. By granting institutions more autonomy, the Minister expected to create a situation in which institutions, through direct interaction with societal subsystems, will react to the signals they receive, engaging themselves in policy-making. Strong and effective institutional management was necessary for this to occur. The HOAK document provided a new image of administrative thought and action. Institutions are expected to operate more in accordance with market developments. Attention is focused on profiles, improvements in performance, a decrease in drop-out rates, a diversified student supply, and better adjustment of course supply to labour market demands.

In order to facilitate these shifts in institutional behaviour, governmental steering will no longer be directed at the discipline level, but at the newly introduced sector level, i.e. an aggregated discipline level. Sectors will be designated to institutions, and within the boundaries of the sector, institutions are free to determine the actual subjects of teaching and research, thus increasing the adaptive capacity of institutions to meet changing environmental demands. Governmental interference below the sector level is limited to the following circumstances:

- if macro-efficiency is reduced, for example, by an institution introducing a new course in a field where capacity already far exceeds demand;
- if a course is clearly of sub-standard quality;
- if a course clearly does not fall into an assigned sector (for example, if a medical programme is offered within the law sector) (DMES, 1988, 29).

The nine distinguished sectors are: education, agriculture, science, engineering, health, economics, law, behaviour and society, and language and culture. Each discipline is assigned to one of these sectors.

As a major condition for increasing institutional autonomy a formal system of quality control had to be developed (Goedegebuure/Maassen/Westerheijden, 1990). It is left to the institutions themselves to develop an evaluation system which will generate both quantitative and qualitative information. However, if institutional efforts are below standard, the government can take over monitoring standards through an independent higher education inspectorate (Maassen, 1989).

The third basic change in governmental policy-making presented in the HOAK document is the new system of planning and funding. With the publication in 1987 of a draft version of the first Dutch *Hoger Onderwijs en Onderzoek Plan* (*Higher Education and Research Plan*; the Dutch abbreviation for this document is HOOP) the Ministry of Education and Science started the first cycle of a new biennial planning system. In this system, in year one a draft version of a governmental plan (i.e. HOOP) and in year two institutional documents, called development plans, are to be published.

The introduction of this new planning cycle can be considered as an important step in the development of the new governmental strategy towards higher education. The HOOP document includes all governmental higher education documents that previously appeared separately. It offers an image of the future of the higher education system as desired by the government. The institutional development plans are expected to be a reflection of the institutions' intentions, of the influences of their environments (including government policies) and of their internal activities and developments.

The basic assumptions underlying the new planning system can be summarised as follows (Maassen/Potman, 1990). The Ministry of Education and Science makes information on the higher education system and its environment easily accessible. Information on threats and opportunities in the environment can be found throughout the HOOP document. Institutions only have to add information that is specific for their task environment. In addition, they have to add up-to-date information on their performance in teaching and research. Institutional profiles are expected to be developed expressing differences between institutions. A more diversified system is assumed to be more likely to improve the quality of higher education and research. Facts and arguments given by the government are supposed to influence the perceptions of the universities with respect to the needs for planning in such a way that their plans and activities will fit the new governmental strategy towards higher education.

In the first HOOP document attention is focused on institutional outputs. It introduced, amongst other things, the notion of a student voucher system (Maassen/Van

Vught, 1989) as an expression of the quasi-marketing approach the government has turned to.

The new planning cycle can be regarded as an important policy instrument for formalizing the replacement of central government regulation with decentralisation of power to higher education institutions. For the legislative translation of the new government strategy towards higher education presented in the HOAK document in 1989 a comprehensive higher education bill, known by its abbreviation as the WHW bill, was introduced in parliament. However, in the period between publication of the bill and parliamentary discussion, some important events occurred.

As a result of strong dissent within both the higher education community and parliament, the idea of a student voucher system was dropped for the time being. In addition a new government came to power, resulting in a new minister of education and science. Even though the new minister indicated that in general he would follow the overall policy direction developed by his predecessor in terms of 'government at arm's length', he amended the WHW bill in some fundamental ways.

Firstly, he suggested that the concept of 'sector' should be removed from the bill and be replaced by a 'central register of higher education courses', which should include a database containing information on the quality of programmes and subject areas. Only those programmes registered, will be funded by the government and can award certified degrees. Students are eligible for student support (grants and loans) only for registered courses. If quality assessments result in negative judgments for a number of years (not further specified!) a course will be dropped from the register, implying no government funding, student support and certified diplomas.

Secondly, the annual student tuition fee should no longer be fixed. Institutions should be able to vary the amount below a maximum of Dfl. 1750 per year, which equals the present amount.

Thirdly, institutions should have the right to determine yearly entrance numbers, on the condition that these numbers will not be less than 70 per cent of the average inflow during the last three years. If student demand exceeds available places, institutional capacity for those areas should be expanded to at least 125 per cent of the average capacity over the last two years.

Fourthly, the *numerus fixus* possibilities on the basis of labour-market developments should be enlarged. Parliamentary approval for fixing a *numerus fixus* remains necessary.

Fifthly, in the original WHW bill possibilities for institutional co-operation between HBO institutions and universities were limited. The Minister proposed to enlarge these possibilities. However, separate programmes and degrees, in terms of the binary distinction, must remain visible.

Finally, neither approval in advance of an institutional budget nor publication of a biennial institutional development plan should be legal requirements. Control should be based on yearly institutional reports, which should incorporate a section containing institutional plans for future developments. Elimination of the development plan as an institutional document would remove the foundations for the planning cycle discussed above.

The arguments for these rather drastic changes in the WHW bill are that the minister considered the concept of the 'sector' as not workable in practice. Not only would it prohibit flexible institutional adaptation to changing needs in society (an institution would be confined in its 'adaptive responses' to allocated sectors), but it would also fail to clarify the educational programmes available. Programmes with the same name could be completely different at different institutions, and programmes with different names, for example because they are located in different sectors, could basically be very similar.

The 'register' system would, according to the minister, more adequately describe the similarity and diversity of higher education programmes.

Be this as it may, it represented a substantial change in the steering level of higher education policy. The original reason for introducing the sector concept was that through it governmental steering would no longer be directed at the programme level, since such detailed review did not correspond to the overall philosophy of 'government at arm's length'. The proposed change again redirects governmental steering to the programme level, especially because of the proposed connection between quality assessment and governmental funding.

Regarding the 'liberation' of student tuition the argument is that institutions will be able to offer a favourable price/quality ratio to students, with the government database providing the possibility for students to check this ratio. In this way some room for competition among institutions is created, enlarging the dynamics of and diversity in the higher education system. A critical element in this debate is the 'purity' of the information available through the assessment procedures.

With respect to both the *numerus fixus* and entrance level changes, it should be noted that, because of the rise in participation rates and the student's right for financial support, the Minister confronts a large budget deficit, that appears to become larger rather than smaller because of this connection. It is conceivable that the proposed changes in this area have more to do with hidden attempts to reduce higher education participation (which would imply a fundamental shift away from 'open access') through both institutional and governmental action, than the argued 'optimal allocation of governmental funds'.

In the first discussion (November 1990) on this matter between the minister and parliament all ministerial amendments have been rejected by the latter. Parliament wants to stick to the original WHW bill. The ministerial amendments would give the institutions too much freedom in the eyes of parliament. What the outcome of the discussion to follow between the minister and parliament will be is not clear.

Restructuring of University Education

A clear pattern can be distinguished in the general policy developments on higher education in the Netherlands since the mid-1970s. This pattern has been described above: starting with more or less *ad hoc* restructuring and retrenchment operations the minister of education and science introduced a new governmental strategy towards higher education in 1985. This strategy was introduced in the HOAK document, and successively translated into an important policy instrument, i.e. the new planning system, and a higher education bill, i.e. the WHW bill.

An important part of this development has been the restructuring of university education through the introduction of the two-tier structure in 1983 and the developments that followed. Three successive ministers have focused on a different part of this new structure. The first one, Minister Pais, designed it and succeeded in getting it accepted by Parliament. During his period of office only the first tier was made concrete. The second one, Minister Deetman, introduced a new staff position: *Assistent in Opleiding*, (AIO: *Assistants in Training*).

AIO's are appointed for four years during which they are supposed to write a dissertation. Although officially they are part of the academic staff, they can be considered as students enrolled in the second tier. During Minister Deetman's period of office the structure of the second-tier in which the AIO's and other second tier students were supposed to work received little attention. One of the main complaints as regards the second tier was that the facilities for the students, for example, with respect to guidance, were completely inadequate.

The third minister, Ritzen, is trying to finish the work of his predecessors by designing an adequate structure for the second tier. One of the ideas being discussed at the moment is the introduction of research schools for talented second-tier research students. In each of these schools 40 to 50 AIOs and other two-tier students could be trained and guided adequately. It is proposed that one or a number of universities should take the initiative for establishing and designing a research school. The universities will be responsible for the research schools, although close co-operation with business will be possible, if not stimulated. The idea of a research school is based on the assumption that talent and resources should be concentrated instead of fragmented. This concentration should add to making Dutch higher education more diversified.

The topic of diversity or differentiation is not a new one. In the next section it will be discussed on the basis of the concept of isomorphism.

Diversity and Isomorphism in Dutch Higher Education
Since the end of the World War II 'diversity' has been an important policy issue in Dutch higher education. Like many of his predecessors, the current Minister of Education and Science wants to enlarge diversity in higher education. He has even indicated that in the coming period diversity will be the main characteristic of the Dutch higher education system.

Unfortunately, the concept of diversity has not been defined in the policy context, so it is not clear what exactly is meant by it. In addition no empirical studies on diversity in Dutch higher education have been conducted. In order to shed some light upon the realisation of the policy goal, we will give a modest attempt to analyse some recent developments by using the concept of isomorphism.

In discussing diversity in higher education one has to be aware of the fact that in organisation literature most authors focus on the differences between organisations (Birnbaum, 1983) and they try to explain variation in, for example, organisational structure (Hannan/Freeman, 1977). A striking feature of many populations or systems of organisations, however, is the homogeneity of structures and practices. DiMaggio and Powell (1983) have argued that once an organisational field is established the organisations constituting that field as well as new entrants to it will become more and more homogeneous. They have formulated the paradox that those who act rationally make their organisation increasingly similar to others even as they try to change it.

The concept of isomorphism is suggested to capture best the process of homogenization. Hawley (1968) has described isomorphism as a process that forces one unit in a population to resemble other units that face the same set of environmental conditions. Two types of isomorphism can be distinguished. Competitive isomorphism concentrates on market competition, niche change, and fitness measures. DiMaggio and Powell suggest this view to be 'most relevant for those fields in which free and open competition exist' (Hannan/Freeman, 1977).[2] As an alternative to competitive isomorphism institutional isomorphism can be distinguished. The latter suggests that organisations compete for resources and customers, as well as for political power and institutional legitimacy, i.e. for social as well as economic fitness.

---

2   For an application to the field of higher education see Maassen and Van Vught (Maassen/Van Vught, 1988).

Institutional isomorphism takes place through three mechanisms: coercive isomorphism, mimetic processes, and normative pressures. *Coercive isomorphism* results from formal and informal political and other pressures put on organisations by other organisations upon which they are dependent. A common law for an organisational field, for example, influences the structure and behavior of the individual organisations to a considerable extent.

Mimetic processes stand for imitation between organisations, resulting from uncertainty. When organisational technologies are poorly understood, when goals are ambiguous, or when the environment creates symbolic uncertainty, organisations may model themselves on other organisations. One of the assumptions underlying this mechanism is that a skilled labour force of experts may encourage mimetic isomorphism. Mimetic isomorphism can also stem from the fact that there is little variation to be selected from. New organisations are modelled upon old ones, and managers actively seek models upon which to build (Kimberly, 1980).

Normative isomorphism stems from professionalisation. Various kinds of professionals within an organisation will differ from one another. They will, however, resemble their professional counterparts in other organisations. This kind of isomorphism is caused by professionalisation through the professional training of specialists, and through the communication and affiliation of specialists in professional networks, associations, etc. These mechanisms create a pool of almost interchangeable individuals who occupy similar positions across a range of organisations. Personnel flows are further encouraged by structural homogenisation, for example, the existence of common career titles and paths with meanings that are globally understood (e.g. assistant, associate, and full professor) (DiMaggio/Powell, 1983, 152/153).

Various processes of isomorphism can be detected in Dutch higher education. There are several mechanisms that facilitate this process.

Firstly, the Dutch Ministry of Education and Science puts pressure on all higher education institutions to behave according to its wishes. In doing so it uses one common legal framework for all comparable institutions. In the near future, one common law (WHW) for the entire higher education and scientific research field will replace all present higher education laws. This may increase coercive isomorphism.

Secondly, the most important policy issues presented in the first HOOP document were applied to all institutions. Institution-specific issues were underdeveloped in the first episode of the new planning system (Potman/Binsbergen/ Van Vught, 1989). This is inconsistent with the underlying ideas of the new governmental steering strategy towards higher education in which central regulation and funding are to be less prominent and coercive than before. Coercion should become less through the replacement of direct regulation and funding at the institutional level by persuasion and through stimulating the development of institutional missions and profiles.

Mimetic isomorphism is also encouraged. Especially institutions for higher vocational education are confronted with uncertainty. Most of them were recently established as multisectoral institutions; they still have to find their way (both internally and externally). Furthermore these institutions for the first time face a comprehensive national planning system. These uncertainties stimulate imitation behaviour. The higher education system as a whole is confronted with far-reaching political, economic, technological and social developments that create uncertainty and hence stimulate mimetic isomorphism.

Thirdly, normative isomorphism might be increased as a spin-off of the new steering and planning system. The planning system includes consultations among professional peers, that are institutionalised in special sections of the Association for Co-operating

Dutch Universities. Hence the communication of specialists in professional networks is not only directed on specific policy issues, but on research and teaching matters as well. The emerging quality control system for higher education, being part of the new strategy, relies heavily on peer review. This implies that professionals with a specific disciplinary expertise assess performance in education and research within this discipline. This also stimulates a focus on disciplines, instead of a focus on institutions.

It appears that the governmental aim to diversify the higher education system, in order to improve its flexibility and to be better able to achieve the goals of the system, is not very successful so far. The differences that already existed may continue, but most of the recent innovations in higher education seem to increase the homogenisation of the system (Maassen/Potman, 1990).

Conclusion

Dutch higher education is going through an important transition period. On the one hand, the Dutch government wants to stimulate the transformation of the current higher education system into a more flexible, adaptive, and effective one. It wants to achieve this goal mainly by giving the institutions more autonomy, which should in its turn result in a more diversified system of better quality. On the other hand, there are a number of political and social circumstances that make it difficult, if not impossible, for the government to be consistent in trying to reach the aforementioned goal.

Firstly, the budgetary problems of the minister of education and science were created, amongst other things, by the growth in enrolments. The government cannot guarantee that in the years to come there will be no new retrenchment operations. The cut-backs of the 1980s have seriously damaged the relationship between the government and the institutions. As a consequence there exists a mutual lack of trust between the institutions and the government.

Secondly, higher education, and especially the universities, have become less important on the political agenda. Members of parliament are not really involved or interested in the transformation of higher education. In general, they do not trust the institutions and are not willing to give them as much autonomy as the current minister has proposed in his amendments to the WHW bill.

Closely related to the second point is the third factor, namely that especially the universities have been too inwardly oriented. They have not been able to change their public image which has become relatively negative during the past decade.

Finally, up to now the institutions have not yet optimally used their new autonomy. There are a number of indications that Dutch higher education is becoming less, rather than more diversified. If this situation continues the Minister of Education and Science could feel the need or be put under pressure by Parliament to interfere in the newly emerging autonomy of the institutions. This could strengthen the mistrust between the Minister and the institutions with all the accompanying negative consequences.

Next to these negative circumstances, there are a number of positive developments. First of all, higher education has become more productive, more efficient and more effective. For example, the average length of study has dropped rather sharply, the productivity of the university academic staff (e.g. the number of Ph.D.s) has increased enormously, and the average costs per student have dropped. Secondly, the introduction of a formal quality control system has created a situation in which discussion on and improvement of the quality of higher education is no longer a political utopia. Thirdly, as a consequence of a number of developments, Dutch higher education has become more and more internationally oriented.

While, until the end of the 1980s, in some respects it was the most 'provincial' of all EC higher education systems, the situation has changed rather dramatically. 'Internationalisation' has become almost a magic term. From various sources funds have been created and now suddenly every self-respecting institution is looking across the Dutch border.

As indicated above, Dutch higher education is going through a transition period. What the outcome of it will be, is not clear. It is still very well funded, enrolment projections indicate that in the near future no serious drop in student numbers has to be expected, the current minister of education and science is rather favourable towards higher education, and most of those involved agree that higher education should be left alone for some while, in order to be able to learn how to deal adequately with the new freedom. Whether higher education will get enough societal and political freedom of movement for this 'experiment', is one of the main issues it confronts at the beginning of the 1990s.

References

Bijleveld, R.J. (1989) 'The Two-Tier Structure in University Education. An evaluation of a major restructuring operation' in P.A.M. Maassen and F.A. van Vught (eds) *Dutch Higher Education in Transition. Policy-issues in Higher Education in the Netherlands.* Culemborg: LEMMA.

Bijleveld, R.J. and L.C.J. Goedegebuure (1989) 'The Paralysing Effects of a Balanced Power System' in P.A.M. Maassen and F.A. van Vught (eds) *Dutch Higher Education in Transition. Policy-issues in Higher Education in the Netherlands.* Culemborg: LEMMA.

Birnbaum, R. (1983) *Maintaining Diversity in Higher Education.* San Francisco: Jossey-Bass.

DiMaggio, P.J. and W.W. Powell (1983) 'The Iron Cage revisited: institutional isomorphism and collective rationality in organisational fields' in *American Sociological Review* Vol 48, 147–160.

Dutch Ministry of Education and Science (1985) *Hoger Onderwijs: Autonomy en Kwaliteit (HOAK).* Den Haag: SDU.

Dutch Ministry of Education and Science (1989) *Dutch Higher Education and Research.* Den Haag: SDU.

Dutch Ministry of Education and Science (1990) *HOOP. Feiten en Cijfers.* Den Haag: SDU.

Goedegebuure, L.C.J. (1989) 'Institutional Mergers and System Change' in P.A.M. Maassen and F.A. van Vught (eds) *Dutch Higher Education in Transition. Policy-issues in Higher Education in the Netherlands.* Culemborg: LEMMA.

Goedegebuure, L.C.J., P.A.M. Maassen, and D.F. Westerheijden (1990) *Peer Review and Performance Indicators. Quality assessment in British and Dutch higher education.* Utrecht: LEMMA.

Hannan, M.T. and J.H. Freeman (1977) 'The population ecology of organisations' in *American Journal of Sociology* Vol 82, 929–964.

Hawley, A. 'Human Ecology', in D.L. Sills (ed) (1968) *International Encyclopedia of the Social Sciences.* New York: MacMillan, 328–337.

Kimberly, J. (1980) 'Initiation, innovation and institutionalisation in the creation process' in J. Kimberly and R.B. Miles (eds) *The Organisational Life Cycle.* San Francisco: Josey-Bass.

Kouwenaar, K. and J. Stannard (1989) *Higher education in the Netherlands.* Zoetermeer.

Maassen, P.A.M. (1987) 'Quality Control in Dutch Higher Education: internal versus external evaluation' in *European Journal of Education* Vol 22 No 2.

Maassen, P.A.M. (1989) 'Quality Assessment in Higher Education: The Dutch Experience' in M. McVicar (ed) *Performance Indicators and Quality Control in Higher Education.* Portsmouth: Portsmouth Polytechnic.

Maassen, P.A.M. and H.P. Potman (1990) 'Strategic decision-making in higher education. An analysis of the new planning system in Dutch higher education' in *Higher Education* Vol 20, 393–410.

Maassen, P.A.M. and F.A. van Vught (1989) 'An Intriguing Janus-head: the two faces of the new governmental strategy for higher education in the Netherlands' in *European Journal of Education* Vol 23, 65–77.

Maassen, P.A.M., and F.A. van Vught (eds) (1989) *Dutch Higher Education in Transition. Policy-issues in Higher Education in the Netherlands.* Culemborg: LEMMA.

Pfeffer, J. and G. Salancik (1978) *The External Control of Organisations: A Resource Dependence Perspective.* New York: Harper and Row.

Potman, H.P., P.A. Binsbergen and F.A. van Vught (1989) *Geplande plannen? Onderzoek naar de doorwerking van het HOOP in de ontwikkelingsplannen van universiteiten en hogescholen in Nederland.* Enschede: Centre for Higher Education Policy Studies, University of Twente.

Spaapen, J.B., C.A.M. van Suyt, A.A.M. Prins, and S.S. Blume (1988) *Evaluatie Vijf Jaar Voorwaardelijke Financiering; de Moeizame Relatie tussen Beleid en Onderzoek.* Den Haag: DOP.

Vught, F.A. van (1989) 'Collective Rationality and Retrenchment' in P.A.M. Maassen and F.A. van Vught (eds) *Dutch Higher Education in Transition. Policy-issues in Higher Education in the Netherlands.* Culemborg: LEMMA.

CHAPTER 11

New Tasks and Roles for Higher Education in Belgium and Luxembourg[1]

Willy Wielemans and Johan L. Vanderhoeven

Introduction

Although Belgium is a small and rather young European country (established in 1830), it has its own typical educational history. As far as universities are concerned it has an old and very rich tradition reaching far beyond the historical and geographical boundaries of the present nation-state. In this paper a brief description and political-historical overview of Belgian higher education will be given, followed by an analysis of changes currently taking place within the system.

Structure of Belgian Higher Education

Historical Overview

Generally speaking, policy in Belgium, including higher education policy, is determined by two politically heavily charged items, i.e. the (strained) relations between ideological groups, and the relations between the two language communities (Van De Vijvere, 1977). Policy-making is at its best when a reasonable equilibrium has been reached in each of these problem areas.

Recently a new phase of the reform of the Belgian State (initiated in 1970) has been implemented. One of the most important elements of this phase was a shift of power with regard to education policy from the national level to the community level. Now the three Communities (Dutch-speaking Flanders, the French-speaking and the German-speaking Communities of Wallonia) can autonomously and independently define and implement their education policy. Until then important policy options could only be taken if there was a national consensus. The new arrangement, the 'communitisation' of educational power, was preceded by laborious negotiations to safeguard national balances between different ideological groups as far as their participation in education policy is concerned.

As a consequence of this development, educational policy and administration have been (almost) completely transferred from the national to the regional level. As to scientific research, this redistribution of power has been carried through in a less radical way. Of the total budget allocated to science in 1989 (i.e. 59.3 billion BEF), 35.3 billion

---

1   Since the establishment of higher education in Luxembourg is rather modest, only an appendix will be devoted to this Grand Duchy.

BEF (59%) is reserved for the 'Communities', 4.1 billion BEF (7%) for the 'Regions' and the remaining 20 billion (34%) will still be administered by national authorities. This situation implies some problems, especially as far as the credit facilities of scientific research at universities are concerned, and appropriate solutions have not been found yet.

Political-Historical Overview of University Education

Since independence in 1830, universities have always been treated separately in Belgian educational policy (Vanhove, 1985). Until 1965, universities could escape from societal debate on education (Knowles, 1977, 608). For more than a century the ideological equilibrium between the four traditional Belgian universities Gent (public), Liège (public), Leuven (Catholic) and Brussels (liberal latitudinarian), has always been maintained.[2] The so-called 'free' universities, Leuven and Brussels, were not recognised nor subsidised by the government, but because of the constitutional freedom of education the development of 'free' universities was guaranteed.

The autonomy of universities has been enlarged since the 1950s. Thus free universities acquired corporate capacity and public universities were granted extensive administrative autonomy. In the 1970s, a new funding system was introduced under which free institutions were to be treated in the same way as public universities, on exchange of acceptance of a number of administrative principles such as budgets, accounts, personnel regulations etc.

Since then, laws on university education have not been changed considerably. The most important changes are carried out by means of budget laws. This kind of narrow budgetary policy might be evaluated as 'the non-policies of university education' (Molitor, 1983). However because of their importance for the changing relationship between government and universities, we will deal with them separately below.

Political-Historical Overview of Higher Education Outside the University (HEOU)

Belgian law makes a distinction between 'higher education outside the university' (HEOU) and 'universities'. Legislation on 'higher education' has in general not a direct impact on universities. The main reason for this has to be found in a separate development of both forms of education. HEOU originated mainly from higher levels of secondary (technical) schools (De Block, 1974; D'Espallier, 1951; Verheyen/Casimir, 1939). Up to the present, this historic connection is still very noticeable, especially in the higher technical institutes. Nowadays, HEOU is organised in two different forms, i.e. a short-term and a long-term as will be explained below.

As far as organisation of budgeting, appointments, curricula etc is concerned, HEOU is covered by the School pact Law of 1959. After an acute and ideologically loaded debate on school, a political agreement had been reached concerning the basic principles of educational policy. One of the main principles was the splitting up of the educational system into three networks: a public (state) one (neutral education) of which the central authority is the organising body; an officially subsidised one, organised by municipalities and provinces; and a so-called free network, set up and run mainly by catholic authorities.[3] In exchange for the subsidy (full allowance for salaries, grants

---

2 At the four universities the teaching language was French. Only since 1930, Dutch has been accepted as teaching language, first in Gent and subsequently also in Leuven and Brussels.

3 Apart from these three networks a few schools are entirely private. They do not receive any grant at all, nor are their certificates homologated by the government. Their existence is irrelevant to the theme of this article.

for running costs and favourable terms for building loans) on account of the government, subsidised schools must accept a number of legal controls.

In practice, as to the content of courses, institutions for higher education of each network have a high degree of freedom, and are able to take up their own full responsibility. This freedom is equally large concerning the appointment of staff in subsidised institutions. The organising committee is fully forced to appoint on condition that the minimal prescriptions concerning the certificate requirements are respected. One problem concerning staff appointments has to be mentioned, viz. the politicisation in the public or State run institutions. Recently, and as a consequence of the new federalised policy structure of this latter educational network, an agreement between all political parties has been reached in order to break the politicisation of this network. This will probably open up new perspectives.

Present Structure

In Belgium higher education includes university education and several forms of applied higher education outside the university (HEOU). The essential task of university education is to conserve, dispense and advance scientific progress and therefore university teaching and research are closely linked. The principal aim of higher education outside the university (HEOU), on the other hand, is to dispense scientific knowledge and its application in the various professions. Both types of advanced education have their own particular goals, which determine the different structures and teaching methods. Higher education, in general, is organised in cycles and study years.

University Education

The French Community includes four Universities and six University Centres, in which education is limited to a certain number of disciplines. The Flemish Community comprises three Universities, three University Centres (which together constitute the University of Antwerp), and two University Centres which are again only active in a few subjects.

The characteristic feature of university education is that studies are quite stringently subdivided. Each study period or cycle is confirmed by the award of a degree to the student, which is a requirement for admission to the following study cycle. The first university degree is usually that of *candidate*, obtained after two or sometimes three years. This constitutes the essential basis for the continuation of studies. The second degree, that of *licentiate*, which is obtained after two or three years of study, includes specialised instruction and submission of a thesis at the end of the course. In certain disciplines (in medical and applied sciences), this second degree results also in the title of *doctor*, but in this case it is awarded after a longer period of study. The teaching at these levels comprises lecture courses, practical exercises and supervised work. Second cycle degrees usually qualify the holder to practice in a profession. Access to teaching posts in secondary education is subject to the possession of a supplementary degree, that of qualified teacher in higher secondary education, which may be granted immediately upon the award of a licentiate degree.

The third degree, that of *doctor*, may be obtained no sooner than one or two years after the award of a licentiate degree. The examination involves the presentation of an original dissertation and an accompanying thesis which the candidate must justify in public. The doctorate may be prepared only by candidates who are considered to have an aptitude for personal intellectual work and scientific research.

The highest degree is that of Professor in higher education. This degree may be obtained no sooner than two years after the candidate has obtained the corresponding degree of *doctor*. It involves the presentation and justification of an original dissertation and three topics or additional questions chosen by the candidate, together with an oral lesson on a subject indicated by the jury.

University degrees are divided into three major categories: legal degrees, scientific degrees and legal degrees awarded as scientific degrees. Legal degrees, first, are awarded for studies in which conditions of admission, programmes and duration are fixed by law. They correspond to traditional study courses. Scientific degrees, second, are awarded for studies where conditions of entry, programmes and duration are fixed directly by the university. These are mainly university studies which have developed in addition to traditional faculties, to cater for new demands and which concern such varied fields as economics, sociology, psychology, educational sciences, criminology, Oriental philology, African philology, physical education, geology, political science and computer sciences. Legal degrees awarded as scientific degrees, third, are degrees granted to candidates (notably foreigners) who do not fulfil all legal requirements for entry to university and/or who do not wish to practise their profession in Belgium. As far as academic quality is concerned, (course contents, duration and difficulty of studies) there is no difference whatsoever between legal degrees, scientific degrees and legal degrees awarded as scientific degrees.

Higher Education Outside the University (HEOU)

HEOU covers an extremely wide field of applied training, in preparation for various occupations mainly those in industry, commerce, transport and agriculture, together with auxiliary medical and social professions, teaching, translation and interpreting, applied arts and the media. These institutions are thus not dissimilar to the German *Fachhochschulen* or the British polytechnics.

This type of education may be either short-term or long-term. Short-term higher education consists of a three- or four-year study cycle. Long-term higher education is of university level; it consists of two cycles and is of at least four years duration. The short-term higher education cycle consists of a study programme which gives scientific and technical training leading to a professional qualification in a specific field. Long-term higher education consists of an initial cycle of general theoretical and scientific training, in preparation for a second specialised cycle, at the completion of which the student has to submit and justify his personal work (thesis, project and/or studies work).

HEOU confers, in particular:

- graduate diplomas (in various disciplines) as midwife, nurse, social worker, librarian, archivist, nursery school teacher, primary school teacher, lower secondary school teacher, in short-term courses.
- diplomas and qualifications as industrial engineer, licentiate in nautical science, commercial engineer, teacher in upper secondary education and architect, in long-term courses.

Transfer from one Type of Higher Education to another

Transfer from university education to long- or short-term non-university education is accompanied by a dispensation for one or more courses. Transfer from HEOU to the university is also possible.

Universities are more and more frequently availing themselves of the opportunity granted by law to allow students from long- or short-term higher educational establishments to make partial use of their studies when progressing to university education. The problem of transitions between the different types of HE is legally arranged, but only in a limited way. Since the federalisation of the educational authority in 1989,

Flanders has taken the first legal measures in order to create more coherence and flexibility in this respect (De Leeuw/Geivaerts, 1985–86, Geivaerts/Joly, 1990; Veny, 1988–89).

Recent Changes in Belgian Higher Education

Changes in the Relationship with the Government

As to HEOU it is important to mention that the Ministry of Education has promulgated two plans in 1986: measures within the framework of the general policy austerity plan (the so-called 'Saint Ann Plan') and a rationalising and programming plan for HEOU. This included the introduction of norms for establishing and maintaining educational institutions as well as an increase of the required minimal number of students per field of study.

Before, HEOU institutes were subsidised on the basis of a fixed cost price per student, in combination with fixed minimal numbers of students per class. This system has been complemented with a 'package' of fifty-minute periods, the volume of which relates to both number of students and field of study. Each institute has the freedom to spend this volume on the different educational activities it likes to develop. Officially, the government has called this intervention 'responsibilisation and flexibilisation of schools'. But it seems that the policy of austerity has been compensated and legitimated by a kind of increased local autonomy.

As to universities a number of initiatives have to be mentioned which could be of special importance for the changing relationship between government and universities. A Royal Decree of 1976 promulgated the financing of 'concerted research activities' in fully fledged universities. During a period of at maximum six years projects were financed with the following aims: to develop university centres of excellence in the field of fundamental research, or to develop analogue university centres, or to finance centres of excellence which intend the economic and social valorisation of research. Two years later, it was decided that universities should each have a research council. This council has to watch over application of research money as well as to co-ordinate all requests for subsidy and to advise on it inside each university. In this context the question may arise whether this council either has a task to fulfil between university and government or, much more, is functioning as a filter inside its own institution. The ambiguous role of this council becomes more transparent when we describe the financing of research.

Between 1981 and 1988, in the centre-right governing coalitions, the conservative Minister of Budget was also responsible for Science Policy. Anticipating the austerity plan, he proposed a new financial source for so-called 'university high-tech attraction poles' (UHAP). Those poles should be the basis for science parks near universities. During a period of five years each pole should receive an annual subsidy of 20 to 25 million BEF (25% of it to be invested in inter-university cooperative contracts).[4] When the first subsidies were being distributed it appeared that the advice of research councils was not compulsory. In 1989, the new (national) Minister of Research Policy announced in 1989 that the operative capital of the UHAP's should be increased. An amount of 150 million BEF would be provided annually. At the same time also 'impulse pro-grammes' were launched concerning artificial intelligence, bio-sciences and teledetec-tion (150 to 200 million BEF over five years).

---

4   Approximately 12 UHAP's are subsidised.

In all this, human sciences were moved to the backyard. Reacting to this, the National Council for Science Policy in April 1987 published a note entitled 'Recommendations for the promotion of human science research'. Yet it has to be noticed that this note is only focusing on the policy serving function of human sciences. There is no room for a policy questioning role for those disciplines. This impression is reconfirmed by new initiatives in the framework of the new social and socio-economic oriented programme 'Social Research' upon which the (national) Council of Ministers has decided in 1990.

In fact a seemingly paradoxical situation has been created: whilst the Saint Ann Plan was meant to save 9 per cent on the budget for science,[5] it announced that the amount spent on research from 1.47 per cent of GNP in 1986 had to be increased to 2 per cent at the same time. But this should now be achieved not through government expenditures, but by private investment in research reinforced by fiscal measures.

This policy seems to fructify. At the end of 1988 the expenditure for science stood at 1.62 per cent of GNP. 70 per cent of this amount is private investment. The pure government expenditure for science actually stands at only 0.54 per cent of GNP (De Strooper/Van Langenhove, 1988, 6–7). At the time these financing measures were taken, elsewhere means have been cut. Especially savings have been pursued via a reduction of the fixed cost price per student and making use of the demographic decline. Other measures have excluded certain categories of students from being 'subsidisable students'. At the moment about 14 per cent of the student population of the Flemish Community are actually not subsidisable; in the French and German speaking Communities the proportion reaches approximately 8 per cent.

After the announcement of the Saint Ann Plan, universities have argued they had to concede comparatively more than other levels of education (Baeck, 1987).

At the same time, subsidies for the social sector have been reduced systematically. As a consequence of this, enrolment fees have been increased. Some are now afraid that

Table 1: Survey on expenditures in Belgium by pupil/student

	1975	1980	1985	1987
HEOU				
means (in mil.Bfr)	5874,5	8209,6	8059,1	8201,0
student numbers	72181	96845	11450	114779
means/students	81385,7	84770,8	72966,4	71450,1
index means	100	139,75	137,19	139,60
index students	100	134,17	153,02	159,02
index means/students	100	104,16	89,66	97,79
University				
means (in mil. Bfr)	17604,3	16942,5	14828,1	15258,0
student numbers	73847	81793	89087	90251
means/students	238388,8	207139,2	166445,4	169061,6
index means	100	94,24	84,23	86,67
index students	100	110,76	120,64	122,21
index means/students	100	86,89	69,82	70,92

Source: Ministerie van Onderwijs, 1988.

5   These figures include all science expenditure of the private and public sector related to research in university laboratories or elsewhere in firms or research institutes.

a planned establishment of a social sector in HEOU would be at the cost of the university social sector (De Vuyst, 1988, 29). In the education budget of 1990, expenditure for running costs in higher education in general has not been increased.[6] The university expenditures remained blocked at the level of 1985.

Meanwhile the Flemish autorities have developed a new method of financing the Flemish universities (Vlaamse Raad, 1988–89). In future, education and research are to be financed according to separate mechanisms: educational costs should be tightly linked to student numbers, while research financing should be determined separately within the framework of science policy. Evolution of budgets in comparison with evolution of student numbers is obviously different in the French-speaking Community as shown in Table 2.

Table 2: *Evolution of the budgets from 1989 to 1990 in comparison with the evolution of student numbers*

Section	Flemish Community		French Community	
	Budget*	Student numbers	Budget*	Student numbers
Primary	+2.5%	-0.4%	+4.2%	+0.4%
Secondary	+1.8%	-2.3%	+5.7%	-1.0%
Special	+2.4%	0	+4.3%	+0.5%
HEOU	+2.3%	+1.5%	+8.4%	+4.0%
University	-0.6%	+0.3%	-8.5%	+5.2%
Social Promotion	+5.8%	+7.4%	+6.8%	unknown
Global	+2.2%	+2.6%		

* Initial budgets, after deducing budgets for school building funds.

Source: Ministerie van onderwijs, 1989, 1990.

New Research Priorities

Since the promulgation of the measures mentioned above, higher education tried to 'digest' these reduced government subsidies. This digestion by Belgian institutions has been processed in a different way. Thus, *inter alia*, the research councils set up in each university since 1978 function both as interpreters and as intensifiers of government policy. The uniform priorities of central authorities, reinforced by the requirements of the labour market, are thus transformed into internal criteria as well as into preferences for scientific projects. As a consequence of this, not only faculties inside each university are pushed to enter into mutual competition, but also universities have to compete with each other. What has been in the custody of ideological and language equilibria earlier, is now forced to a permanent competition due to an interplay of policy and market.

Changes in Student Numbers and Study Choices

Belgium opts neither for an explicit educational planning, nor for any kind of *numerus clausus*. The agreed fixed cost price per student forms the basis of the grant that higher education receives. Therefore changes in student numbers per institution and per field of study are very important. The profile of student numbers is determined by demo-

---

6   Included here is all science expenditure, by the private as well as by the public sector, concerning research at universities and at other (industrial) laboratories.

graphic factors and by the coefficient of schooling. In Table 3 we register the size of the age groups from which students in higher education are recruited.

Table 3: Age cohort 18–20

	Men	Women	Total
1970	217,676	209,646	427,322
1980	242,938	234,265	477,203
1984	242,745	232,941	475,688
1990	207,324	199,386	406,710
2000	176,089	170,065	346,154
Decline 1980–1990	-14.7%	-14.9%	-14.8%
Decline 1980–2000	-27.5%	-27.4%	-27.5%

Source: National Institute of Statistics, 1985.

From this table we learn that the peak of the 18–20-year-old age cohort was 1980, and that it has since been declining. A drop of 14.8 per cent was forecast for 1990 and 27.5 per cent for the year 2000. Thus the decline in the birth rate, which began about 1965, will mean a distinct narrowing of the base for recruitment of students for higher education.

The other important variable of demand is the schooling coefficient, i.e. the percentage of young people from a given age group who wish to go on to higher education. Because of the unlimited access to any kind of higher education[7] (and because of the increasing impact of the market mechanism), we have to register the fact that increasing numbers of youngsters are choosing the non-university sector, while the demand for university courses seems to be satisfied. The gradual trend towards stability in numbers of university students is *inter alia* a result both of longer courses of study and of larger numbers of female students. At the beginning of the 1980s, female students were only 40 per cent of the university population. At the moment there are more than 50 per cent in the first years of the Flemish universities. In Wallonia their participation stabilises at approximately 46 per cent.[8]

Table 4 shows the evolution of student numbers in higher education in the two main Communities of the country. It appears that the participation at HEOU is considerably higher in Flanders than in Wallonia. The reverse phenomenon applies to universities. Moreover, two other facts should be taken into consideration: (1.) the number of foreign students in Wallonia is more than double that of Flanders; and (2.) the criteria for the counting of students are not harmonised sufficiently (Hendrickx, 1988, 2–7).

It is generally recognised that the contraction in university enrolments is not accidental or temporary, but must be considered as lasting (Baeck, 1987, 10–15). This

---

7   As to the entrance conditions for higher education, in general a homologated certificate of higher secondary education is required. Entrance to long-term HEOU and to universities requires an additional proficiency diploma delivered at the end of secondary education. This diploma is not delivered to pupils of professional secondary schools.

8   As far as Flanders is concerned it has to be noted that the participation of females to the engineering faculty is rather weak (16.3%). In economy and in mathematics/informatics, they comprise respectively 40 per cent and 36 per cent of the population. In the faculties of law, medicine and chemistry, their percentage fluctuates between 51 per cent and 65 per cent. Psychology, educational sciences and pharmacy have 75 per cent female students. In dentistry, they are rising to 82 per cent (VLIR, 1989).

Table 4: Evolution of enrolments in higher education
(in % and in absolute numbers)

Year	1983–84	1985–86	1987–88
French- and German-speaking Communities			
HEOU	46,638 (48.98%)	46,496 (48.19%)	48,557 (48.81%)
University	48,587 (51.02%)	51,126 (52.37%)	50,934 (51.19%)
Total	95,223	97,622	99,491
Flemish Community			
HEOU	68,413 (56.24%)	70,242 (56.46%)	77,247 (58.73%)
University	53,239 (43.76%)	54,159 (43.54%)	54,275 (41.27%)
Total	121,652	124,401	131,522

Source:　Ministerie van Onderwijs, Statistisch Jaarboek van het Onderwijs, 1989.

hypothesis however, should be reconsidered since enrolments are increasing again from 1988–89 onwards (VLIR, 1988–89, 4–8).

Shifts between sectors in non-university as well as university higher education are striking. In HEOU, and especially in short-term courses, there has been a massive shift towards economics, with an increase of 34 per cent during the past three years. This evolution can partially be explained as a consequence of the organisation of new courses after the promulgation of the rationalising and programming plan in 1986 (Ministerie van Onderwijs, several volumes). In technical subjects, too, the student population has been growing slowly but steadily since the beginning of the 1980s. With the exception of similar increases in the small agricultural sector, a falling trend has emerged in the first-year enrolments of all other short-term HEOU.

It is also noteworthy that girls traditionally make up the majority in short-term courses; more than 60 per cent of first-year students are girls. Moreover, the percentage of girls is increasing in fields of study where employment prospects are particularly poor and that in general face falling enrolments. In HEOU as a whole, student numbers are rising in institutions established by private initiative, primarily Roman Catholic associations (which at present account for more than 60%); Community (State) establishments have become less popular.

Relationship to the labour market

In the labour market, graduates of short-term HEOU courses are encountering increasing competition from graduates of the long-term courses and from allied branches of study at universities. These threats are strongest in the fields of economics and commerce, where a rapid rise in enrolments has taken place at all levels of higher education (Ministerie van Onderwijs, different volumes).

Furthermore, the universities are experiencing very important shifts in demand. In the industrial sector, especially processing industries, employment is decreasing (from 37.7% of the active population in 1960 to about 25% currently), while the service sector has grown from 46.4 per cent in 1960 to 65 per cent now. Belgium, like other countries, is launching a strategy of reindustrialisation called 'the third industrial revolution', with the aim of producing high-tech goods. However, this innovation-intensive industry cannot be relied upon to generate massive amounts of employment. Jobs for graduates in the industrial sector may therefore be relatively limited in the (near) future.

In addition to the private sector, the subsidised tertiary sector has until recently provided substantial openings for graduates because Belgium, after the Netherlands, has the second most highly developed welfare state in the EC.[9] Faculties producing graduates for this very well-protected sector enjoyed a remarkable expansion during the 1960s and 1970s, but the drastic cuts in social welfare programmes as well as the austerity measures imposed by the Saint Ann Plan in 1986 have marked a turning-point in staffing of the welfare state.

These changes in the labour market have mainly led to a corresponding redistribution of students across the various faculties. Thus, it appears that the decline of the welfare state has mainly affected those faculties whose graduates traditionally work in the subsidised tertiary sector such as dentistry, pharmacy, and the fields of physical education, arts and philosophy, psychology and educational sciences (VLIR, 1989). Likewise it is striking that in Flanders the fields of study most prone to unemployment have the highest proportion of female students (VLIR, 1989). In Wallonia, a comparable tendency exists.

All the indicators suggest that the labour market for graduates has changed profoundly. Unemployment has devalued some degrees, while others are still much sought after, including economics, business studies, law and sciences. A split has occurred in the broad field of humanities: 'hard' and 'useful' subjects like economics, certain branches of sociology and psychology, provide increasing employment stakes, especially in fields relating to social control; they derive their status from their contribution to the successful breakthrough of 'social technology'. On the other hand, 'softer' and more critical/reflective fields of study are apparently less desirable as suppliers of capable and useful manpower.

Graduates in the so-called 'cultural sciences', or the fields of study of the faculties of arts and philosophy, are affected most adversely by this trend, and there has been an alarming decline in the student population in these areas since the beginning of the 1980s[10]. This massive fall-off, which was also due to the Saint Ann Plan for education, could lead to the marginalisation of cultural studies in universities and the loss of good students to fields with better prospects. This development could well result in a significant cultural impoverishment of society.[11] In addition, recent studies confirm that under-employment is an alarming phenomenon, e.g. approximately 15 per cent in social sciences and approximately 30 per cent in criminology and in arts and philosophy (Gent, 1990; Schodts et al, 1989–90).

In conclusion, the mutations in the labour market for graduates and the choices made by students at enrolment are bringing about profound changes in the self-conception of both HEOU and universities, of the authorities responsible for educational policy, of students and their 'clients'. Two developments are already clear: firstly, many

---

9   Social transfers reached in 1983 the following figures (indicated as % of GNP): 34.4 % in NL; 31.9 % in B; 30.2 % in DDK, 29.2 % in L; 28.9 % in D; 28.8 % in F; 24.6 % in I and 23.7 % in GB. (Eurostat, 1985).

10   Since 1980–81, in the three largest Dutch-speaking faculties of arts and philosophy, the number of first-year students has dropped by 30 per cent in Leuven, 38.5 per cent in Gent and nearly 40 per cent in Antwerpen (Bonte, 1987, 7).

11   For unemployed philologists and historians, there is little consolation. The opportunities for employment in the medium term are extremely limited because of both a falling birthrate and the low rate of turnover and replacement of teachers. A society which has to retrain nurses to become assistants for the elderly is not in the best position to offer a bright future to its youth. More than half the teaching body is aged under 40; only 11 per cent is over the age of 50. Major needs for replacements will emerge only at the end of the 1990s.

young people have lost confidence in the university as the guarantor of satisfying and well-paid employment; secondly, there have been increasing complaints about the failure of the higher education system to cope with the changes in the labour market and in economic, social and cultural needs. The criticism expressed by academics of the cuts has had little effect on policy-makers or on industrialists as long as no serious attempts were being made towards future needs for higher education and research. In other words: the market dictates, and policy follows.

The Changing Process of Democratisation of Higher Education

A recent study of 'Social Inequality and Universities' (Lammertyn, 1987) shows that trends in university admissions over the last 20 years have been markedly in favour of middle-class students and women: the policy of democratisation pursued has definitely operated to the advantage of these groups. Matters are very different for young people with working-class backgrounds and the children of low-paid white-collar employees, especially in the categories 'clerks' and 'craftsmen', who have lost ground since 1975.

An analysis of the figures shows clearly that the lower the socio-professional category of origin, the sooner the trend towards greater university attendance was reversed. For male students this turning-point occurred for children of 'clerks'in 1967, for unskilled workers in 1968, for 'artisans' in 1973, for 'draughtsmen' in 1979 and for skilled workers in 1982. The turning-point for women followed a couple of years later in each case.

Statistics also show that the reversal of the trend towards democratisation in universities was accompanied by wider participation in non-university higher education, with lower-income groups being especially concerned by this switch. Children from working-class families (skilled and unskilled) make up 25.9 per cent of the total student population in the non-university sector and only 13.6 per cent in universities (Deleeck, 1987).

Critical Interpretation of These Changes

Remote Control

Without minimalising the importance of the above-mentioned government policy until now, it has to be noted that the central authorities have not considered any other interventions concerning the structure, the organisation and financing, the management and the autonomy of Belgian higher education.

Notwithstanding the prevailing 'ideology' of selectivity and differentiation, the traditional free access to all forms of higher education remains unchanged. *Numerus clausus* measures *stricto sensu* have not been taken. There is no policy plan trying to influence the input or output of certain fields of study. Qualitative evaluations of institutions, e.g. via accreditation procedures or via certain forms of inspection, are nothing but echos from abroad. Indicators to measure the efficiency of (certain sections of) higher education to be used to determine the distribution of funding, are unknown in Belgium. Equally we do not see any increase or changes in the functions of intermediate bodies which are responsible for co-ordination and/or supervision between government and higher education.

On these grounds we have to conclude that 'remote control' concerning higher education is and still remains very typical in Belgium, and that consequently the autonomy of especially universities is not (or almost not) curtailed by direct government interventions.

Limits of Belgian Educational Policy

Pursuing educational policy in Belgium is limited by two very delicate equilibria, those of ideology and language, and is only possible on condition that these are not disturbed at all. Per language territory (Flanders/Wallonia) all possible levels and sectors of education and of research centres have to be equally supported and developed. Moreover, the institutionalisation and financing of education (including higher education) inside each language community has to be the expression of the ideological heterogeneity of the people. As to education, this diversity concentrates mainly in two very important historical-sociological pillars, the so-called Catholic pillar and the other pillar traditonally inspired by the latitudinarians.

As mentioned above this bipartition is expressed in the structure of Belgian higher education: higher education, organised by the Flemish or Walloon Community, is based on the principle of ideological neutrality. Higher education, established by private initiative, has the opportunity to create a clear ideological or religious profile. Higher education in Belgium is run by the (so-called ideologically neutral) Community, or established and run by 'Catholics' (e.g. the Catholic University of Leuven), by 'latitudinarians' (e.g. the Free University of Brussels), or by decentralised public authorities (e.g. municipalities and provinces). The equilibria between these ideological and language groups are so delicate that the government policy always has to start from the assumption that all institutions of higher education are equal, and this with respect to all disciplines and study programmes.

For these reasons competition between Belgian institutions of higher education is not very strong. Education as a public service is prevailing over (increasing) market orientation.

From the foregoing it appears that Belgian government policy can hardly be more than financially distributive. As has already been said, one of the most fundamental changes in higher education policy is the reduction of government expenditure. This reduction has been legitimised as an aspect of an overall austerity plan to seek solutions to the country's economic difficulties. Notwithstanding some contestation, these imposed savings have been carried out without noticeable difficulties, especially in higher education.

The evidence for this can be found in the fact that HEOU and more specifically universities, can hardly call on any kind of political support. The attitude of a good deal of Belgian politicians towards universities is, on the contrary, most ambiguous. On the one hand, a certain admiration is expressed for universities and for scientific research. On the other hand, they hold the view that universities live in grand style and thus have make concessions in times of economic crisis. Moreover, often the idea is put forward that the university represents a privileged world and that university education is not preparing students students enough for the real requirements of professional life.

Therefore, the government links more and more its research 'financing' with a central research 'policy', whereby certain priorities are described more precisely. Thus also in Belgium, as in many other countries, the need to be competitive is tackled through more mandated research at least in some fields of future oriented knowledge and skills. Stimulating the private sector contribution to global expenditure for scientific research, the previous and present governments have intentionally forced higher education to attune its research to the needs of the society. The requirements of sponsors will, consequently, be more influential to the choices of research projects. Private financing is henceforth co-determining the survival as well as the success of research centres.

Conclusions

From the foregoing analysis and interpretation, it appears that the Belgian government in its relation to higher education is almost 'forced' into non-action or is only able to intervene via incremental policy, mainly because of the typical ideological and language equilibria. The most used, as well as the only tolerable and still legitimate, policy channel seems to be subsidisation. With the exception of the still historically important interventions in science policy, the Belgian government has not explicitly or intentionally changed its relationship to higher education.

As we have seen, economic market requirements influence to a high degree student numbers, study choices, the budget for education and research, even the democratisation of higher education. Market-oriented utilitarianism resounds in the new curricula and in the development and ranking of knowledge, skills and attitudes. The service function ranks highest in the hierarchy of goals for the university. The humanities face the difficult choice between, on the one hand, being more useful, more valued and successful, and on the other, acting as a source of critical-reflective questioning of the many problems of (post-)modern society.

Undoubtedly the mentioned effects of the market also have an impact on the relationship between government and higher education, as the following examples show:

By granting per number of students, the Belgian authorities (since 1971) have confirmed market tendencies. At least implicitly they signal to higher education that market mechanism is a serious indicator which can/ought to be active in the relationship between government and higher education. Also the almost excessive choice of certain fields of study under the influence of the labour market is not corrected by the Belgian policy makers. Once more higher education is obliged to prepare for the whimsical dirigisme of the labour market, assuring at most the subsidy for education as well as the private financing for research. Because of the increasing significance of this market mechanism in the 1980s, as a regulator between government and higher education, universities especially will be but little inclined to embark on self-correcting initiatives, i.e., to maintain the cultural pluriformity of society.

As to research, in recent years a more intentional interplay between government and market has occurred. The budgets for education and research are more and more linked to one another and interventions of the central authorities in the science policy of Belgian universities are increasing.

Lastly the question has to be asked about the pros and cons of this reduced or incremental government intervention. It seems that neo-liberally inspired governments (like the ones in Belgium from 1981 till 1988) should intervene as little as possible in order to create a maximum governing role for market mechanisms. It is questionable whether such governments (we have in mind certain foreign cases) sometimes do not slow down and waste energy more by strong central steering than by giving free play to the unplanned market mechanism. For, the market compels to flexibility, breaks unwieldy systems open, making them more sensitive to external incentives, pounds against protecting self-complacency, intensifies the interaction between sub-systems, pushes systems out of balance and makes them 'dissipative structures' searching for new dynamic interactions. The apparent chaos of incrementalism acquires a creative chance when policy is limited to a remote control or to a necessary policy action on the basis of accidents and incidents. The market requirements to a large extent handle the conductor's baton which otherwise would be taken by the more rational-synoptical policy.

As has been argued in this contribution, the Belgian government has not intentionally integrated the requirements of the market into its relation to higher education (with the exception of science policy). However the question may be put whether Belgium, compared to other European countries, has scored in a negative way because of indication or because of incrementalism as far as higher educational policy is concerned.

A concluding evaluation concerning the relationship between government and higher education in Belgium could be that during the last decades creative dynamics between government, market and local relative autonomous institutions have emerged. True enough, in this triangle the fanciful market has apparently become dominant. Maybe in this respect it is not completely utopian to expect that the government as well as the (relatively autonomous) higher educational institutions will intervene and restore the power balance of the mentioned triangle. Strangely enough, it seems they will be supported in this by what we have repeatedly referred to as the dominant factor, i.e. the requirements of the labour market. This expectation can be deduced from a recent inquiry organised by the university of Ghent (Belgium) concerning the employment situation of 4000 university graduates (Bossiers, 1989). The result of this inquiry shows an increasing disconnection between diploma and job, or between education and allocation. Tasks performed by university graduates correlate less and less with their studies completed earlier. This disconnection is partly brought about by the ever-swelling numbers of training programmes organised by industries and banks. Perhaps this will result in a situation whereby higher education institutions – and in particular the universities – become less directly dependent on the fluctuating requirements of the labour market and will again be capable of developing their own identity as well as of defining specific goals and functions.

Appendix
HIGHER EDUCATION IN THE GRAND DUCHY OF LUXEMBOURG

Higher Education

The Grand Duchy of Luxembourg has approximately 356000 inhabitants, of which 26 per cent are foreigners. The number of foreigners is increasing, especially in the 0–14 age group. Compulsory education is still from 5 to 15 years of age, although, in effect, education lasts from the ages of 5 to 18 years for most children; vocational education, for the majority of students, will take place from the age of 15 or 17 onwards. The languages of instruction are French and German.

Strictly speaking, Luxembourg does not have a university with programmes of study leading to a degree or diploma. Higher education takes place in the Institute of Technology, where engineers are trained, the Pedagogical Institute, where teachers are trained, and in university courses. Some university courses are taken in universities in other countries, primarily Belgium and France (61 per cent), but also in the Federal Republic of Germany, Switzerland, and Austria (see Table 5). Some 35 per cent of university students are female. The number of higher education students has risen from 2000 in 1970 to 2500 in 1980. This is only 2 per cent of the working population. However, numbers are growing and university students encounter problems in obtaining employment after their studies.

Teacher training

The Pedagogical Insitute is responsible for all theoretical and practical pre-school and primary-school teacher training. Until 1982, this training lasted two years, but since

**Table 5: Number of students in universities outside Luxembourg
by discipline and sex, 1978–79**

	Male	Female	Total	Percentage
Pure sciences	132	64	196	7.6
Engineering	272	8	280	10.9
Medicine	413	252	665	25.9
Language	191	226	417	16.2
Social sciences	278	136	414	16.1
Law	122	63	185	7.2
Architecture	39	12	51	2.0
Others	192	171	363	14.1

then it has been three years. Only about 40–50 students per year are selected, on the basis of results in the national examination taken at the end of the general secondary school.

Secondary-school teachers are trained abroad for their subject matter training: they must complete four years of study and obtain a degree in order to be accepted by the Ministry of Education for a teacher-training course. This course comprises two phases. The first is a general pedagogical training at the teacher-training department at the Centre Universitaire de Luxembourg and the second is a five-term practical course in a secondary school. Moreover, each teacher candidate has to write a short thesis in a special subject and complete educational work drawn from an official programme. A final practical examination must be taken. This is evaluated by a jury of secondary-school teachers and comprises two model lessons (which the student teaches), the correction of two sets of homework, and two inspection visits. There is a *numerus clausus,* and when demand exceeds supply in any particular discipline, entrance is by competition. Teacher training for secondary technical school is similar to the above.

Educational research

In general, the evaluation of specific programmes for research into various aspects of the school system takes place in the Service de Recherches Psychopédagogiques of the Pedagogical Institute. Most of the studies are concerned with problems in primary school: difficulties of foreign children in learning mathematics, psycho-pedagogical problems at the *kindergarten* level, etc.

References:

Baeck, L. (1987) *Universitaire opleiding en arbeidsmarkt.* Brussels: Universitaire Stichting.

Bonte, A. (1987) 'Kultuurwetenschappen ontvolken'. *De Standaard,* 28 februari, 7.

Bossiers, G. (1989) 'RUG-enquête over de tewerkstelling bij ruim 4000 universitair afgestudeerden'. *Intermediair* (20) nr 43, 1–4.

De Block, A. (ed) (1974) *Standaard encyclopedie voor opvoeding en onderwijs* Deel I (entry 'tertiair onderwijs'). Standaard-Kirnheim, Antwerpen-Hoorn, 192–202.

D'Espallier, V. (ed) (1951) *Katholieke encyclopedie voor opvoeding en onderwijs* Deel I (entry 'België'). Pax 't Groeit, Antwerpen-'s Gravenhage, 191–228.

Deleeck, H. (1981) 'De democratizering van het hoger onderwijs'. *De Gids op Maatschappelijk Gebied* Vol 72 Nos 6–7, 507–533.

De Leeuw, E. and M. Geivaerts (1985–86) 'Overgangsmogelijkheden vanuit het hoger onderwijs buiten de universiteit naar het universitair onderwijs'. *Persoon en Gemeenschap* Vol 38 Nos 4, 149–158.

De Strooper, B. and L. Van Langenhove (1988) 'Het wetenschapsbedrijf in België: financiering en struktuur'. *Focus Research* Nos 6–7.

De Vuyst, J. (1988) 'Op de drempel van hogere studies' in Van HoestenBerghe, L. (red) *Studentenrecht. Sociale en juridische gids voor de student hoger onderwijs.* Acco, Leuven-Amersfoort, 29.

Eurostat (1985) Statistisch Bulletin No 1.

Geivaerts, M. and C. Joly (1990) 'Overgangsmogelijkheden in het hoger onderwijs'. *Universiteit en Beleid* Vol 4 No 2, 10–14.

Hendrickx, V. (1988) 'Statistische gegevens betreffende de studentenbevolking aan de Vlaamse universitaire instellingen'. *Universiteit en Beleid* Vol 3 No 1, 2–7.

Knowles, S. (ed) (1977) *The International Encyclopedia of Higher Education.* Vol 3 and 6. London. Jossey-Press.

Lammertyn, F. (1987) 'Sociale ongelijkheid en universiteit'. Onze Alma Mater Vol 41 No 3, 151–185.

Ministerie van Onderwijs, Secretariaat-Generaal, Dienst Begroting en Programmatie (1988) *Allocatie van de nationale educatieve middelen per onderwijsniveau: een evolutieschets.* Brussels. (0/3.2/HD/MS/0050).

Ministerie van Onderwijs, Statistisch Jaarboek van het Onderwijs. Brussels. (Several volumes).

Molitor, M. (1983) 'Les non-politiques de l'enseignement universitaire'. *La revue nouvelle* Vol 39 No 11, 363–376.

NIS (1985) Bevolkingsvooruitzichten 1981–2025. Brussels.

Postlethwaite, T.N. (ed) (1988) *The Encyclopedia of Comparative Education and National Systems of Education.* Oxford: Pergamon Press, 451–454.

R.U. Gent (1990) *Adviescentrum voor Studenten. Tewerkstellingsenquête,* Rapport 1.

Schiepers, G. (1979) 'Enkele aspecten van en problemen i.v.m. het toezicht op de universitaire instellingen'. *Tijdschrift voor Bestuurswetenschappen en Publiekrecht* Vol 34 3–17.

Schodts, L., D. Smedts and J. Hoornaert (1989–90) *Arbeidsmarkt voor universitairen* (several volumes).

Van Den Poel, Th. (1988) 'Begrotingsprogramma voor wetenschapsbeleid 1989'. *Universiteit en Beleid* Vol 3 No 2, 8–10.

Van Den Vijvere, J. (1977) 'L'enseignement post-secondaire en Belgique. Entre l'évolution et la mutation'. *Paedagogica Europea* Vol 12 No 1 41–43.

Vanhove, L. (1985) *Inleiding tot de wetgeving op het universitair onderwijs* Acco: Leuven-Amersfoort, 9–39.

Veny, L. (1988–89) 'Bedenkingen omtrent de wederzijdse doorstroming tussen het hoger onderwijs buiten de universiteit en de universiteit'. *Persoon en Gemeenschap* Vol 41 No 6, 219–229.

Verheyen, E. and R. Casimir (eds) (1939) *Paedagogische encyclopedie* Deel I (entry 'België'). Antwerpen: De Sikkel, 173–207.

Vlaamse Raad (1988–89) Gedr. St. 19/2.

VLIR (Flemish Inter-university Council) (1989) *Bruggen van hoger onderwijs korte en lange type naar universiteiten.* Brussels: VLIR, 1989.

VLIR (1989) *Statistische Gegevens Betreffende de Studentenbevolking aan de Vlaamse Universitaire Instellingen Academiejaar* 1988–1989 Brussels.

CHAPTER 12

Reform and Differentiation in the Danish System of Higher Education

Poul Bache

Higher Education in Denmark

In this paper, the term 'higher education' is defined as tertiary education in general, i.e. all formal education based on 12 years of primary and secondary education. The most important channels of access to higher education are four streams of secondary education which lead to examinations, giving access to higher education:

Table 1: Access-giving examinations 1990

Numbers of leavers 1990:	
The *studentereksamen* from the *gymnasium* (three year academically oriented secondary school)	18,600
The HF (higher preparatory examination)	5,000
The HHX (higher commercial examination)	7,100
The HTX (higher technical examination)	1,000
Total	*31,700*
Per cent of age cohort	*44 %*

Source: Ministry of Education.

These examinations give access to higher education in general, but supplementary courses may be required in some cases. Also persons without one of the four access-giving examinations can get admission to higher education, usually on the basis of an evaluation of their individual qualifications. Approximately 60 per cent of the applicants to higher education have passed the *studentereksamen*, while almost 20 per cent of the applicants have not passed an access-giving examination. The number of persons passing the latter examination has been rising constantly since the 1960's. A short decrease in the middle of the 1980's has been followed by a new rise as a consequence of expansion of the HHX and HTX. It is expected that the number of access-giving examinations will decline in the last half of the 1990's, due to demographic developments.

In the Danish system of education, three levels of higher education can be identified:

- Shorter programmes, i.e. educational programmes of 1 to 2 years, very often including practical vocational training.
- Medium-level programmes, i.e. programmes of 3 to 4 years, for example teacher training, engineering, social work or business studies.

- Long programmes, i.e. programmes of normally five years, leading to the *kandidat* degree, which is regarded as an equivalent to the master's degree in the UK. Graduates with the *kandidat* degree can go on with postgraduate programmes leading to the Ph.D. degree.

All higher education is financed by the Ministry of Education, and students in full-time courses do not pay any fees. Some higher education institutions are private or chartered institutions, others are state institutions, but all are funded and administered according to the same criteria.

The Sectors of Danish Higher Education

Higher education is offered at a variety of educational institutions, which can be divided into three main sectors:

The University Sector

This sector consists of the 5 Danish universities and 13 other university-level institutions (*hjere laereanstalter*) concentrated in the larger Danish towns, in particular in the Copenhagen and Århus areas. These institutions are the only institutions which are entitled to offer courses for *kandidat* and Ph.D. degrees, and they undertake research as well as education. Traditionally, the kandidat-degree has been the first degree at Danish universities, and until recently the university sector did not – with a very few exceptions – offer courses shorter than the (minimum) five-year courses for the *kandidat* degree.

The functions and internal administration of the institutions in the university sector are described in the Universities Administration Act of 1973, the main features of which are:

- The tasks of the institutions are both education and research up to the highest level.
- Institutions and academic staff are granted freedom of research.
- The Minister of Education is authorised to issue regulations for the courses offered by an institution.
- The individual institutions are governed by elected bodies, composed of representatives from academic staff, technical-administrative staff and students.
- The head of the institution, the rector, the heads of faculties and the deans, are elected by governing bodies and have limited formal powers.

The other institutions in the university sector, the *laereanstalter,* have traditionally been more oriented towards applied research and professional training than the universities. This difference is not so important today, as universities are now also increasingly labour-market and applied research oriented. The main difference between universities and *laereanstalter* is that the latter are specialised in one or a few fields of education and research, while the former have several different faculties. In most respects a *laereanstalt* has a role that is very similar to the role of a university faculty. A special type of *laereanstalt* is the Business Schools, which were originally established as private institutions, but are now financed 100 per cent by the Ministry of Education and governed in the same way as the other university-level institutions. The business schools traditionally offer short courses (typically 2 to 3 years). In recent years, a very large proportion of the students at the business schools in Copenhagen and Århus have continued their studies after the first degree to take the *kandidat* degree.

The university sector is thus composed of institutions which have very different origins, but have developed in the same direction. As a result, the sector is now rather homogeneous. Although there are still differences between institutions, institutions within a sector now have fairly uniform structures and goals. The model for this development has been the university of the Humboldtian type. The institutions in the Danish university sector identify themselves with basic characteristics of the Humboldtian university:

- the freedom of research
- high priority to basic research
- close association between research and education
- rather long degree courses, based on research
- a high degree of formal autonomy
- no external representation in governing bodies

One of the principles of the classical Humboldtian university, the separation of basic and applied research, has been modified and the distinction between universities and *laereanstalter* has faded.

Table 2: The university sector

Institutions:	Budget 1990 Million DKK	Scientific Staff	Number of faculties
University of Copenhagen	1176	2100	5
University of Århus	669	1270	5
University of Odense	291	509	4
University Centre of Roskilde	153	262	3
University Centre of Ålborg	347	642	3
The Danish Techn.University	564	1065	1
The Royal Veterinarian and Agricultural University	295	502	1
The Royal Dental College of Copenhagen	86	150	1
The Royal Dental College of Århus	77	125	1
The Royal Danish School of Pharmacy	75	129	1
The Copenhagen School of Business Administration, Economics and Modern Languages	240	407	2
Århus School of Business Administration, Economics and Modern Languages	109	233	2
The Royal Danish School of Educational Studies	158	299	2

Source: Ministry of Education

The College Sector

Higher education programmes shorter than long degree courses in the university-sector have traditionally been reserved for institutions, which were specialised in middle-level education programmes. There are 90 of these institutions which are almost all very small compared to the universities, and which only offer education within a very narrow range of subjects. These institutions are distributed over the whole country.

Table 3: The college sector

	The Danish School of Journalism
	The Engineering Academy of Denmark
	Danish College of Librarianship
	Danish College of Physical Education
9	Colleges of Engineering
3	Colleges of Business Economics and Administration
4	Colleges of Social Work
12	Colleges of Physiotherapy and Ergonomy
19	Teacher Training Colleges
21	Pre-school Teacher Colleges
15	Colleges for Social and Child Care Workers
2	Schools of Midwifery
2	Colleges of Home Economics
91	Institutions in total

Source: Ministry of Education

The Vocational Schools

The schools for vocational training have as their main task vocational training and education at upper-secondary level. In addition, these institutions offer courses at tertiary level. An important part of higher education courses at the shorter programme level takes place at vocational schools. Many of the tertiary-level courses are primarily used as further training for persons with a basic vocational training; but in recent years courses of this type have received an increasing number of school leavers from the *gymnasium*.

Table 4: Sectors of higher education

University	College	Vocational
Long Courses	Middle-level courses	Short courses
Research	No research	No research
Relatively large institutions in the larger towns	Many relatively small institutions all over Denmark	Many institutions of various sizes
High degree of autonomy in academic matters	Less autonomous	Increasing autonomy
Governed by bodies, elected by staff and students	Various forms of government	Governed by boards dominated by labour market organisations

Source: Ministry of Education.

Plans for Reform 1974–90

Before 1976, all persons with the *studentereksamen* were entitled to admission to universities, while admission to other institutions of higher education was restricted for capacity reasons. In the 1960's and 1970's, the number of young people completing secondary school was increasing rapidly, as in most other European countries.

Three new universities were established to satisfy the expanding demand for university education. The new university of Odense and the university centres of Roskilde and Ålborg were planned as comprehensive universities with both long degree courses in traditional university subjects and shorter, more labour-market oriented courses. However, as the capacity of the new universities was still limited in the first half of the 1970's, and as students preferred the two older universities in Copenhagen and Århus, the new universities only received a small part of the growing intake of university students.

The influx to long-cycle and medium-cycle higher education grew from 14.1 per cent of the age cohort in 1960 to 26.7 per cent in 1975. The number of students at the universities grew from 9100 in to 54,500 over the same period. The student numbers were also growing in other sectors of higher education, but at a much slower pace. The lack of balance between universities and other higher education institutions became a problem. Not only were universities becoming overcrowded, but labour-market perspectives were frightening, as university graduates were almost exclusively employed in the public sector.

The Planning Council for Higher Education (a body consultative to the Minister of Education in matters concerning the university sector only) recommended expansion of the College sector and implementation of middle level programmes in the university sector. These middle-level programmes, however, were not expanded sufficiently to relieve the pressure on the longer programmes at the universities; and by the beginning of the 1970's the problems became acute. The expanding system of higher education was still dominated by a large and expanding university sector with long degree courses in traditional academic subjects, very high drop-out rates, and little labour-market orientation. Graduate unemployment was rising and became a serious issue. The basic problem faced by the higher education system was how to satisfy both the demand for mass education and the demands from the future labour market within the framework of the traditionally elite-oriented system.

In 1970, Parliament asked the Planning Council for Higher Education to develop a comprehensive plan for the structure and further expansion of Danish higher education. In the beginning of 1974, the Planning Council published the result of its work, titled *Helhedsplanlaegning af de hjere uddannelser 1974–87* (Comprehensive planning of higher education 1974–87), known in the Danish debate as the H-plan. The H-plan recommended a number of reforms in order to deal with the problems of higher education. The most important recommendations were:

1. Centralised regulation of intake of student to all courses in higher education.

2. Reform of educational structures and curricula at the universities in order to obtain more efficient courses (lower drop-out rates) and shorter first-degree courses.

3. Budgetary reform.

4. Establishment of short-cycle courses outside universities as an alternative to university-level courses.

5. Further expansion of the university sector was to be concentrated at the university centres in Roskilde and Ålborg and at Odense University, which was to be turned into a university centre by means of mergers with other institutions in Odense.

The H-plan became the guideline for change in higher education in the period following 1974. The outcomes of these changes will be discussed in the following sections.

Regulation of the Intake of Students

In 1976, Parliament introduced a *numerus clausus* at universities and passed a general regulation of the student intake to higher education in the university and college sectors. Since 1976, the number of places in the different types of study programmes at individual institutions throughout the higher education system has been fixed annually by the Ministry of Education. This has been one of the most important tools in the steering of higher education during the 1980's. The main purpose of this steering has been to direct the flows through the higher education system:

- from courses traditionally leading to public sector employment to courses aiming at the private sector;
- from long *kandidat*-degree courses in the university sector to shorter programmes in the College or Vocational sectors.

This process was an exercise in manpower planning. The background was growing unemployment for graduates, and the goal was to achieve a better balance on the graduate labour market.

Table 5: Intake to higher education 1977–90.
University and College sectors.

	1977	1990	Index 1977=100%
University sector:			
business economy	880	2248	255
social science	2034	4174	205
humanities	2797	2880	103
business language	2272	2056	90
engineering	916	1523	166
health	1251	1011	81
science	1805	2842	157
architecture	534	275	51
Total University Sector:	*12,489*	*17,009*	*136*
College sector:			
business language	658	292	44
business economics	67	469	700
social work	445	368	83
engineering	1275	2781	218
health	324	500	154
teacher-training	6346	4887	77
journalism, librarianship	548	426	78
Total College Sector:	*9663*	*9723*	*101*
Total Both Sectors	*22,152*	*27,218*	*123*

Source: Ministry of Education.

The result of this policy has been a considerable switchover in the intake of students to higher education. Student numbers in engineering, science, social science and business economy have expanded. The increase in student intake has been especially high in business economy, which has almost tripled, and in engineering, where the intake in the colleges has been doubled.

Intake to a number of courses preparing for public sector employment (social work, teacher training and librarianship) has been cut. Also the intake to the humanities at the universities has been reduced considerably in the first half of the 1980's, when unemployment rates were high and rising. By the end of the 1980's the intake to these courses has been increased again as the employment situation improved.

Unemployment of higher education graduates was highest during the first half of the 1980's and has been declining since:

Table 6: Graduate unemployment in per cent

	1982	1985	1987	1989
Social Sciences				
K	3.6	4.1	2.7	4.0
M	4.1	3.8	2.9	3.5
Humanities				
K	15.3	22.1	15.5	13.1
M	10.0	9.7	8.7	7.7
Engineering				
K	2.9	2.0	4.9	5.8
M	3.6	2.0	2.9	4.0
Natural Sciences				
K	5.1	6.2	4.8	4.9
Health				
K	2.1	3.5	3.5	2.8
M	0.2	0.6	0.8	1.3
Education and psychology				
K	14.9	18.5	15.6	14.3
M	3.2	6.6	5.5	5.5
Graduates in total				
K	5.4	7.9	6.1	6.1
M	3.2	4.7	4.1	4.3
Total workforce	*9.8*	*9.1*	*7.9*	*9.4*

K = *Kandidat*-degree graduates M = Medium-level graduates

Source: Ministry of Education, Statistical Division.

The goal of the entrance regulation policy, i.e. to reduce unemployment, has to some extent been achieved. It is, however, important to note that the regulation of the intake has been accompanied by further measures to improve the employment situation. The most important of these measures were:

- introduction of new courses and curricula;
- better information to students on employment prospectives;

- projects, sponsored by the Ministry of Education, fortraining and private sector-employment of unemployed graduates.

Although the number of places in higher education has been increased during the last half of the 1980's, there is annually a large number of applicants to higher education who are refused admission for capacity reasons. In the summer of 1990, 14,000 of 45,000 applicants to higher education were refused. The limited capacity of the higher education system is given much attention in the media and by the politicians. The result is a growing political pressure for more places at low costs.

Table 7: *Applications to higher education 1990*

	Applicants	
	Accepted	*Refused*
University Sector:		
Engineering	1523	15
Science	2842	589
Health	1011	656
Social Sciences & business economics	6422	1594
Humanities & business language	4936	1796
Architecture	275	400
Total university sector	*17,009*	*5050*
College Sector:		
Business languages & economics	761	200
Engineering	2781	113
Health	500	1008
Social Work	368	300
Librarianship & journalism	426	87
Teacher Training	4887	3952
Total college sector	*9723*	*5660*
Vocational Sector:		
Commercial	3119	1446
Computer	1086	207
Health	2045	1650
Total vocational sector	*9250*	*3303*
Total all sectors	*32,937*	*14,013*

Source: Ministry of Education.

Changes in Curricula and Educational Structures 1975–90

The H-plan recommended not only an expansion of shorter programmes in the college and vocational sectors, but also the establishment of new middle-level and short-cycle courses within the university sector. The idea of introducing a bachelor's degree (i.e. a first degree on a lower level than the *kandidat* degree) into the Danish universities has emerged regularly during the last 30 years. However, firm resistance from the universities prevented the idea from being realised.

In 1988, however, the bachelor's degree was established by decree from the Ministry of Education. According to the decree, all students who successfully completed the first three years of the course for the *kandidat* degree were awarded the bachelor's degree.

In addition, it was made possible for universities to establish new courses on bachelor's degree level. This was – not without hesitation – accepted by the universities, as free access of all enrolled university students to the *kandidat*-degree courses was left untouched.

In 1989, the ministry announced that all further expansion of the number of places in higher education would be placed at medium- or short-cycle courses. This meant that expansion in the university sector would happen only if institutions offered courses for the bachelor's degree. As a result of this, the universities introduced programmes for the bachelor's degree in science and the humanities in 1990.

The Funding of Higher Education

Budgetary Reform

In 1981, the Ministry of Education introduced a new budgetary system, common to both the university sector and a large part of the college sector. This system is – with some minor changes – still in force. The main principles are:

- Resources are allocated separately for research and teaching.
- Funds for teaching are allocated by a formula depending on the number of active students (i.e. students who pass examinations) and a student/teacher-ratio, fixed by the Ministry. There are different ratios for different types of courses.
- Funds for research are allocated independently of funds for teaching.
- In principle, funds are given as a lump sum to the institutions, but some funds may be earmarked for special purposes. The bigger institutions in the university sector with several faculties do not receive an overall lump sum, but each faculty gets its own budget from the ministry. Only funds for buildings and administration are at the disposal of the institution as a whole.

Budget Cuts

In Denmark, as in many other European countries, a reduction of public expenditure has been an important goal for the government. As a consequence, higher education institutions have experienced a series of reductions in funding of research and – especially – in funding of education.

The development is illustrated by these figures for the student/teacher ratios in different types of higher education:

Table 8: Student / teacher ratios 1982–1991

Subject area	1982	1985	1991
Humanities	13.0	13.5	20.6
Business language	15.0	15.5	20.6
Social science	20.0	20.0	24.9
Business economics	17.0	20.0	24.9
Science	7.0	8.5	11.5
Medicine	13.0	13.5	17.0
Engineering	7.5	9.0	12.2

Source: Danish government budgets, 1982, 1985, 1991.

Demand for Bigger and More Efficient Units

With increasing concern about costs and quality, the question of institutional size has come into focus. Many institutions are so small that the relationship between educational quality and economic efficiency becomes a problem. A number of teacher-training colleges have been closed or merged in the last few years. In general, the pressure on smaller institutions is growing. The pressure for bigger units is not only felt at institutional level, but also by institutes and departments within universities. Many university departments have been merged, some even closed, most often on the initiative of the institutions themselves. This development is expected to continue. The ministry and its advisory bodies are looking with increasing criticism at departments where staffing and equipment are too meagre to serve as a basis for good research and education. There is growing support for the point of view that too many small departments work within the same academic subject. If this is true, there is an obvious need for concentration of academic resources, not only within individual institutions, but also on a national level. To what extent this will be achieved through voluntary co-operation between institutions, or will require intervention from central authorities, remains to be seen.

The Funding of Research

Research at the institutions in the university sector encompasses both basic and applied research. The budgets of research and education are separated, but research and education are closely associated, as the two activities are carried out by the same people. Danish research policy has been based on a dual system of research funding. The universities receive funds for research from two sources: funds for basic research from the Ministry of Education, and funds for research programmes from the Research Councils and other public or private sources.

The importance of the external funds, i.e. funds from other sources than the basic grants from the ministry, has been considerably increased during the 1980's. With the exception of the Technical University, where external funds have played an important role for a long time, the volume of external funding of research was marginal 10 years ago. Today up to 20–25 per cent of university budgets is financed by external sources. This development means that the role of universities as research institutions is changing, as institutions must increasingly 'earn their living' by competing for external funds.

The close association between research and education is probably the most fundamental principle of the university sector. Nevertheless the traditional links between research and education are being threatened in at least two ways:

1. The growing importance of externally funded research forces universities to do research in fields where the money is, which is not necessarily where the students are.

2. The introduction of shorter educational programmes in universities means that there will probably be a growing number of university courses which are not associated with research.

The budgetary separation of education and research means that some academic fields have experienced substantial growth in student numbers without increase in resources for research. Other fields have, as a result of the *numerus clausus,* substantial research resources, but very few students. Taken together, these developments lead to a growing imbalance in the relationship between research and teaching at universities.

Expansion of the Non-University Sector

The H-plan suggested an expansion of middle-level courses outside the university sector in order to direct a growing number of students to the non-university sectors. In accordance with the intentions of the plan, the influx to business and technical colleges has increased considerably since 1974. However, during the same period the intake to a number of other institutions in the college sector, in particular the teacher-training colleges, has been much reduced. The net result is that the total numbers of enrolments in the colleges in 1990 were at the same level as in the middle of the 1970's.

The main reason for this development is that a large part of the colleges are small and offer only a few, specialised courses preparing for employment in various parts of public service with decreasing needs for new recruitments. The attempts to establish new short-cycle courses in the vocational sector, as alternatives to courses at colleges and universities, were for a long period a very limited success. The courses at tertiary level at the vocational schools were primarily structured as further education for persons with a secondary-level vocational training from within the sector, and great plans for new curricula, which were to recruit school-leavers from the *gymnasium*, gave very limited results.

Only at the end of the 1980's were the short-cycle courses at post-secondary level being expanded in the vocational sector, and student numbers are expected to increase substantially over the years to come.

The University Centres

When the two newest universities in Roskilde and Ålborg were established in the 1970's, they were called university centres to emphasise that these institutions were not meant to be copies of the older universities. The university centres were intended to offer curricula which were derived from the needs of the topical labour-market, and middle-level courses should be offered, as well as courses for the *kandidat* degree. However, the two university centres in Roskilde and Aalborg never managed to function as the intended centres of expansion. Firstly, the idea of a comprehensive university offering both traditional long-cycle and new shorter-cycle courses was not realised, as the long-cycle courses came to be as predominant at the university centres as they were at the traditional universities. Secondly, until the beginning of the 1980's, the number of students choosing the university centres was rather modest, and when enrolments started to increase substantially, budget cuts rather than investment in new university facilities were on the political agenda.

The Governance of Higher Education

In 1974, the administrative responsibility for higher education in the university-sector and a large part of the college-sector was placed in a new directorate of higher education within the Ministry of Education. The Planning Council for the universities was replaced by new consultative bodies (National Planning Committees), which were advising the minister in matters concerning higher education in the university sector and a large part of the college sector. Thus, the first steps were taken to bring the sectors of higher education into one coherent system.

During the 1980's, colleges which had previously been under the authority of other ministries (colleges with programmes in health and social work) or other departments in the Ministry of Education (teacher-training colleges), were brought together under the directorate of higher education (or the Department of Higher Education, as it is called now). In 1990 the national planning committees have been restructured, and these new, restructured consultative bodies advise the Minister of Education on matters concerning the three higher education sectors in general.

In this way there has been a gradual development of a coherent system of administration that covers all three sectors of higher education.

Demand for Management and Accountability

In the last half of the 1980's, it has been the policy of the Ministry of Education to decentralise decision-making and to give educational institutions higher degrees of freedom, both in educational and administrative matters. The policy of decentralisation and institutional autonomy is followed by increasing demands on the outputs of the educational system. The outputs are to be accounted for by the institutions – both in qualitative and quantitative terms. As a consequence of this, procedures for systematical evaluation of educational programmes are being prepared by the ministry. While the need for qualitative evaluation generally seems to be accepted by higher education institutions, the ministry's recent plans for a computerised information system for the university sector have met fierce opposition from the universities. The opposition is especially directed against proposals for the establishment of performance indicators for research and educational activities at the institutions.

The policy of decentralisation puts greater demands on institutional management. It has now been generally recognised that educational institutions, too, need efficient management. Thus, autonomy, management and accountability have been the leading concepts in reforms of institutional structures in the college and – especially – the vocational sector in recent years. Compared to the degrees of freedom granted to the schools of vocational training, the time-honoured autonomy of the universities is beginning to look like a rather theoretical concept.

The law which regulates the university sector, the University Administration Act, has for 20 years been an untouchable holy cow in Danish education. However, in 1990, the Minister of Education has proposed a revision of the Act, and there seems to be widespread support in favour of a revision, both in academic circles and in Parliament. The main purpose of the revision is to provide structures for better management and accountability, which are to pave the way for higher degrees of freedom for the universities. So far all parties seem to agree. Which management structures the universities are going to have, on the other hand, is a matter of fierce dispute. A central issue in the ongoing debate on the Act is the relationship between university and society. One view is that universities ought to be governed by boards with substantial external representation, like many of the institutions in the college sector. The idea behind this is that only when representatives of 'the interests of society' have been included in governing bodies, can universities be granted that high degree of autonomy they ought to have. The opposite view, supported by a large part of the academics, is that university autonomy and freedom of research require governing bodies composed of university staff and students only.

The result of this debate is not yet known. Yet it seems certain that future university autonomy will depend on the ability of the universities to respond to societal needs in a way that can secure public confidence in the value of the university.

Higher Education in the Beginning of the 1990's

The massive growth of higher education since the 1960's has created a dilemma concerning the role of the university-sector in Danish higher education: is it the mission of universities to provide education for the masses, i.e. one-third of an age cohort passing the access-giving examination? Or is the task of the universities to educate the much smaller elite of students who are motivated towards, and capable of, studies at *kandidat* and doctoral level?

The answer of the universities to this dilemma has been ambiguous. On the one hand, the universities generally have wanted to take in as many students as possible, not surprisingly, since money followed the students. On the other hand, the universities until recently have maintained that the *kandidat* degree generally should be the first degree, and shorter degree courses accordingly have not played a significant role at universities.

This might have been justifiable 20 years ago, when less than 10 per cent of an age cohort went to university. Now the mass intake of students has created a growing mismatch between student qualifications and academic requirements, which is illustrated by high drop-out rates (40–60%), especially in sciences and the humanities. The new regulation of access by the ministry has to some extent solved the problem. In medicine, law and a number of other courses, admission requires rather high marks in upper-secondary school examinations, and as a consequence, drop-outs have decreased considerably. Albeit in other fields, such as science, where the universities have been able to accept most of the applicants, the drop-out level is still high.

So the problem is still there, and the dilemma has been accentuated as the number of places in higher education has increased in response to the growing number of refused applicants. In addition, further expansion is presently discussed in the Danish parliament.

It is far from clear which role the university sector is going to play in this game. The Ministry has clearly indicated that owing to both financial and labour market considerations the number of students at *kandidat* degree level is not to be increased. It also recently established new short-cycle courses in the vocational sector, which are expected to expand rapidly in the coming years. This expansion is to be financed in part by a reduction of the number of places in the university sector, especially in social science and business administration, where the increase in student intake to the universities has been especially high.

The universities are now beginning to establish courses at bachelor degree level, more suitable for mass education. As most institutions in the college sector are much smaller and less flexible than the universities, it is difficult and costly to establish many new places in that sector. This means that the universities will be in a good position in the coming competition for places in medium-cycle courses, if they decide to give priority to shorter mass-education courses.

Conclusions: Reform and Differentiation

From the middle of the 1970's, the Danish Ministry of Education has attempted to implement plans for change in higher education. The main objective has been to develop a coherent system of higher education, which could fulfil both the needs of the labour market and the need for mass education.

The results have been considerable changes in the distribution of students on various types of courses, and a better balance on the graduate labour-market. However, the large number of refused applicants represents a growing problem.

The endeavours for expansion of short- and medium-cycle courses, both in and outside the universities, have only succeeded to a limited extent. In spite of an adverse ministerial policy, the university sector has in the 1980's received a growing share of the influx to higher education.

The colleges, mostly small and rather specialised institutions, have not been a competitive alternative to the universities, although short-cycle courses in the vocational sector are expected to receive an increasing share of the students in the 1990's.

References:

Blume, S. (1974) 'New teaching-research relationships in mass post-secondary education' in *Structures of Studies and Place of Research in Mass Higher Education*. Paris: OECD.

Christensen, J.P. (1982) *Den hjere uddannelse som politisk problem*. Kbenhavn.

Christensen J.P. (1986) De unges uddannelsesvalg. Uddannelse No 6, oktober.

Finansministeriet (1990) *Finanslov for finansåret 1990*.

Planlaegningsrådet for de hjere uddannelser (1974) *Helhedsplanlaegning af de videregående uddannelser 1974–87*. Kbenhavn.

Tversted, L. (1988) *Planlaegningen af de videregående uddannelser. Fra 1960' erne til i dag*. Århus Universitet.

OECD (1988) *Reviews of National Science and technology policy: Denmark*. Paris: OECD.

Undervisningsministeriet og Finansministeriet (1989) *Budgetanalyse vedr. de videgående uddannelser og forskningen*. June 1989.

Undervisningsministeriet (1988) *De videregående uddannelser 1987–88* July 1988.

U91 (1990) *Det nye mnster i dansk uddannelses- og forskningspolitik*. Undervisningsministeriet.

Vohn, L. and M.M. Jensen (1978) *De videregående uddannelser 1966–75*. Hovedtendenser for udviklingen i tilgang. Undervisningsministeriet.

Part III

Policy Impacts and Institutional Change

CHAPTER 13

Higher Education and the Constitution of the European Community

Bruno De Witte

Introduction

The European Community does not have a fully-fledged higher education policy of its own, for which it lacks the necessary powers. Yet higher education policies of the Member States[1] are affected by EC measures in a variety of ways. One reason is that the central economic policies of the European Community necessarily spill over into the educational sector. Furthermore, the recent moves of the EC to extend its policy objectives beyond the economic sphere and build the basis for a European citizenship have found specific expression in the field of higher education. Quite simply said, the European Community is irresistibly becoming an all-purpose organisation and thereby also embraces within its scope of activity a fundamental social institution like higher education.

In the first part of this paper, an inventory will be made of the various ways in which the national systems of higher education are influenced by European Community rules. A distinction will be made between, on the one hand, legal rights based on EC law that can be invoked against either the higher education institutions or the national authorities, and, on the other hand, financial incentive schemes of the European Community and intergovernmental co-operation developing in the shadow of the EC system. Particularly the first category, that of legal rights, will be emphasised. They have the most incisive impact on national systems of higher education and their role is often underrated in policy analysis. Moreover, they clearly show the indirect nature of EC influence on the educational systems: the EC does not have an explicit educational policy as such, but pursues a number of other policies and objectives that do have an important side-effect on the educational system, and particularly on higher education.

In the second part of the paper, then, the significance of those various elements will be examined by relating them to what may be called the 'constitution' of the European Community. What are the basic policy objectives of European integration that have been invoked in support of EC initiatives related to higher education? How do those acts fit within the legal division of powers between the EC and the Member States as laid down

---

1   This paper only discusses the impact of the European Community on its own Member States. However, higher education policies of third States may also be affected (Guinand, 1990).

in the EEC Treaty? How, finally, does educational policy fit within the uneasy federal partnership between Europe, the nation state and regional institutions?

Forms of European Community Involvement

Legal Rights

Individuals participating in the educational process have been granted rights, either by the EEC Treaty itself or by secondary legislation based on this Treaty, which can be invoked by them against educational institutions or educational authorities of the single countries. Those rights have one thing in common: they are all based on the principle of non-discrimination on grounds of nationality. In the context of higher education, four rights may be singled out: the right for persons and organisations to set up educational courses or institutions; the right to teach; the right to study; and the right to recognition of studies.

The Right to Provide Higher Education

Education may be provided by self-employed persons or organisations, who may wish either to 'establish' a private school in another EC country, or else deliver educational 'services' to another EC country. As the Court of Justice held in a case brought by the Commission against Greece, those activities are covered by the Treaty provisions on freedom of establishment (article 52 ff.) or freedom to provide services (article 59 ff.),[2] whenever remuneration is sought for them. The practical consequence of those rights is a prohibition of discrimination on grounds of nationality. If a country allows the provision of private education by its own citizens, then it should allow, under the same conditions, schools set up by EC citizens, or long-distance education provided from another EC country. If, on the other hand, a country excludes private activity in a certain type of education (as is the case, in Greece, with university education), then this prohibition equally holds for EC citizens. In other words, there is not really a 'common market for university studies' as far as the supply side is concerned. The various States can freely decide if, and to what extent, private initiative is admissible in this sector.

The Right to Work for Higher Education Institutions

More often, persons who earn their living in the educational sector do so as teachers, that is, on the basis of a contract of employment with either a private or a public institution or as civil servants. They are to be considered as workers in the sense of the EEC Treaty and may invoke the right to live and work in EC countries other than their own.[3]

However, because most of those teachers are called to work in the public sector, the crucial question from the point of view of EC law has been whether those public schools are part of the 'public service' to which, according to article 48(4) the right of free movement does not apply.[4]

---

2   Case 147/86, *Commission v Greece*, judgement 15 March, [1988] European Court Reports 1637.

3   The argument presented by the German government, that education was not an economic activity, and that teachers could therefore not be 'workers', was given short shrift by the European Court of Justice in case 66/85, *Deborah Lawrie-Blum v Land Baden-Württemberg*, [1987] 3 Common Market Law Reports 389, para 13 and ff.

4   For a survey of this question and of the various arguments that could be invoked either way, see John Handoll (Handoll, 1989, 31–50).

In a series of judgments, the European Court of Justice has drastically limited the scope of the exception in article 48(4). Workers from other EC countries can only be excluded from public sector jobs that are concerned with the exercise of state authority (justice, police, central ministerial departments), but not from the more numerous jobs in public service sectors such as health care, transport or education (Handoll, 1988) . This rule was explicitly confirmed by the European Court of Justice in the case of a British trainee teacher in Germany,[5] and that of two foreign lecturers at the University of Venice.[6]

The right granted by article 48 is not simply a right to teach, but more broadly a right to work in higher education institutions. It also includes researchers who do not teach. The Court of Justice decided, in a case involving the Italian 'Consiglio Nazionale della Ricerca', that foreign researchers could not be excluded a priori from employment in that organisation, although leading or politically sensitive functions within such an institutions could still be reserved for nationals.[7]

To conclude, the fact that the scientific staff of higher education institutions have, in some countries, the status of *fonctionnaire* or *Beamte* is not a valid reason to exclude candidates coming from other Member States (Putzhammer, 1989). Of course, there remain other obstacles of a more indirect nature for foreign teachers. First of all, employment as a teacher is often made dependent on possession of a particular national diploma; as will be explained further on, the right to recognition of studies may soon alleviate, if not entirely eliminate this obstacle. Another indirect obstacle, namely the requirement of proficiency in the national language, was recently considered by the European Court of Justice in the *Groener* case. Anita Groener is a Dutch national who was a part-time teacher of painting at the College of Marketing and Design in Dublin. In order to be appointed on a permanent basis, she had to show an adequate knowledge of the Irish language. This is a general requirement for most appointments in the public educational system of the country (but not for universities), which therefore does not constitute a direct discrimination on grounds of nationality. Yet it is obviously a severe obstacle for foreigners seeking permanent employment.

A European Community Regulation of 1968 provides that linguistic requirements of this nature will be acceptable only if they are justified by the nature of the post to be filled (Council, 1968, article 3). The Court accepted that this was indeed the case; it held:

> The EEC Treaty does not prohibit the adoption of a policy for the protection and promotion of a language of a Member State which is both the national language and the first official language. (. . .) The importance of education for the implementation of such a policy must be recognised. Teachers have an essential role to play, not only through the teaching which they provide but also by their participation in the daily life of the school and the privileged relationship which they have with their pupils. In those circumstances, it is not unreasonable to require them to have some knowledge of the first official language.[8]

---

5   European Court of Justice, case 66/85, *Deborah Lawrie-Blum v Land Baden-Württemberg*, [1986] European Court Reports 2121.

6   Case 33/88, *P.Allué & C.M.Coonan v University of Venice*, judgment of 30 May 1989 (not yet reported).

7   Case 225/85, *Commission v Italy.*

8   European Court of Justice, case 371/87, *Anita Groener v Minister for Education and City of Dublin Vocational Education Committee*, judgment of 28 November 1989; not yet published in

The Rights of Students

The basic right of students under EC law is that of non-discrimination on the ground of nationality or, positively formulated, the right for students from other EC countries to be treated on equal terms with their guest country's own students. While the rights of teachers can rather easily be related to the economic freedoms of the common market, students do not seem to be concerned by the establishment of a common market. After all, they do not normally play an active role in the economy. The relevance of the EEC Treaty for their position has, however, been affirmed in a number of recent judgements of the European Court of Justice, which have been the object of ample and controversial commentaries in the legal literature (Lonbay, 1989; Arnull, 1988; Traversa, 1989; Lenz, 1989; Hartley, 1989; De Witte, 1989).

A basic distinction has to be made between two categories of EC students: those residing already in another EC country than their own ('migrant workers and their families') and those who first move to another EC country for the purpose of studying there ('other students').

Migrants and their Families

Migrants from EC countries, and above all their children, have been granted rights as a consequence of the free movement of workers recognised by article 48 and following of the EEC Treaty. It was not altogether obvious, at the time the EEC Treaty was adopted, that the right of EC nationals to take up employment in another Member State should be accompanied by rights in the educational sphere. Indeed, earlier bilateral conventions on labour migration usually did not include provisions pertaining to education. Article 48 of the EEC Treaty itself only guarantees non-discrimination in respect of conditions of work.

Yet a Regulation adopted by the Council of Ministers in 1968 recognised that genuine mobility of 'persons' (as opposed to 'labour force') between EC countries required equal treatment not only in the employment sphere itself, but also in the surrounding social system, including particularly housing and education. Article 7 of that Regulation provides that workers who are nationals of other Member States shall 'under the same conditions as national workers, have access to training in vocational schools and retraining centres'. Next to the rights granted to the workers themselves, Article 12 of the same Regulation provides that the children

> of a national of a Member State who is or has been employed in the territory of another Member State shall be admitted to that State's general educational, apprenticeship and vocational training courses under the same conditions as the nationals of that State, if such children are residing in its territory.

This initial legislative framework has been completed through the creative interpretation by the European Court of Justice in a series of cases. In essence, the Court has developed the limited right of equal access of EC workers and their families into a much broader guarantee of equal treatment in education. Article 12 was interpreted as covering not only formal admission to schools but also all 'general measures intended to facilitate educational attendance',[9] including, among other things, educational grants. Later on, the Court of Justice held that the term 'general education' used in the same article, although it might have been intended above all for primary and secondary

---

the Official Report, but see the commentary by Bryan M.E. McMahon (McMahon, 1990).

9   ECJ, case 9/74, *Donato Casagrande v Landeshauptstadt München*, [1974] European Court Reports 773.

education, referred in fact to any form of education, including university and other post-secondary studies.[10]

Another relevant provision of the same Regulation is article 7(2) which guarantees to EC workers 'the same social and tax advantages as national workers'. The concept of 'social advantages' has gradually been broadened; it refers, in the current definition of the European Court, to all the advantages which

whether or not linked to a contract of employment, are generally granted to national workers primarily because of their objective status of workers or by virtue of the mere fact of their residence on national territory, and the extension of which to workers who are nationals of other Member States therefore seems suitable to facilitate their mobility within the Community.[11]

Most welfare benefits are covered by this definition, and the fact that educational advantages of various kinds are covered as well was established, again, by the European Court. In the *Lair* case, a French national who had worked and had become unemployed in Germany, had started language studies at the University of Hanover and applied for a study grant, which was refused by the German authorities. Once persons are workers in the sense of the EEC Treaty, the European Court held, they have an equal right to 'all advantages designed to enable them to improve their vocational skills and achieve social advancement, in particular, a maintenance grant for the pursuit of university studies'.[12]

Equal treatment does not only extend to financial support schemes but also, as was decided in *Matteucci*, to scholarships for specialised studies abroad, even if those scholarships are attributed within the framework of a bilateral cultural treaty which explicitly restricts this benefit to citizens of the two contracting States (and would therefore seem to exclude nationals of other EC States).[13]

Formally, all those educational benefits accrue to the migrant workers themselves and not to their families. Yet such a restriction would be anomalous within the overall scheme of the Regulation which is concerned above all with the educational rights of the migrant children. Therefore, the Court held in another recent case that all those educational benefits qualifying as social advantages (in the case at hand, the right to global study financing in Dutch higher education) should be granted not only to the EC workers but also to their children; and, indeed, to all the members of their family.[14]

As a result of those various developments, EC workers and members of their family can now claim full equal treatment with nationals in the educational sphere, including higher education. Given the fact, on the other hand, that the conditions for being considered as a 'worker' in the sense of the EEC Treaty are very liberal, students from EC countries could decide to fake an employment relationship (or independent

---

10 European Court of Justice, joined cases 389 and 390/87, *Echternach and Moritz v Netherlands Minister for Education and Science*, judgment of 15 March 1989.

11 ECJ, case 207/78, *Ministère Public v Even and ONPTS*, [1979] European Court Reports 2019, at 2034.

12 ECJ, case 39/86, *Sylvie Lair v Universität Hannover*, judgment of 21 June 1988, [1988] European Court Reports 3161.

13 ECJ, case 235/87, *Annunziata Matteucci v Communauté française de Belgique*, [1988] European Court Reports 5589. Miss Matteucci was an Italian national living and working in Belgium who had applied for a scholarship attributed on the basis of the cultural agreement between Belgium and the Federal Republic of Germany.

14 ECJ, joined cases 389 and 390/87, *Echternach and Moritz*, footnote 10 supra.

economic activity) in another Member State, in order to gain access to the educational system of that country, with all the accompanying benefits.

This further development was, however, discouraged by the Court of Justice in the *Brown* case in which it held that there is no equal claim to a study allowance when the employment relationship of the claimant is 'merely ancillary to the studies to be financed by the grant'.[15] This barrier erected by the Court maintains a basic distinction between two types of EC nationals: on the one hand, those residing in another Member State (migrants with their families); on the other hand, EC nationals ('students') who move to another Member State primarily for study purposes. The latter also derive rights from the EEC Treaty, but to a lesser extent.

Other Students

Citizens of one Member State who go and study in another Member State, will be called 'EC students' here. Their rights are not based on the chapters of the Treaty dealing with free movement of persons, but on article 128, dealing with vocational training, in combination with the general non-discrimination principle of article 7.

The application of this general non-discrimination clause gives EC students a right of equal access to education which, unlike that of EC workers and their families, is limited to particular courses, namely those qualifying as vocational training in the sense of article 128. However, in the *Gravier* case, the Court did not define vocational training in its original narrow and 'technical' sense, but included under that heading any study programme which 'prepares for a particular profession, trade or employment or provides the necessary training and skills for that profession, trade or employment'.[16] The Court clearly held that practically all types of university or higher education courses are covered by the European Community notion of vocational training.[17] All university studies lead, if nothing else, to a career of teacher of the particular study discipline, and therefore qualify as vocational training (except for students who have reached pensionable age).

Yet this right of equal access to higher education is still limited in some respects. Only conditions of access based on nationality or country of origin are prohibited. General conditions of access like study qualifications, linguistic proficiency or *numerus clausus* rules are still permissible as long as their purpose is not to discriminate against EC students.

EC students' right to equal treatment is also less extensive than that of migrant workers and their families, because it is limited to formal conditions of access, including the payment of tuition fees, but excluding the right to financial support by the host State during their studies. The latter restriction, which was decided by the European Court of Justice in the *Lair* judgment, is open to a number of criticisms. First of all, conditions of access cannot easily be distinguished from additional support. Thus, in the Netherlands, students receive a global grant which serves both as a reimbursement of tuition fees and as a maintenance grant. Should one cut this global grant into pieces, and give to EC students one part but not the other? (Drijber, 1988, 1638) The distinction made by the Court also contradicts its own earlier reasoning in *Casagrande* where it held that,

---

15 Case 197/86, *Brown v The Secretary of State for Scotland*, [1988] European Court Reports 3205.

16 Case 263/86, *The State (Belgium) v René Humbel*, para.12.

17 Case 24/86, *Vincent Blaizot v University of Liège and others*, [1988] European Court Reports 379; and even more strongly in ECJ, case 242/87, *Commission v Council*, para.27.

in the case of migrant children, there was an intimate connection between formal rights of access and a study grant.

The Court probably acted here out of considerations of judicial policy. *Gravier* and subsequent decisions had already raised many eyebrows among national educational authorities. There, the Court had unexpectedly recognised the right of equal treatment of EC students as regards tuition fees, with the possible consequence that students would start to move 'en masse' to countries (such as Belgium) with unlimited access and low tuition fees.[18] The Court may have chosen not to extend the *Gravier* non-discrimination rule into the field of maintenance grants in order to spare those countries any further financial risks.

The Right to Recognition of Studies

Citizens from other Member States do not only have equal access to higher education, they logically also have the right, upon completion of those studies, to have their diploma recognised by their host State under the conditions applying for that State's own citizens.

More important is the question whether countries also have to recognise diplomas of higher education awarded by other countries of the European Communities. This is a precondition for an effective free movement of professionals within the European Community, and the EEC Treaty explicitly refers to the need of adopting directives in order to organise such a system of recognition of diplomas for professional purposes. During a first period, EEC directives were adopted for the recognition of specific diplomas for the medical and paramedical professions and for architects; they were accompanied, each time, by a 'co-ordination directive' in which national programmes of study were harmonised to a certain extent. This 'vertical' approach proved to be too slow and was replaced by a new, 'horizontal', approach. In December 1988, a so-called 'general' directive was adopted which provides for the recognition, without prior harmonisation, of diplomas awarded on completion of higher education studies of at least three years' duration. It will allow every EC citizen holding a higher education diploma, in any subject, to practice his/her profession, either under contract or independently, in other EC countries than the one in which his/her study was completed. Only in the case of important differences in education and training or in the organisation of the profession, may the host country require evidence of professional experience or impose a supervised training period or an aptitude test (Council, 1989a; 623; Laslett, 1990).

The consequences of this new approach for higher education systems are, of course, quite different. Study programmes are not directly affected by the new directive. Yet one may wonder whether the indirect consequences will not be more important in the long run than with the earlier sectoral approach. The creation of a European market for professionals may well motivate the various countries to improve the quality of their higher education systems and, thereby, the professional chances of their own citizens. A more quantitative effect may already be witnessed. Countries like Belgium and France that have higher education studies of two years' duration, think of upgrading them to three years, so as to bring them within the scope of the recognition directive (Teichler, 1990, 31).

Recognition for professional purposes is often distinguished from academic recognition of diplomas and periods of studies.[19] Academic recognition may take place at

---

18   For a discussion of the consequences of the *Gravier* doctrine, from the point of view of public finances, see Jean-Claude Scholsem (Scholsem, 1989).

various stages of the higher education curriculum; it may relate to entrance qualifications, to intermediate qualifications, to periods of study, and to final qualifications (for postgraduate purposes). Academic recognition may be problematic even within a single State (as, for instance, in the UK), but much more so at the international level.

In contrast with professional recognition, there is no explicit mandate in the EEC Treaty in this respect, and the EC has been entering this area only very recently, and still timidly, with the experimental European Community course credit transfer system (Action 3 of the ERASMUS programme), and with the creation of a network of National Academic Recognition Information Centres (NARIC) whose role is of an advisory nature. Yet, because the lack of academic recognition affects the professional careers of those involved, it is arguable that more general European Community measures would be justified in this area.

Other Forms of Community Involvement

Financial Incentives

The European Community had adopted, in recent years, a large number of programmes in which EC funds are earmarked for specific projects in higher education. The Commission of the European Communities has played a very active role in developing those programmes and in negotiating the necessary agreement of the Member State representatives in the Council. Once the programmes are adopted by the Council, the Commission also exercises control over their implementation and decides on the attribution of financial subsidies. A rough distinction can be made between mobility programmes and research and technology programmes, although some programmes combine both.

The purpose of the first category is to promote the mobility of higher education students and/or teachers across intra-Community borders. The most well-known among those programmes is ERASMUS.[20] This programme was adopted in 1987 and mainly involves the establishment and operation of a European co-operation network between universities and direct financial support for students pursuing a period of study at a university in another Member State. It does not, however, give every single student a right to spend a period of study abroad. The long-term objective is that 10 per cent of all students in higher education should spend such a period abroad; in the year 1990–91, about 40,000 students received a Community grant.

Erasmus had been preceded by COMETT (Community Action Programme in Education and Training for Technology)[21] whose purpose is to strengthen co-operation between higher education institutions and industry. One of its main aspects is the placement, with Community grants, of students in firms located in other Member States.

---

19   For this distinction, and for a general survey of both academic and professional recognition, see Chiara Zilioli (Zilioli, 1989, 52); See also the survey of existing mechanisms of academic recognition by F. Dalichow (Dachilow, 1987).

20   Council Decision of 15 June 1987 adopting the European Community action scheme for the mobility of university studies (ERASMUS) *Official Journal of the European Communities* 1987, L 166. This programme has been amended and extended by a Council Decision of 14 December 1989, *Official Journal* 1989, L 395.

21   Council Decision of 24 July 1986, *Official Journal of the European Communities* 1986, C 222. See also the revised version ('Comett II'): Council Decision of 16 December 1988, *Official Journal* 1989, L 13.

The Lingua programme is a multi-annual scheme of EC grants which is rather similar to Erasmus but limited to one particular area of higher education, that of foreign language education; the mobility of both students and teachers of European Community languages is to be promoted.[22]

The last of the mobility programmes is TEMPUS, which was adopted in 1990.[23] It combines features of ERASMUS, COMETT and LINGUA, but with specific reference to Central and Eastern Europe. It offers financial support to Joint European Projects linking universities or enterprises (or both) from those countries with partners from at least two EC countries; it also offers mobility grants for the staff and students of the participating institutions.

As for the research and technology programmes of the European Community, they practically all involve universities and research institutes for carrying out various projects. Two programmes directly aim at promoting the mobility and co-operation of researchers themselves, namely SCIENCE (for the natural sciences) and SPES (for economists).

None of those programmes directly regulates educational structures or educational programmes. Participation in all those financial incentive schemes is on a voluntary basis. Yet, the choice whether to participate in a programme is not left to the Member States but to the institutions of higher education themselves; the decision on attribution of EC funds is, again, not controlled by the educational authorities of the member countries, but by the Commission. It is therefore undeniable that those subsidy programmes potentially affect national policies of higher education. For instance, within the ERASMUS scheme, participating universities have the obligation to recognise the periods of study abroad, and this may upset a rigid curriculum imposed by the educational authorities (Lenaerts, 1989, 123). Another noticeable effect of ERASMUS is that smaller countries, in particular, tend to offer more and more courses in foreign languages in order to attract sufficient interest from students of their partner universities.

The steering function of grants-in-aid in a federal system has often been noticed. By attributing money for specific purposes, the EC encourages the Member States to take initiatives for those purposes. If the Member States choose to apply for Community funds, they also have to respect the conditions attached to it and, if necessary, modify their educational rules so as to comply with those conditions.

Intergovernmental Co-operation

The generally accepted view had, for a very long time, been that educational policy 'as such', that is, a policy not directly related to the guarantee of one of the common market freedoms, was not a proper object of action by the European Community. It could, if necessary, be discussed by the governments of the Member States, but only in the margin of the EC structure. An early example of such intergovernmental co-operation was the creation of the European University Institute of Florence in 1972; the political decision was taken by the governments of the Member States of the EC, but the legal form was that of an agreement under international law rather than an act of EC law.

---

22 Council Decision of 28 July 1989 establishing an action programme to promote foreign language competence in the European Community (LINGUA) *Official Journal of the European Communities* 1989, L 239.

23 Council Decision of 7 May 1990 establishing a trans-European mobility scheme for university studies (TEMPUS) *Official Journal of the European Communities* 1990, L 131.

From 1971, the education ministers of the Member States started to meet regularly; yet, unlike their colleagues of foreign affairs, economic affairs or agriculture, their meetings did not take place within the formal structure of the Council of Ministers but were 'ordinary' diplomatic reunions in the 'shadow' of the EC. The advantage of this approach is that it ensures flexibility; the ministers can freely discuss any matter they like and adopt concluding resolutions if they like.[24] Yet they do not have to respect the formal rules of decision-making of the Council and, above all, do not need to adopt formal acts of EC law which would be binding for the States which they represent. This absence of binding legal effects does not make this form of co-operation utterly meaningless. The resolutions express a political understanding and their content may slowly trickle down into national policy-making through a process of learning and expectation building.

Moreover, intergovernmental co-operation does not mean that 'genuine' EC action is excluded once and for all. It would rather seem, from past experience, that intergovernmental resolutions are used for starting preparatory measures and pilot actions; if those actions develop into large scale programmes, they have to be incorporated within the EC framework for obvious reasons of democratic accountability and judicial protection (Van Craeyenest, 1989).

Many items from the basic resolution of 1976 that were listed under the heading 'co-operation in the field of higher education', have by now been turned into solid programmes like COMETT, ERASMUS and LINGUA. Other points, like the development of a common policy on admission of students from other Member States, have been rendered obsolete by the case law of the European Court of Justice described above. Still other points (like the question of academic recognition of diplomas and periods of study) are still in the intergovernmental pipeline but may soon emerge in the Community decision-making structure.

The Constitutional Dimension

The Objectives

A People's Europe

The political theme of a 'people's Europe' (*l'Europe des citoyens, Das Europa der Bürger*) was launched in 1984 as a response to what was perceived as a serious crisis of the European integration process. Voter turn-out in the second direct elections to the European Parliament in 1984 was very low, which seemed to confirm what opinion polls kept indicating, namely, that there might be considerable support for the idea of European unity but no enthusiasm for the European Community as an organisation. The EC appeared as a technocratic and/or business oriented organisation, offering little tangible benefits for individual citizens.

A remedy was sought in the adoption of symbolic policies designed to strengthen feelings of loyalty to and identification with the European Community. The Fontainebleau European Council meeting shortly after the elections considered that it was 'essential that the Community should respond to the expectations of the people of Europe by adopting measures to strengthen and promote its identity and its image both for its citizens and for the rest of the world' and set up, in order to prepare such action,

---

24   Those resolutions are collected, together with binding acts of Community law, in a publication of the Council of the European Communities, (Council, 1987).

an ad-hoc Committee on a People's Europe (also known as the Adonnino Committee, from the name of its chairman). In two reports submitted in 1985, the Committee listed thirteen pages of proposals for bringing about a 'people's Europe' (Adonnino, 1985).

The general thrust of the report was that progress in economic integration had to be accompanied by visible progress in other fields as well. One of the areas in which, according to the Committee, actions could be developed was that of 'youth, education, exchanges and sport'. Proposals relating specifically to higher education advocated an increase in university co-operation, and promotion of transnational mobility and language teaching. The Committee also (but separately) suggested the adoption of a system of general recognition of diplomas of higher education.

Those ideas bore fruit, though not immediately. The Milan meeting of the European Council in June 1985 considered the reports with favour, but the minds of the Heads of State and Governments were preoccupied with other things. At that meeting, the internal market of 1992 was adopted as the primary objective of the Community, and the decision was taken to convene an intergovernmental conference which, less than one year later, was going to adopt the text of the Single European Act, the most important revision of the EEC Treaty to date. '1992' took over, in a much more effective way, the role of mobilising myth which had been sought in the idea of a 'people's Europe'. The proposals of the Adonnino Committee were piloted on a side track. The European Council agreed with the tenor of the Adonnino report, and gave a mandate to the Commission of the European Community to ensure, within the limits of its powers, the implementation of the Committee's proposals. Yet, those limits were not in any way extended by the Single European Act, which did not even mention the objective of a people's Europe and did not attribute new powers to the Community in fields, like education, that had been covered by the Adonnino report.

The objective of a people's Europe was therefore not incorporated in the EC's constitution. While the Commission, in the following years, continued to cherish the idea, it had to find the ways and means for achieving progress without such constitutional legitimation. The Commission's major resource was that at least some of the proposals of the Adonnino report had an economic flavour and fitted within the internal market programme. The prime example was that of the mutual recognition of diplomas. The Directive on that subject perfectly fits within the internal market programme; indeed, it was one of the first proposals submitted by the Commission in that context. But neither the text nor the preamble of the directive which was finally adopted in December 1988, refer to the objective of a people's Europe. It is far from evident that the concept played any role in the final stages of negotiation.

In the ERASMUS programme, adopted one and a half years earlier, the reference to the people's Europe is much more direct. In the text of the Decision itself, one of the objectives of ERASMUS is said to be 'to strengthen the interaction between citizens in different Member States with a view to consolidating the concept of a People's Europe'.[25]

When assessing the follow-up of the Adonnino reports in 1988, the Commission was able to indicate two programmes in higher education (ERASMUS and COMETT) as two of the major successes achieved so far (Commission, 1988, 12). LINGUA was announced as a further project in the same vein, but its adoption in 1989 seems to have exhausted the 'people's Europe' theme as far as education is concerned.

---

25   Council Decision of 15 June 1987, article 2(iv).

At the European Council of Dublin, in June 1990, the Heads of State and Government revived once more the idea of a people's Europe (because the impetus provided by '1992' is decreasing?), by discussing 'a number of themes of particular relevance to the individual citizen including the free movement of persons, the environment, drugs and their links with organised crime, and anti-semitism' (European Council, 1990). No mention is made of education, and the impression prevails more than ever that the 'people's Europe' is an empty vessel to be filled by whatever theme currently concerns public opinion in Europe. Higher education measures, in the mean time, have found a more solid ideological foundation in other EC objectives.

The Internal Market

The Commission's White Paper on the Completion of the Internal Market, which was issued in 1985, started a new chapter in the history of European integration. The 1992 deadline, which the Paper happily proposed, was quickly adopted by the Governments at the Milan meeting of the European Council mentioned above, and proved to be the driving force behind the moves for institutional change introduced by the Single European Act in 1987. Since then, considerable progress has been made in the removal of the remaining barriers to the free movement of goods, persons, services and capital.[26]

Yet, this process had been under way since the signature of the EEC Treaty in 1957. The four 'common market freedoms' mentioned above had been essential elements of European integration since the very beginning, and had been partially realised in the course of the years through the legislation adopted by the Council and the dynamic jurisprudence of the European Court of Justice. It was shown, earlier on in this paper, that one of those freedoms, the free movement of persons has become the vehicle for a series of individual entitlements in the field of higher education.

In this sense, the Commission's White Paper and the Single European Act, by introducing the concept of 'internal market' and the 1992 deadline, have only given a further impetus to a process already well on its way. There is, however, one piece of EC legislation which is more directly linked to the philosophy of the White Paper, namely the directive on recognition of diplomas. In the White Paper, the Commission officially announced the shift in its approach to the problem of recognition of diplomas, which was mentioned above, from recognition of specific diplomas with harmonisation of study programmes, to general recognition of broad categories of diplomas without prior harmonisation. This was an application of the more general principle of mutual trust which had first been coined in relation to the free movement of goods and now became the overall philosophy of '1992'.[27]

The new strategy has been very successful generally speaking, and the adoption of the directive on diplomas according to the model delineated in the White Paper is one of its main achievements. Attention is, however, increasingly shifting now to a new

---

26   See the definition of the 'internal market' in article 8A of the EEC Treaty (newly introduced by the Single European Act): 'The internal market shall comprise an area without internal frontiers in which the free movement of goods, persons, services and capital is ensured in accordance with the provisions of this Treaty'.

27   The principle of mutual trust in the context of circulation of goods meant quite simply that a product lawfully manufactured and marketed in one Member State should be taken in principle to be of sufficient quality to be sold throughout the Community. The diversity of existing national rules should be respected and harmonisation of national rules by the EEC institutions should be limited to essential aspects of consumer protection. One may note the parallel with the basic approach of the general directive on recognition of diplomas.

challenge: that of the implementation of the internal market programme by the Member States (Schwarze et al, 1990). The new division of labour between Community and Member States has led to the adoption of Community legislation of a different type, in which only basic elements are regulated, while a large measure of discretion is left to the Member States with a corresponding risk of slow and distorted implementation (Dehousse, 1989, 131). The diploma directive may soon prove to be an illustration of both the success and the pitfalls of the new strategy. The Member States seem to want to exploit fully the possibility of imposing adaptation measures and aptitude tests upon migrant professionals, a possibility which was originally intended only for exceptional cases.

More broadly speaking, attention is shifting from the establishment of the internal market to the consequences of this establishment and the functioning of this market after 1992. When assessing the most recent Commission plans in the field of education, the Council of Ministers for Education drew attention to 'the consequences of the establishment of the internal market which will affect the educational policies of the Member States and mark a new stage in the Community co-operation initiated in this field by the resolution of 9 February 1976' (Council, 1989b).

In the Commission's plans themselves (Commission, 1989), educational and training policy are still very much seen from an economic perspective. But the context is not so much that of the creation of an internal market, but rather that of the development of 'human resources' as an important factor in stimulating the overall performance of the European economy and producing a better economic and social cohesion within Europe. The internal market, then, would seem to require both, the elimination of obstacles to economic integration in the higher education system (equal access of students and teachers, recognition of diplomas), and the creation of the educational skills necessary for the effective functioning of the market (mobility and research programmes).

Educational Policy for its own Sake?

In recent years, the Ministers of Education of the Member States no longer meet entirely outside the Community structure, as they did before. Rather, they have one foot inside and one foot outside. Their meetings, twice a year, are now systematically called reunions of the 'Council and the Ministers for Education meeting within the Council'. The representatives of the governments are wearing two hats; with their Community hats on, they can adopt formal decisions of the Council of Ministers of the European Community (for instance, the ERASMUS and LINGUA programmes); with their intergovernmental hat on, they can continue to adopt, as before, resolutions and conclusions expressing political commitments devoid of binding effects.

The fact that Ministers of Education take binding decisions in the name of the European Community is an institutional sign that educational policy is now pursued as such at the Community level. But there are other indications in the same sense. In a recent overall policy statement, the Ministers of Education of the Member States adopted conclusions 'on co-operation and Community policy in the field of education'. The existence of a genuine Community educational policy is thereby clearly confirmed; the Ministers also agree in the same document on the objective of 'bringing about a Europe of knowledge and cultures'. But at the same time, they affirm that EC action 'must be based on two fundamental principles – respect for linguistic and cultural diversity, and affirmation of the subsidiarity of Community activities – and must respect the fundamental powers of the Member States in matters of general educational policy' (Council, 1989b). The Ministers, with those words pointed to the continuing existence of both political and legal constraints to EC action in the field of (higher) education. Those will be examined in the concluding section of this paper.

The Constraints

Legal Constraints: the Problem of Community Competence

The EC institutions are not free to act as they choose for the achievement of the objectives which they have set themselves. They have to respect the limits imposed by the EEC Treaty. The powers of the institutions are enumerated in this Treaty (and also the, less important, ECSC and Euratom Treaty), and every act of the EC must find an appropriate legal basis in it.

Yet, the EEC Treaty (unlike most federal constitutions) does not have a provision which neatly lists a number of policy sectors attributed to the EC. Scattered articles of the Treaty do transfer decision-making power for some such sectors, like agriculture, transport, or external trade policy. Yet, the Treaty also attributes (more important) powers of a different nature. They can be called functional powers, because they are defined in terms of an objective to achieve, rather than in terms of a substantive policy to develop. The overall functional objective is, of course, the establishment and functioning of a common market; partial objectives within this overall goal are the achievement of the fundamental common market freedoms (movement of goods and persons, provision of services, movement of capital).

In implementing those objectives, the EC institutions necessarily have to cut across the boundaries between substantive policy areas which the individual states are used to trace for their own internal purposes. In this way, many public policies which were not transferred as such to the Community have, nevertheless, in the course of the years, become constrained by Community rules and Community action. Thus, harmonisation for the purpose of ensuring the free movement of goods and services had led to the emergence of a European consumer policy; the free movement of services had led to the emergence of a Community media policy; pursuit of the common market objectives had prompted the adoption of environmental protection measures at EC level long before environmental policy was formally recognised as an EC policy by the Single European Act.

The same process has happened with the free movement of persons and education. Already in a judgment of 1974, the European Court of Justice considered whether the Council, by including provisions on the education of migrant children in a regulation implementing the free movement of workers (Regulation 1612/68, analysed above), had not overstepped the substantive limits of EC competence. Its answer was that 'although educational and training policy is not as such included in the spheres which the Treaty has entrusted to the EC institutions, it does not follow that the exercise of powers transferred to the EC is in some way limited if it is of such a nature as to affect the measures taken in the execution of a policy such as that of education and training'.[28]

While the free movement of persons has been a rich source of individual rights for participants in the higher educational process, the main legal lever for the EC in recent years has been article 128 of the EEC Treaty. The article provides that the Council shall lay down general principles for implementing a common vocational training policy

---

28   Case 9/74, *Donato Casagrande v Landeshauptstadt München*, [1974] European Court Reports
      1974, 773, at 779. This 'Casagrande formula' has been repeated several times since; see e.g.
      case 242/87, *Commission v Council*, judgment of 30 May 1989, para.31 (not yet reported).

capable of contributing to the harmonious development both of the national economies and of the Common Market.

For a long time, this was a 'dormant' provision of the Treaty. It was thought that the words 'general principles', used in the article, prevented the EC from adopting any detailed and/or binding rules in this area (Hochbaum, 1989, 152ff). But the European Court of Justice has vitalised the article by its judgments. As mentioned before, *Gravier* and subsequent cases gave a definition of the words 'vocational training' which is 'extremely wide, wider than the phrase's meaning in everyday speech and in technical use by education policy makers' (Flynn, 1989, 99) and now includes all higher education studies. In the later ERASMUS judgment, the Court made it clear that the words 'general principles' do not prevent the EC from adopting binding and detailed rules in this broad area.[29] A genuine EC policy on higher education has now become possible, albeit under the unalluring heading 'vocational training'.

Wide as it may be, the concept of vocational training only covers the teaching part of higher education. That does not matter so much because the EC has received the legal competence to deal with the research side elsewhere in the Treaty, namely in the articles 130F and 130G which were added by the Single European Act of 1986. Those articles describe a common policy of research and technological development. Universities are, for the first time, mentioned in the EEC Treaty. It is said that the EC will encourage their research programmes, particularly when they co-operate with private enterprises. The EC is also instructed to take action for stimulating the training and mobility of researchers in the EC.

It should be noted that the whole policy of research and technological development is made subservient to the overall aim of strengthening the scientific and technological basis of European industry.[30] This might well limit the type of university research which the EC is going to encourage, and more particularly inhibit support, on this basis at least, for the arts and social sciences. But this is not yet the end of the legal resources offered by the EEC Treaty. There is also a general so-called 'gap filling' clause in article 235. It allows the Council to adopt EC acts for which the necessary powers are not available elsewhere in the Treaty, whenever such acts are necessary 'within the operation of the common market'.

This possibility has been widely used by the EC in a number of fields. Its use within the area of education is still politically controversial, but seems to be legally possible. The reference, within the article, to the operation of the common market does not mean that article 235 actions must be justifiable in terms of economic efficiency, but merely that they must have an impact on economic activity, even if their primary purpose is non-economic.[31] The effective 'operation of the common market' might indeed require the adoption of regulatory measures that do not fit within a strict *logique du marché*. Taken in this sense, article 235 may precisely be a way of incorporating considerations of a purely educational nature in acts which might otherwise be constrained by their terms of reference to the free movement of persons, vocational training, or research and technology.

---

29 Case 242/87, *Commission v Council*, judgment of 30 May 1989. See the (critical) comment by C.D. Classen (Classen, 1990).

30 Article 130F (1).

31 Earlier Community practice with article 235, for instance in the environmental area, provides an excellent illustration of this approach. See, generally, J.L. Dewost (Dewost, 1987).

If article 235 has such a wide scope, the conclusion would seem that there is no effective legal limit to EC action in the field of education. Yet legal considerations remain important, because the EC institutions do not have a free choice among the various legal options. More particularly, the question whether a proposal fits within the scope of article 128 of the Treaty (vocational training policy) or has to be based on article 235, has important consequences for the decision-making progress. In the first case, decisions can be taken, and have been taken, by a simple majority of the votes within the Council (that is, 7 votes out of 12), while in the second case decisions can only be taken unanimously, which constitutes a solid protection of national (educational) sovereignty.[32]

Political Constraints

Even when legal powers are available for a given activity in the area of education, it may not always be politically expedient or feasible to exercise them. Education is a rather sensitive area in which Member States increasingly resent Community involvement and stress the need for 'subsidiarity'.

There is a diffuse unrest in many Member States, but three States in particular have expressed considerable reluctance to move forward in this area: Denmark, the Federal Republic of Germany, and the UK. Denmark and the UK generally resent the extension of Community powers and the corresponding loss of 'national sovereignty', and the resentment is particularly vivid when this happens in policy areas that are not explicitly mentioned in the Treaty. In both countries, this reluctance is further strengthened by the fear that Community educational policy might erode existing privileged links with non-Member States (the Commonwealth in the case of Britain; Scandinavian countries in the case of Denmark).

Further, there is the concern of the German *Länder* that growing involvement of the EC may seriously affect their autonomy in an area which they had hitherto been able to shield against interference by the *Bund* (Hochbaum, 1987; Eiselstein, 1989; Konow, 1989). The same situation could arise as regards Belgium, where the constitutional reform of 1988 has attributed full legislative competence for education to the three autonomous Communities of the country (Verstegen, 1990; Bourtenbourg, 1988). In Spain, there are more timid moves of devolution of educational authority to the Autonomous Communities (Garcia Garrido).

Not all those misgivings about a European Community seriously threatening well-established policies of higher education, seem well founded. They often disregard the potential for innovation and development of national policies offered by EC initiatives. Yet they certainly affect the possibility for further developments at EC level. The circumstances in which the LINGUA programme was adopted illustrate those difficulties (Janssen, 1988/89, 195).[33]

It would seem, however, that the existing tension should not be solved by insisting on a rigid system of division of competences between the various layers (EC – member

---

32 Because of this political importance, the apparently technical dispute about the appropriate legal basis for the (first) Erasmus programme was submitted to the European Court of Justice (case 242/87, *Commission v Council*, see above).

33 The part of the Lingua proposal dealing with school exchanges was deleted by the Council on the insistence of the British and German governments that it constituted undue interference with matters of general educational policy.

state – region), but rather by a federal partnership model in which each of the relevant actors participates in a joint policy-making mechanism (Mayntz, 1990). It would seem unfeasible, and unwise, to stop the European Community from encroaching upon national prerogatives in higher education. Yet, it is important that the Community, whenever it acts, shows sensitivity to the idiosyncratic nature of the institutional structures and educational traditions of the various countries.

References:

Adonnino Committee (1985) 'A People's Europe'. *Bulletin of the European Communities* Supplement 7/85.

Arnull, A. (1988) 'Of strip cartoonists, vets and gunsmiths'. *European Law Review*, 260–267.

Bourtembourg, J. (1988) 'L'enseignement et la communautarisation'. *Administration publique*, 183–199.

Classen, C.D. (1990) 'Bildungspolitische Förderprogramme der EG – Eine kritische Untersuchung der vertragsrechtlichen Grundlagen'. *Europarecht*, 10–19.

Commission (1988) 'A people's Europe', Commission communication transmitted to the European Parliament on 24 June 1988. *Bulletin of the European Communities* Supplement 2/88, 12.

Commission (1989) Communication from the Commission to the Council. *Education and training in the European Community: guidelines for the medium term (1989–1992).* COM(89) 236 final (2 June 1989).

Council (1968) Council Regulation 1612/68 of 15 October 1968. *Official Journal of the European Communities* L 257.

Council (1989a) Directive 89/48 of 21 December 1988. Official Journal of the European Communities. L 19/16.

Council (1989b) 'Conclusions of the Council and the Ministers for Education meeting within the Council of 6 October 1989, on co-operation and Community policy in the field of education in the run-up to 1993'. *Official Journal of the European Communities* C 277/5.

Council of the European Communities (1987) *European Educational Policy Statements*, 3rd ed. Luxembourg: Office for Official Publications of the European Communities.

Craeyenest, F. van (1989) 'La nature juridique des résolutions sur la co-opération en matière d'éducation' in De Witte, B. (ed) *European Community Law of Education.* Baden-Baden: Nomos, 127–133.

Dalichow, F. (1987) 'Academic recognition within the European Community'. *European Journal of Education*, 39–58.

Dehousse, R. (1989) '1992 and beyond: the institutional dimension of the internal market programme'. *Legal Issues of European Integration* 109–136.

De Witte, B. (1989) 'Educational Equality for Community Workers and their Families' in De Witte, B. (ed) *European Community Law of Education.* Baden-Baden: Nomos, 71–79.

Dewost, J.L. (1987) 'Décisions des institutions en vue du développement des compétences et des instruments juridiques' in R. Bieber and G. Ress (eds) *Die Dynamik des Europäischen Gemeinschaftsrechts/The Dynamics of EC-law.* Baden-Baden: Nomos, 321–340.

Drijber, B.J. (1988) 'Gelijke behandeling van studenten uit de EEG – zijn er nog grenzen?'. *Nederlands Juristenblad*, 1635–1640.

Eiselstein, C. (1989) 'Verlust der Bundesstaatlichkeit?'. *Neue Zeitschrift für Verwaltungsrecht*, 323.

European Council (1990) Conclusions, Dublin, 25–26 June 1990. *Europe – Documents* No 1630/1631, 27 June 1990.

Flynn, J. (1989) 'Gravier: suite du feuilleton' in De Witte, B. (ed) *European Community Law of Education.* Baden-Baden: Nomos, 95–112.

Garcia Garrido, J.L. (1988) 'Regionalism and cultural pluralism in the Spanish educational system'. *West European Education,* 20–34.

Guinand, J. (1990) 'The implications of European integration for higher education institutions in non-EEC countries'. *Higher Education Management,* 202–212.

Handoll, J. (1989) 'Foreign Teachers and Public Education' in De Witte, B. (ed) *European Community Law of Education.* Baden-Baden: Nomos, 31–50.

Handoll, J. (1988) 'Article 48(4) EEC and Non-National Access to Public Employment'. *European Law Review* 223–241.

Hartley, T.C. (1989) 'La libre circulation des étudiants en droit communautaire'. *Cahiers de Droit Européen,* 325–344.

Hochbaum, I. (1989) 'The Federal Structure of Member States as a Limit to Common Educational Policy: the case of Germany' in De Witte, B. (ed) *European Community Law of Education.* Baden-Baden: Nomos, 145–158.

Hochbaum, I. (1987) 'Politik und Kompetenzen der Europäischen Gemeinschaften im Bildungswesen'. *Bayerische Verwaltungsblätter,* 481–490.

Janssen, B. (1988/89) 'Bildungs- und Kulturpolitik'. *Jahrbuch der Europäischen Integration,* 192–198.

Konow, G. (1989) 'Bildungs- und Kulturpoltik in der Europäischen Gemeinschaft'. *Recht der Jugend und des Bildungswesens,* 118–129.

Laslett, J.M. (1990) 'The mutual recognition of diplomas, certificates and other evidence of formal qualifications in the European Community'. *Legal Issues of European Integration* 1, 1–66.

Lenaerts, K. (1989) 'ERASMUS: Legal basis and implementation' in De Witte, B. (ed) *European Community Law of Education,* Baden-Baden: Nomos, 113–125.

Lenz, C.O. (1989) 'Die Rechtsprechung des Europäischen Gerichtshofs im Bereich des Bildungswesens'. *Europa-Archiv,* 125–134

Lonbay, J. (1989) 'Education and Law: the Community Context'. *European Law Review,* 363–387.

Mayntz, R. (1990) 'Föderalismus und die Gesellschaft der Gegenwart'. *Archiv des öffentlichen Rechts,* 232–245.

McMahon, B. (1990) Case note on case 371/87, *Common Market Law Review,* 129–139.

Putzhammer, H. (1989) 'EG-Ausländer im deutschen öffentlichen Dienst?'. *Recht der Jugend und des Bildungswesens,* 157–169.

Scholsem, J-C. (1989) 'A propos de la circulation des étudiants: vers un fédéralisme financier européen?'. *Cahiers de Droit Européen,* 306–324.

Schwarze, J. et al (eds) (1990) *The 1992 Challenge at National Level.* Baden-Baden: Nomos.

Teichler, U. (1990) 'Hochschulen in Europa. Studiengänge, Studiendauer, Übergang in den Beruf'. *Das Parlament, Beilage: Aus Politik und Zeitgeschichte* No 50, 25–39.

Traversa, E. (1989) 'L'interdiction de discrimination en raison de la nationalité en matière d'accès à l'enseignement'. *Revue trimestrielle de droit européen,* 45–69.

Verstegen, R. (1990) 'De Gemeenschappen bevoegd voor het onderwijs'. *Tijdschrift voor Bestuurswetenschappen en Publiekrecht,* 3–36.

Zilioli, Ch. (1989) 'The recognition of diplomas and its impact on educational policies' in De Witte, B. (ed) *European Community Law of Education.* Baden-Baden: Nomos, 51–70.

CHAPTER 14

Developments in European Community Politics of Higher Education
Observations from Outside[1]

Erich Leitner

Introduction

The debate on the development of the European Community has for some years been marked by enhanced attention to education, science and university policy. This is based not only on economic considerations such as the connection between education and the labour market, but also on perceptions of the importance to be attached to culture, of which science and universities are essential factors, for the process of European integration.

The following is written from an Austrian university perspective. Although Austria is not yet part of the EC, its system of higher education has greatly been influenced in its development, and not just because the country aims at joining the EC, by the state of debate in the EC countries and the recognisable trend to greater internationalisation of the tertiary education sector. While scientific research has an international orientation in its projects and methods, the institutions that carry it out, namely the Austrian universities and colleges, see themselves as, and are structured as, clear reflections of educational developments specific to a cultural identity and a nation-state. This is true particularly of the role of science in society, the relationship between State and university, the objectives and organisation of studies and the position of university teachers in administrative law.

While the higher education policy of the European Community does not aim at intervening in university structures of Member States, nor at making the European university scene uniform, there is, nevertheless, a trend, discernible at least in outline, towards bringing national university systems closer together through Community initiatives. Ladislav Cerych points to this fact in the following words: 'A certain number of binding decisions already exist, and others will undoubtedly become enforceable in the future' (Cerych, 322).

In a common economic area with freedom of movement and freedom of settlement for citizens, universities will have to face up to a more intensified climate of comparison and competition in their activities. As regards the effects of EC regulations, may one in

---

1   Translated by Iain Fraser, Florence.

this context accept the statement that 'such a framework – a single internal market – means by definition a situation of increased competition' (Cerych, 325)

Despite all national ties of the European university systems, the tendency towards internationalisation of universities is also clearly discernible, even in functional fields which are not, like research, international by definition; even if one still has to agree with the critical observation by Clark Kerr that despite all the calls for internationalisation, the situation of an 'intellectual Golden Age of a single civilisation-wide (...) learning community' (Kerr, 18) is still far from being reached.

The increasingly clear trend towards an international orientation in scientific, teaching and research activities in the context of the European integration process brings out the tension between an international orientation and national ties in the divergencies in university development among EC Member States themselves, but also between the EC and its neighbouring countries. In this paper, the challenge EC university policy presents for a small country outside the Community framework will be analysed from an Austrian perspective. It is divided into three parts. Firstly, the educational and higher education policy of the European Community is presented in outline; then follows a description of the Austrian university system; in conclusion comes an analysis of Austrian university policy from the viewpoint of incorporating this university system in the European integration process.

The Education and Higher Education Policy of the European Community

In the process of European integration, education policy long played rather a subordinate role, if one takes the relevant enactments as a basis. Education policy was in principle largely regarded as a matter for the Member States. One exception here from the outset was the sphere of vocational qualification. Article 57 of the EEC Treaty has as its object the mutual recognition of diplomas, certificates and other evidence of formal qualifications, in particular concerning the medical and allied, and pharmaceutical, professions in the Member States. Article 118, one of a number of social provisions, contains a reference to basic and advanced vocational training. Article 128 gives the Council the possibility of laying down general principles for implementing a common vocational training policy. Article 9 of the Euratom Treaty addresses the foundation of university training schools and that of an institution of university status. This mandate has in part been accomplished through the foundation of the European University Institute in Florence.

It is only since the early 1970s that one can see increased Community involvement with questions of education, undoubtedly encouraged by the great social policy importance that the debate on education questions has taken on in Member States since the late 1960's. One feature of this is that education ministers of Community countries have met regularly since 1971, though not in a formally regulated context since education is not a sphere of Community policy laid down in the Treaties. The results of their discussions, declarations of intent and resolutions have nonetheless brought some approach to concord in the development of national education systems, or as Bruno de Witte puts it: 'It would rather seem, from past experience, that intergovernmental resolutions are used for starting preparatory measures and pilot actions' (De Witte, 1992).

In 1973 an expert commission mandated by the Commission of the European Communities produced a programmatic paper 'Towards a Common Education Policy' stating, with reference to Articles 118 and 128 of the EEC-Treaty, that 'the Community's education policy is closely bound up with areas in which the Community acts because of the Treaty alone' (Commission, 11). Apart from this formal statement according to which a Community education policy is indeed legitimated by the sphere of application of the EEC Treaty, the document states that the vocational training that has to be considered in the context of the economic prerequisites of integration (including right of settlement, occupational mobility, mutual recognition of certificates etc) cannot be seen separately from the education system in general (Commission, 11).

While this claim in an EC mandate in the field of education is to be treated as merely a declaration of intent, the insight that questions of vocational training cannot be treated in isolation in the context of developing national education systems but are EC-related issues, would lead at least to a continuing informal dialogue between Member States and the EC on education questions. Though this does not make education policy a component part of EC policy, like economic policy or agricultural policy, it has been developed into a broad field of action whose essential importance for achieving the integration objectives of an economic community and a cultural community has been identified. The statement made in 1980 by Wolfgang Buss, that co-operation in the educational sphere was a 'necessity accepted' by all Member States, in line with the desires of all Member States (Buss, 23), has since been appropriately confirmed by decisions taken by the education ministers of the Community Member States, in which Bruno de Witte sees 'the existence of a genuine Community educational policy (...) clearly confirmed' (De Witte, 1992). The education ministers also stated in a 1989 resolution that co-operation in the educational sphere 'must be based on two fundamental principles – respect for linguistic and cultural diversity and affirmation of the subsidiarity of Community activities – and must respect the fundamental powers of the Member States in matters of general educational policy' (Council, 1989).

The EC's policy in the field of education is not approved equally by all Member States today. Resistance comes particularly from states with a decentralised or federalist education structure, like the Federal Republic of Germany, where the *Länder* see their cultural sovereignty, including all educational matters, as a 'core of their autonomy' (Cludius, 34ff; Hochbaum, 1989) and wish to allow the EC room for manoeuvre only in the area of vocational training, but also by Belgium and Spain (Garcia Garrido, 20–34). Denmark and Britain fear that a common education policy may interfere with sovereign rights, with effects on their special treaty links with third countries (Scandinavian countries or Commonwealth countries respectively) (De Witte, 1992).

It would be an impermissible curtailment of the notion of science and education policy, were it to be interpreted solely as one segment of general education policy. While the EC's education policy goals and intentions have a far from negligible influence on science and university policy too, the universities and colleges, as institutional supports for science and for its teaching, are structured, apart from by the influences operating on them from the general educational system and the employment system, above all by the processes of the creation of knowledge. The academic teaching and learning process is an inseparable component of the process of knowledge. Teaching and research, in their unity, constitute the centre of university action. The 'picture of the university (is) characterised by scholarship as the leading axiom of all universitarian activities' (Leitner, 1990).

In the process of diversification of the university sector which has become increasingly effective in recent years in national education systems, institutional forms of tertiary education have emerged which often do not primarily set knowledge at the core of their activities but have been principally created in order to provide training for specific highly qualified professions. The university sector today *de facto* includes on the one hand institutions that feel themselves committed to science, like the universities, and on the other institutions which primarily engage in high-level vocational training tasks, such as technical colleges of various types. The institutions of the university sector differ in work profile and ambition, and not in degree only, but substantively too. Common to all these institutions, and thus to the whole education sector, is, however, that at all levels and stages there is a link to the economy and the employment system, to the socio-political system (education of human beings and citizens) and to the cultural environment (regional, national, international).

The education policy of the European Communities, defined by the Community's general political goals, namely the creation of a single European economic area and a 'citizens' 'Europe', operates at two levels. The first level covers all common initiatives by Member States or the Community itself, among them the foundation in 1972 of the European University Institute in Florence, and special Community programmes to promote mobility in the university sphere (ERASMUS, COMETT, LINGUA, TEMPUS) and the co-operation programmes in the research and technology area. These EC-financed programmes, in which individuals and university institutions from Member Countries, but on a voluntary basis also from non-Community Countries, can take part, though they do not have any direct influence on the university policy of Member States, do have an undeniable indirect influence. Bruno de Witte also reaches this conclusion: 'It is therefore undeniable that those subsidy programmes potentially affect national policies of higher education' (De Witte, 1992).

The second level of initiatives in the university sphere is based on statutory provisions and their interpretation and application, which may be of considerable effect on national university systems. Particularly Article 48 of the EEC-Treaty, which lays down non-discrimination on grounds of nationality, creates regulations here, following the case law of the European Court of Justice (ECJ) with far-reaching consequences, that considerably affect Member States' sovereignty on university issues. For EC citizens, there today exists in all member countries a legal entitlement to:

- offer study courses and set up corresponding academic institutions on a private basis;
- work in teaching and research in institutions in the university sector, if appropriate language knowledge is shown;
- be treated equally as a student in all member countries, as if in their own country;
- have qualifications following at least three years of study recognised throughout the EC.

Restrictions on these rules exist in respect of work in public institutions and of recognition of qualifications for particular occupations, where additional qualifications may be required.

The process of European integration is intentionally inseparably bound up with the creation of a European labour market guaranteeing free exercise of their profession for all people in all Member States. This applies in particular to the academic professions, where mobility at the moment finds its limits, apart from the requirement for linguistic capacity, chiefly in specific national regulations (vocational entrance requirements) for individual groups of academic occupations, particularly in the public service. This partly divergent legal situation between the EC and the member countries leads to the position that demands are coming from various quarters to fill the gaps in statutory provisions in the area through lawmaking by the ECJ (Cludius, 1988).

To date, ECJ decisions have had effects particularly for access to studies in Community Member States, especially in *numerus clausus* subjects and for study fees. EC law, but also the ECJ's caselaw, has brought an element of specific provisions on the structure of university study in the Member States, the effects of which on national university structures, in particular the vocational training function of studies for a European labour market, is yet to be seen. Clerk Kerr's assumption 'that for the EEC the idea of a common market for learning may be welcomed in principle, but resisted in detail' (Kerr, 17), cannot be unreservedly followed in the light of the legal situation that is emerging.

The Austrian University System

The conception of Austrian universities is based on the philosophy of Wilhelm von Humboldt, adopted by the Austrians after the Prussian model in 1848. The notions of university autonomy, unity of research and teaching, education by scholarship, freedom of teaching and, with some restrictions, freedom of learning, are still the guiding principles at Austrian universities today.

Distinct departures from Humboldt's philosophy in Austria, contrasting with the Prussian model, include the constant stress on vocational education, and the relationship between State and university. The Austrian university centres round scholarship, and all other functions of the university are oriented around the scholarly process. 'To pursue scholarship simply means to search for truth, to question the existing knowledge and to gain new knowledge by means of rationality' (Leitner, 1990, 89). In this search for truth, research is a fundamentally open process.

This concept is in a way an obstacle to the students' direct training for professional purposes, which mainly takes place in professional life outside the control of the universities. Teaching and learning at Austrian universities are mainly oriented towards two interrelated tasks, namely on the one hand to educate through scholarship, while on the other preparing students in a general way for the professions (Leitner, 1979, 59–67).

The Austrian universities are centrally-governed federal institutions and have rather a small margin of autonomy in financial and personnel matters. All nominations and appointments of professors and the acceptance of teachers in higher education for tenure by the Secretary for science and research follow an appropriate procedure established by the government for all areas of the public service.

Austrian universities and colleges are predominantly financed from taxes, raising only a small budget themselves through contract research grants, gifts and tuition fees from foreign students. Nationals do not pay tuition in Austria. The foregoing applies to institutions in the Republic of Austria authorised to award academic degrees, namely the 12 universities and 6 art academies.

Aside from the universities and art colleges, there are various forms of public tertiary education institutions, called academies, for the training of State-school teachers (primary and secondary level), social workers, military officers and medical professionals other than physicians. These institutions are not connected with the universities or art academies either organisationally or administratively. A wide range of possibilities of further professional training is available through professional associations or a number of private organisations.

The Austrian system of tertiary educational institutions, a term used here as a collective expression for all institutions offering a formal course after school-leaving qualifications (*Matura*) that can be completed no earlier than the age of 18, covers, under Government administration, institutions in the academic sector (universities and art colleges) and institutions of other public administrative bodies, having the status of non-academic higher educational institutions. The system of tertiary educational institutions can be portrayed graphically as follows:

Figure 1: The Austrian higher education system

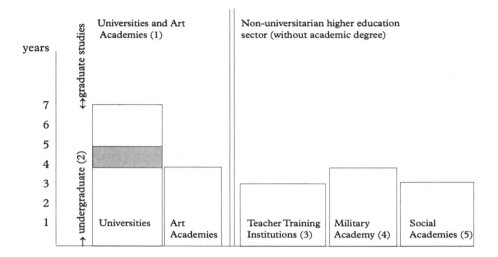

1) Administered by the Federal Ministry of Science and Research
2) In Human Medicine the undergraduate programme leads directly to the doctorate
3) Administered by the Federal Ministry of Instruction and Culture
4) Administered by the Federal Ministry of Defence
5) Administered by the Federal Ministry of Social Affairs

The Austrian higher education system so far lacks the type of tertiary institutions which in other countries offer three or four-year preparatory courses for practical requirements of technical and commercial professions (Gellert, 1991a). This gap is partly filled by those completing the vocational colleges, who take their leaving qualification at the age of 19 and have very good chances on the labour market, in other German-speaking countries too (Germany, Switzerland) – especially those from the Higher Technical Colleges (HTLA).

The basic question here, though, is whether the training of those completing a *höhere Sekundarschule* (Higher Secondary School) can be thorough enough to meet the requirements of a labour market that is increasingly demanding higher-level qualifications. Meeting this perceptible requirement from the economy would be the task of the new type of *Fachhochschule* to be set up, the creation of which would at the same time free the university sector of the burden of students who are aiming primarily not at an academic but at a vocational higher education (Gellert, 1991b).

Alongside this question currently under debate, of setting up *Fachhochschulen*, there have been efforts for years to diversify courses offered by universities in line with labour market requirements. While short courses – as a rule four semesters – are still a marginal phenomenon in the Austrian range of courses, in recent years the mostly two-to-four-semester diploma courses, in part in co-operation with bodies outside the universities, have been meeting with lively demand, and are likely to increase still further in coming years (Bundesministerium, 1990, 142).

According to the definitions in the General University Study Act (1966) studies at Austrian universities have the following goals:

- promotion and development of scholarship, and the education of junior scholars;
- education through scholarship;
- advanced preparation for occupations;
- further education of graduates (Bundesministerium, 1988, 18ff).

Anyone who is an Austrian citizen and who has completed an upper-secondary schooling can take any major of his/her choice at any university without restrictions. Only art academies limit the number of students for admission and require corresponding admission tests. Austrian universities offer 110 different courses of study plus some additional combination and specialisation possibilities.

The courses at Austrian universities are divided into Master's courses and Doctoral studies. Master's courses are composed of two stages, each of which is completed after a diploma examination has been passed in one or several disciplines. Before the final diploma examination can be attempted, a thesis has to be submitted. Students with a Master's degree are admitted to doctoral studies, which require the submission of a thesis and the passing of an oral examination (Bundesministerium, 1988, 18ff).

Students at Austrian universities may organise their studies themselves in a system of considerable freedom and possibility of choice. This requires great discipline and independence of each student in his behaviour in connection with his studies and his own organisation of study, if he does not want to suffer delays in studies. The curriculum and the regulations for exams include usable information for the continuation of studies; however, there is no set timetable for when individual sections have to be finished or when the exit exams to these sections have to be taken. A tremendously high number of drop-outs – about half of all college students do not graduate – is a consequence of this system.

The growth of student numbers at Austrian universities and colleges has been extremely expansive over the last 30 years. The number of students grew from 25,000 in 1957–58 to 173,000 in 1987–88, amounting in the winter semester 1989–90 to 188,360, 170,913 of them Austrians. 49 per cent of students today are females. The proportion of those embarking on studies among the 18–26-year-old resident population is 17.2 per cent (Bundesministerium, 1969–90). The age structure of students has clearly shifted over the last decade in the direction of increased involvement with education by higher age groups. While in 1980–81, 74 per cent of Austrian students were in the age group 18–25, in the academic year 1989–90 this proportion was only 64.5 per cent (Bundesministerium, 1990, 171ff). Accordingly, over one third of students at Austrian universities today are older than 25.

The expansion of universities and colleges, particularly in premises, staff and subjects covered, has not kept pace with this development. The exorbitant growth in student numbers, in a university system conceptually oriented towards manageable numbers and at the same time allowing students great freedom in organising their courses, creates a situation of great anonymity and inadequate guidance of students.

Despite these problems, there is a considerable over-supply of academically qualified teachers for secondary schools, physicians, lawyers and humanities and social science graduates. At the same time, a clear lack of graduates of technical courses is perceptible. Information to new students on job prospects has not yet brought about the expected shift of student flows to courses with better chances on the labour market. The outcome is a considerable number of unemployed university graduates unable to find a post in line with their education.

Austrian science and university policy is endeavouring to bring about a qualitative improvement of research and teaching at universities, despite the quantitative problems. Ways of reaching this are seen in the reduction of high student numbers by shortening excessively long study times and in the setting-up of formal qualifications at lower levels. In research, all efforts are directed at guaranteeing Austrian science its place in the international scientific world, and in the technological sphere, where the possibilities of a small country in basic research and in development work are limited, at keeping a link with international developments through appropriate funding and staffing concentrations, promotion measures and involvement in major international projects.

Austrian Education Policy Faced with the Challenges of the European Community

For a country like Austria, which can be equated in cultural, economic and social levels with the standard of the Community countries the international interwovenness of life makes any debate on reform in education into a dialogue between national requirements and international necessities. For Austrian university policy this means that the functions and actions of universities and colleges must be in line with internationally recognisable standards. The process of European unification, which is facing a qualitative leap with the year 1992, is a decisive challenge for public life in Austria too. The highly developed Austrian industry and service society can develop its potential further in future only if the country is unrestrictedly linked in with the exchange of persons, goods, services and capital in the European area (De Witte, 1992). To ensure this, Austria submitted an application to the European Community in 1989 for accession as a full member (Wimmer/Mederer, 26).

Austrian university policy relates to the European debate in three basic dimensions. Firstly, it is concerned with the bilateral agreements between Austria and the EC States, along with existing regional agreements; secondly, it deals with the agreements between Austria and the EC in the science and university sector; and thirdly, it comprises pressing problems arising for Austrian universities and colleges in the course of an integration in the EC.

Irrespective of the EC membership application, Austrian science and university policy has for long been concerned to collaborate on supranational initiatives, on a basis of bilateral and multilateral agreements (Bundesministerium, 1987, 401ff; Drischel, 1987). At present all EC Countries are partners to agreements with Austria on the equivalence of study courses at universities and the equivalence of academic degrees and college diplomas. Only Greece has not ratified the two agreements, though it has signed them; Luxembourg has signed but not ratified the agreement on equivalence of academic degrees and college diplomas. At the same time there are special bilateral agreements on equivalences in the university sphere with the Federal Republic of Germany, Luxembourg, the Netherlands, Portugal, Italy and Spain. There is an additional agreement with Luxembourg on postdoctoral training for physicians (Drischel/Kasparovsky, 22ff).

The Republic of Austria, and in some cases its individual federal provinces, are additionally in special treaty relationships with countries and regions of Central, Eastern and South-eastern Europe, which also cover co-operation on science and university issues. These supraregional treaty arrangements are:

- the Adriatic-Alpine-Alliance, involving five Austrian federal provinces, five Hungarian Counties, four Italian Regions, one Swiss Canton, two Yugoslav Republics and the Free State of Bavaria;

- the Pentagonale, a partnership among the governments of Austria, Czechoslovakia, Hungary, Yugoslavia and Italy, concentrating on transport and environment policy; Poland's inclusion is under discussion.

Additionally, rectors of universities in the Danubian area have been engaging in an intensive form of cooperation since 1983. This working community now includes 47 universities and colleges from 9 countries. All three Treaty partnerships already reach into the EC: the Adriatic-Alpine-Alliance includes the Free State of Bavaria and four regions of Upper Italy, Italy is a member of the Pentagonale, and universities in Germany and Italy are involved in the Danubian Rectors' Conference. Co-operation in all three Treaty Partnerships covers joint research projects, the exchange of professors, younger academics and students and the beginnings of common supraregionally-organised courses. Austrian accession to the EC would be a step capable of improving the Community's position in these multilateral partnerships and opening up increased access for the EC to non-EC Countries of Central, Eastern and South-eastern Europe, especially since Austria today plays a central part in all these treaty partnerships. The positive effect for the EC would be comparable with the improved access to the Commonwealth States that resulted from Britain's accession and the opening up to the Latin-American area with the accession of Spain and Portugal.

Austria's dependence on international and supranational cooperation in science and university policy, exists not in areas of basic research. Also of fundamental importance is access to scientific development work in the technological/industrial sector. The EC points of concentration in the educational sphere in the late 1980s particularly the pushing forward of special programmes in the university and science area, created a situation for Austria that could no longer be compensated for by existing bilateral agreements. The recognisable tendency to bar the programmes to third countries would have meant for Austrian science that it would have been largely excluded from one of the most important and dynamic scientific scenes in the world. The Austrian Republic's science and university policy in preceding years was accordingly directed at gaining access to EC research and university programmes even now, irrespective of the accession to the EC to be expected in the second half of the 1990s.

The EC regulates research policy through so-called framework programmes, in which objectives, content and funding of research priorities are laid down, and then fleshed out in specific programmes (Wimmer/Mederer, 87ff). In EC research programmes, a third country can be involved in programme affairs and make a financial contribution to the programme budget, in accordance with the GNP. However, in case of project participation, the project applicant from a non-EC country needs at least two EC partners and receives no EC support funds.

The most important step in Austrian involvement in the EC research market was the 'Framework Agreement on scientific and technical co-operation between the Republic of Austria and the European Communities', which came into force in 1987. This Agreement regulates *inter alia* the objects and modalities of information exchange, joint projects, participation in joint programmes and the exchange of academics.

By an EC Council Decision of 22 May 1989, all EFTA Countries, and therefore also Austria, obtained the possibility of involvement in the second phase of COMETT

(Community Action Programme in Education and Training for Technology). For the Austrian universities this means better conditions for setting up educational partnerships between science and business, including the EC area, and therefore improved access to international possibilities of vocational and further education for college graduates and for vocational and further education programmes in the academic and business sphere. The TEMPUS Programme, which applies to Poland, Hungary and Czechoslovakia, creates the possibility for Austria, where joint academic projects with those countries exist, of benefiting at least indirectly from the EC's mobility initiatives. Austrians, like residents of other EFTA countries, are able to take part in the ERASMUS Programme as from the winter semester 1991–92.

Co-operation in the research and technology sphere based on the provisions of the 1987 Framework Agreement has so far led to involvement of Austrian scholars in 20 projects coming under the EC Research Programmes EURAM (modern materials), RACE (communication technology), ESPRIT II (information technology), BRITE (industrial manufacturing technology) and SCIENCE (co-operation and exchange of European researchers). These types of co-operation guarantee Community access to the Austrian research potential and offer Austrian academics, established and up-and-coming, the possibility of improving their qualifications through involvement in major research projects.

While participation in the European research and technology community that is coming into being is essential for Austrian science and business, it can take place only where corresponding Austrian research initiatives and researcher potential already exist. The limited financial position of a small country like Austria – accompanied by some reluctance on the part of mainly small and medium-sized Austrian business towards international research projects – will always set limits to such involvement and tend to compel selection among priorities. Yet there is no alternative to participation in the EC research programmes for Austria, since as has been correctly pointed out, isolation 'from European research would involve severely weakening its international competitivity' (Wimmer-Mederer, 99). While in research and technology policy there are scarcely any severe problems of fit between Austrian university policy and the Community's, in questions of admission of foreigners to studies and recognition of certificates and academic degrees gained abroad there are national procedural rules which, while they seek to take account of supranational requirements through simultaneously existing bilateral and multilateral agreements, nevertheless meet the limits of their possibilities where the Austrian course and institutional structure has no correspondence in the international context. This range of issues, with its manifold interconnections, will be considered more closely here.

Highly sensitive areas in connection with efforts towards Austria's accession to the Community are those in which there will be replacement or superimposition of Austrian law by Community acts and measures. This applies, on the one hand, to access by foreigners to courses, recognition of certificates gained abroad and recognition of academic degrees, and, on the other, to access to academic professions including the recruitment of scholars and professors for the universities themselves. All these areas are at present subject to Austrian sovereignty in legal and administrative respects, on both governmental and university level.[2] The effects of Community accession are however likely to be considerably more marked for universities and the academic

---

2   The effects of Community university policies on another non-EEC country, Switzerland, have
     been studied by Jean Guinand (1990)

professions than in many other European countries, because Austria belongs to the German language area, so that there is no language barrier with Germany in particular. Austrian considerations of the need for extra university professors, for instance, already take the potential of those qualified in the whole German language area into account in forecasting calculations (Hochschulbericht 1990, 95). The proportion of appointments from abroad, particularly from German-speaking countries, is already considerable at Austrian universities, and between 1987 and 1989 reached a proportion of over 30 per cent of all appointments (Hochschulbericht 1990, 93). The share of students from Germany in the academic year 1989–90 was 25 per cent of foreign attendance at Austrian universities (Bundesministerium, 1990, 182).

The admission of foreign students in Austria at present comes under universities' autonomous sphere of action: applicants must provide evidence of adequate knowledge of German and have school-leaving qualifications equivalent to an Austrian *Reifezeugnis*, entitling them to attend university in their country of origin. The EC countries and Austria are Treaty Partners in the 'European Convention on the Equivalence of Diplomas leading to Admission to Universities' (Drischel/Kasparovsky, 10ff). Courses and examinations at a foreign university may be recognised or credited by Austrian universities insofar as their content and extent are equivalent to Austrian courses, or the examination regulations in force in Austria. The recognition or crediting is on individual application by the student concerned, and is examined and assessed by the course commissions of the individual departments.

The Austrian system of governmentally regulated course regulations, while it leaves individual universities little leeway to develop special course profiles, facilitates harmonisation with international requirements in the European dialogue. How far the system of admission to courses and the recognition of sub-courses and examinations on the individual application procedure can persist in a mobile European student population cannot be seen until Austria's accession to the EEC. Free access to study for Austrians is already facing Austrian universities with a number of problems that are barely being coped with. EC accession will presumably worsen this.

But despite these reservations, there are also positive expectations for Austrian students from the country's accession to the EC. Among these is in particular the possibility of participating in the EC's mobility programmes. Some Austrian universities and departments are already promoting the internationalisation of their course offerings by setting up common course arrangements between Austrian and foreign universities, particularly in Central, Eastern and South-eastern Europe.

Academic degrees taken at foreign universities are similarly recognised in Austria on an individual application procedure. They are subject to a procedure of 'nationalisation' by the university governing bodies if the study completed abroad is to be regarded as equivalent in terms of requirements, extent and content with an Austrian course. For a degree taken at a foreign university, the applicant obtains a corresponding Austrian academic degree if the application is positively received. Certificates which in volume or content have nothing corresponding to them in the Austrian range of courses cannot be recognised; among these are in particular degrees taken at foreign technical colleges. Here, with increasing closeness to the EC, consideration should be given to developing the Austrian university system in accordance with internationally prevalent structures.

Austria is concerned to bring forward the issue of equivalence of certificates, academic examinations and diplomas in a European context. The Austrian ideas here are at present concentrated on working out a harmonised recommendation on the principles for establishing equivalence, on the improvement of co-operation in existing information networks in Europe and on the creation of a comprehensive description of the universities and colleges recognised by governmental authorities on their territories, i.e. the publication of a handbook on universities in Europe (Drischel, 1989, 7).

In parallel with this Europe-wide debate on equivalences, talks are in hand between Austria and the EC on the issue of freedom of movement, freedom of establishment and recognition of university diplomas (Drischel, 1989, 7). The key point here is recognition of university degrees for exercise of a profession, given at the time of entry to the profession. The main issue in the debate is the professions where, between completion of university study and commencement of autonomous professional activity, there is a period of dependent work in preparation for the profession. Austria, which has a dual system of prior training for academic professions, namely theoretical courses at university and then practical formalised completion of training on the job before autonomous professional work as, for instance, physician, lawyer, notary, secondary-school teacher etc can be begun, sees the general EC directives on recognition of university qualifications as a framework that makes special additional provisions necessary at national level.

The debate among Austrian university teachers themselves is at present determined by the ambivalent expectations bound up with EC accession. On the one hand, EC accession would bring an unrestricted possibility of participating in all EC programmes; on the other, an extremely strong influx of university teachers and scholars, particularly from German-speaking regions of the EC, into Austrian universities and colleges is feared. Since however Austrian university teachers, once they have been in office for a while, have the status of civil servants and therefore must have Austrian citizenship, take an oath to the Constitution and be prepared to defend the interests of the Republic of Austria, there are legal possibilities here for Austria to control the influx of foreigners. The present legal position also seems to guarantee the State's sovereignty in this area (Wimmer/Mederer, 165ff). It is only with appointments to full professorships that conferment of Austrian citizenship is *ex lege* bound up with the appointment; but here the Austrian academic administration is at liberty to make an appointment or refrain from it. To guarantee mobility of university teachers in a European framework, it will be indispensable at national level to rethink existing service, pay and social security regulations.[3]

The integration debate, particularly in this area, comes up against intrinsic contradictions in the European university systems, which while largely supra-regionally oriented in their functions or on the road to increasing internationalisation, are nonetheless structurally, particularly in the administration and personnel field, so much subject to national regulations that what we have is an incompatibility of differing structural models. In this question of approximating the legal status of university professors in different countries, the possible formulation of a European standard will thus remain reduced to a smallest common denominator, especially since the weight of historical and cultural aspects in these issues is considerable in all European countries.

Concluding Remarks

The process of European integration has today, despite the continuing dominance of economic shaping forces, reached into all areas of life. Perceptions of the power of

---

3   The EC has decisively pointed to the importance of working times, particularly in connection with the calculation of seniority and the associated entitlements to pension for university teachers, as a problem area in its programmes in the area of education.

culture to promote integration add a non-material, intellectual component to the material aspects of unification; its power to create meaning and its emotional content embody particular integrative force.

The European Community's initiatives in the sphere of education are, however, only partly committed to the idea of Europe as a cultural community. In broad areas they derive from economic, technological, labour-market and social-policy considerations. This is particularly clear in science and research policy, where programmes overwhelmingly show a concentration on technology and industry. Bringing together the scientific potential of the individual countries in the scientific and technological sector within the framework of the EC, opens up possibilities on every national scientific scene that would scarcely be open to any of them alone because of the limitation of resources available on any national territory. This is particularly true of Europe's smaller countries.

However, science and research policy are inseparably bound up with the centres of academic life, namely the universities and colleges, so that science and research policy initiatives at the same time contain far-reaching university policy implications. This fact, bound up with the emergence of an area where national boundaries are being squeezed aside, in which freedom of movement, residence and establishment are being accomplished, is compelling universities and colleges to rethink their position and their task in a united Europe. To this process of internationalisation there corresponds a far-reaching national rootedness and structural fixation of university systems. While university research has always moved within the international discourse of the sciences, in the field of academic studies (admission to courses, curricula, academic degrees) and in the administrative and personnel sphere, there are very divergent national regulations. In the process of European integration, it will be essential at least to agree in a European context on the standards for university work as expressed in the qualification profiles of university and college graduates, and to favour the mobility of university teachers by appropriate statutory arrangements.

In this connection the question arises for the academic development debate whether, say in a process of reform, a structural harmonisation of national university systems in Europe within something like a European framework plan will come about. Irrespective of any possible framework arrangement, quality differences among individual universities, but also among academic scenes in Europe, will no doubt always continue to exist.

For a country like Austria, which, while it has applied for full membership of the European Community, is *de facto* still outside it, this question arises in a comparable fashion. While typologically the Austrian university system is marked by the German university idea of neo-humanism, in historical development it has acquired structural peculiarities, so that in its government-centralised guidance structure, for instance, it is more comparable with, say, the French university system. An unusual feature in the international context is above all the high degree of formal legal regulation of studies. While the government control system favours the possibility of uniform arrangements throughout the country and helps reform moves from above, in connection with the challenges of the European integration process too, there should at the same time be an awareness that the universities and colleges are in structure and form an expression of a specifically national heritage that can be grasped at best only indirectly through the codifying effect of regulation. This heritage, a piece of national identity, moulds the values and world views of scientists working at universities and colleges, university teachers and students in a specific fashion – it has a culture-creating character for the whole of public life. Accordingly, any question of re-shaping the Austrian university system from the viewpoint of European integration must be pursued not only along a line of technocratically functional planning, but always also from the whole depth of the cultural function of science and universities. This may be true of all other national university systems in Europe too, since the concept of a cultural community is aimed at maintaining the multiplicity of differing cultures in a greater unity, and cannot be based on some fiction of uniformisation of the different cultures.

References

Bundesministerium für Wissenschaft und Forschung (1969–90) *Hochschulbericht* 1969, 1972 (Vol 1, 2) 1975, 1978, 1981, 1984, 1987 (Vol 1, 2) 1990 (Vol 1, 2). Vienna.

Bundesministerium für Wissenschaft und Forschung (1988) Higher Education in Austria. Vienna.

Buss, W. (1980) 'Sieben Jahre bildungspolitische Zusammenarbeit in der Europäischen Gemeinschaft. Erfolge und Mißerfolge' in Schmitz-Wenzel, H. (ed) *Bildungspolitik in der Europäischen Gemeinschaft.* Baden-Baden, 17–24.

Cerych, L. (1989) 'Higher Education and Europe after 1992: the Framework' in *European Journal of Education* Vol 24, 321–332.

Cludius, S. (1988) 'Bildungs- und Kulturpolitik in der Europäischen Gemeinschaft', Bericht über die Tagung des AEI (Arbeitskreises Europäische Integration) Vols 8–10. September 1987 in Augsburg' in *Europäische Integration* 14/15.

Commission of the European Communities (19173) 'For a Community Policy on Education' in *EC Bulletin Supplement* 10/73, 11. Luxembourg.

Council of Ministers (1989) 'Conclusions of the Council and the Ministers for Education Meeting within the Council of 6 October 1989, on Cooperation and Community Policy in the Field of Education in the Run-up to 1993' in *Official Journal of the European Communities* C 277/5, 1989.

De Witte, B. (ed) (1989) *European Community Law of Education.* Baden-Baden: Nomos.

De Witte, B. (1992) 'Higher Education and the Constitution of the European Community' in this volume.

Drischel, O. (1987) *Die internationalen Abkommen über Gleichwertigkeiten.* Vienna: Bundesministerium für Wissenschaft und Forschung.

Drischel, O. (1989) *Grundsätzliche Erwägungen zur Feststellung von Gleichwertigkeiten aus österreichischer Erfahrung.* Vienna: Internationale Konferenz: Gleichwertigkeiten in Europea, unpublished manuscript.

Drischel, O. and H. Kasparovsky (1989) *Österreich. Zulassung und Gleichwertigkeiten im Universitätsbereich.* Vienna: Bundesministerium für Wissenschaft und Forschung.

Garcia Garrido, J.L. (1989) 'Regionalism and Cultural Pluralism in Spanish Education' in *Western European Education* Vol 20 No 4 20–34.

Gellert, C. (1991a) *Alternatives to Universities.* Paris: OECD.

Gellert, C. (1991b) 'Entwicklung der Hochschulsysteme als funktionale Differenzierung' in *Plenum,* (Austrian Rectors' Conference) 45–50.

Guinand, J. (1990) 'The Implications of European Integration for Higher Education Institutions in non-EEC countries' in *Higher Education Management* 2, 202–212.

Hochbaum, I. (1989) 'The Federal Structure of Member States as a Limit to Common Educational Policy: The Case of Germany' in de Witte, B. (ed) *European Community Law of Education.* Baden-Baden: Nomos, 145–158.

Kerr, C. (1990) 'The Internationalisation of Learning and the Nationalisation of the Purposes of Higher Education: Two "Laws of Motion" in Conflict?' in *European Journal of Education* 25, 5–22.

Knapp, K. (1990) 'Common Market-Common Culture?' in *European Journal of Education* Vol 25, 55–60.

Leitner, E. (1979) 'Current Trends in Austrian Higher Education: the Call for a New Reform' in *European Journal of Education,* Vol 14, 59–67.

Leitner, E. (1990) 'Scholarship and Professional Education' in Gellert, C., E. Leitner and J. Schramm (eds) *Research and Teaching at Universities. International and Comparative Perspectives* Frankfurt/M: Lang, 66–91.

Teichler, U. (1990) *Europäische Hochschulsysteme. Die Beharrlichkeit vielfältiger Modelle.* Frankfurt/M: New York, Campus.

Wimmer, N. and W. Mederer (1990) *EG-Recht in Österreich. Konsequenzen eines EG-Beitritts in zentralen verfassungs-, wirtschafts- und verwaltungsrechtlichen Bereichen.* Vienna: Manz.

CHAPTER 15

Against the Stream
Australia's Policy of Tertiary Integration

Ingrid Moses

Higher Education in the Commonwealth of Australia – a Unified National System

In 1982 Martin Trow wrote: 'What we see is the centralisation, rationalisation, and bureaucratisation of Australian higher education' (Trow, 1984, 147). It did not seem to represent Australian reality then. Now, eight years later, with a Labour government even more keen on efficiency and amalgamations than the Liberal government was in 1981, no faculty member would deny the reality of the statement.

In 1990, all Australian public universities (there are only two private universities at present, though more are planned) are members of a Unified National System (UNS), created by the Minister for Employment, Education and Training, the Hon. J.S. Dawkins. The UNS replaces a binary system of higher education which has existed for the past quarter of a century – colleges and universities, and the tripartite tertiary system which included also technical and further education (TAFE).

In the UNS colleges have largely been abandoned as separate institutions; the UNS is a system of comprehensive universities formed through amalgamations of different institutions. It is a system where competition is promoted by the Ministry but within a framework devised by the Minister. Indeed, the words which Teichler used to describe the tasks for the *Gesamthochschule* (comprehensive university) in Germany could have been used by the Minister: 'to create a link between the research orientation of the universities and the vocational orientation of the non-university institutions of higher learning; to increase considerably the possibilities for transfer between courses of study; (…) to utilise higher education resources better (…)' (Teichler, 1988, 39).

However, while the German comprehensive universities were to 'bring the non-university sector into closer contact with research' (Teichler, 1988, 39), this was not part of the Australian agenda.

Universities

Universities in Australia see themselves as places of higher learning; they accept as their role the preservation, transmission and creation of knowledge. But throughout Australia's higher education history there is a recurrent theme of vocationalism or utilitarian values overshadowing educative ones. There was for a long time no tradition of local graduate studies; the first Ph.D. was awarded only in 1948. Until then, aspiring scientists tended to go overseas for graduate qualifications.

After World War II, all universities were funded for teaching and research; and faculty staff were mostly teaching-and-research appointments. They followed the British career structure of lecturer, senior lecturer, reader and professor, the latter being until the early 1970's also head of department. All faculty grades were expected to teach and conduct research with little role differentiation between the different faculty grades.

The expansion of the higher education system in the 1950's, 1960's and early 1970's necessitated employing as lecturers some people without the scholarly qualifications previously thought necessary. But these appointments, too, were expected to engage in research, and if appropriate acquire formal research qualifications. Graduate programmes had been developed and all universities provided research training in all their faculties and awarded Ph.D.s. Universities retained the monopoly on Ph.D.s and higher doctorates and research, particularly basic research.

The university system was not stratified in function, although the regional universities tended to be more closely attuned to their local communities and region, and the medical schools tended to stay in the old universities. In each state the oldest universities claimed higher status. They attracted better qualified students, and indeed they only admitted well-qualified students, while the newest universities generally attracted the least qualified students. The old universities attracted highflyers in research; and these staff were able to acquire proportionally more external research funds. However, several of the universities founded in the 1950's, e.g. Monash and the University of New South Wales, successfully competed with these older universities for reputation based primarily on excellence in research. Staff needed and had large-scale autonomy to set their teaching and research priorities, and universities as organisations experienced little interference from external sources despite a centralist government. Both staff and student selection occurred within the university system. External representation was mainly on Council or Senate, and sometimes on faculty boards.

Colleges

The higher education system, in general, was stratified, with a sharp division between universities and colleges. Single purpose colleges have existed in Australia since the late 19th century. They provided vocational training in agriculture, mining, and later teaching. Following the recommendations of the Martin Report (Martin Report, 1964–1967), the concept of 'college of advanced education' was introduced into Australian education in the mid-1960's to cope with increased student enrollment. New colleges or institutes of technology were founded, old ones expanded, to provide advanced technical and vocational training for an ever increasing number of students. The expansion of this sector occurred later than the expansion of the university system, but was no less spectacular.

Table 1: *The expansion of higher education enrolments*

Year	Universities	Advanced Educat.	Total
1971	122,668	70,550	193,218
1975	147,754	125,383	273,137
1981	165,937	171,133	337,070
1985	171,990	195,231	370,048
1989	441,076		

Source: CTEC, 1986, 282; For 1989, DEET, 1990a, 19.

Universities, institutes and colleges of advanced education were institutions of higher education; they were separated until recently by the so-called binary line. Originally funded by State governments, the Commonwealth assumed nearly total financial responsibility for this sector in the mid-1970's. In the 1960's and 1970's many colleges were founded both in metropolitan and rural areas. In the early 1980's the then federal government forced many of the separate colleges in metropolitan areas to combine to multi-campus colleges of advanced education, and several teachers training colleges to amalgamate with adjacent universities.

By the end of the 1980's, much differentiation had taken place in the college sector. The colleges were meant to be 'equal but different'. But colleges were never equal to universities. Colleges and universities differed in their mission and functions, in the composition of their student and staff body, in the amount of autonomy they had in course offerings and course content; colleges were organised more on a hierarchical model, universities on a collegial one. The binary system was designed to provide a vertical line between the universities and the colleges, to have parallel systems. In effect, however, there was a horizontal one as well, though it was a permeable one.

Very soon 'academic drift' made colleges and universities less disparate. Although college degree courses were no shorter than their equivalent university ones, they were required (through external accreditation by state higher-education boards) to be both needed and vocationally relevant. Due to the stagnation in the university system, college staff came increasingly from universities, had Ph.D. qualification and both research experience and expectations. Colleges, with the consent of the governments, both federal and state, started offering postgraduate degrees – first postgraduate diplomas, then Master degrees by coursework, then research masters and in the end even Ph.D.s in conjunction with universities. Thus in function, course offerings and staff, to some extent in the composition of the student body, too, some of the colleges became quite similar to some of the universities.

But the major institutes of technology found that they were disadvantaged in attracting good students and full fee-paying overseas students by not being called universities and by not being funded to do research. The first to challenge their second rank status was the Western Australian Institute of Technology (WAIT) which became by change of state statutes the Curtin University of Technology in 1987.

The academic drift by colleges was paralleled by a tendency in universities to orient some of their courses to labour market needs and to compete with the colleges in the provision of a very diverse range of semi-professional courses and industry consultancies.

Technical and Further Education

TAFE was the third sector of Australian tertiary education. State funded, it is the major provider of technical and further education. Its colleges are more widely distributed to remote areas of Australia than were colleges of advanced education or universities. Its trade courses and sub-degree para-professional and professional as well as preparatory courses, in addition to non-award adult education courses for the general public, reach a large number of Australians. In 1990 close to a million students (of a population of nearly 17 million) are enroled in TAFE vocational courses.

The three sectors of tertiary education were until 1987 overseen by three Councils which advised the Commonwealth Tertiary Education Commission (CTEC). The federal government, in turn, was advised by CTEC. The three sectors constituted a highly stratified system; only the universities were funded for research. Each sector had distinct educational functions but overlapped eventually in their awards: the universities awarded undergraduate and graduate degrees, including doctorates; the advanced education sector awarded sub-degree diplomas and certificates, undergraduate degrees and increasingly graduate degrees bar Ph.D.s; and the TAFE sector offered certificate, associate diploma, and diploma courses in addition to its non-award courses. With the abolition of the binary line from 1988 on, only two sectors remain, Universities and TAFE – a new binary line.

TAFE remains the only post-secondary education sector which is still largely funded by the States. However, the federal government provides substantial funds to increase access, to enhance infrastructure, to foster liaison with industry, to provide staff development and assist with curriculum development.

Table 2: Participation in education (a)

Age	School (b)		TAFE (c)		Higher Education (c)	
	1982 %	1989 %	1982 %	1989 %	1982 %	1989 %
15	87	92	8(d)	8		
16	58	72	25(d)	15		
17	30	48	25	22	3	4
18	5	9	27	27	13	18
19	2	2	22	24	13	19
15–19	36	44	21	19	6	8
20	1	16	19	13	17	
21	1	12	14	11	13	
22	10	12	8	9		
23	9	11	6	7		
24	8	10	5	5		
20–24	11	13	9	10		

(a) Proportion of relevant age cohort as at 30 June

(b) Refers to full-time students only

(c) Includes full-time and part-time students. Latest available TAFE statistics are for 1987. Some of the increased participation in higher education is due to the transfer of basic nurse education from hospitals to higher education institutions.

(d) Estimate

Source: DEET, 1990.

The Unified National System

Australian tertiary education had been tri-partite for 15 years as a result of policy decisions and government regulations. But there was dissatisfaction with the system. In 1986 CTEC released a report, *Review of Efficiency and Effectiveness in Higher Education.* The report acknowledged that higher education needed more funds injected, that there was little scope for further saving, that the utilisation rate for teaching facilities were at acceptable level, that the state institutions' physical facilities gave cause for concern, that infrastructure needed to be provided and more funds be granted for equipment. But there was criticism of management of institutions and of teaching and research resources, and indeed of personnel. Recommendations, if adopted, would have led to the system becoming more adaptable, more accountable and more accessible in an evolutionary process.

But the next year brought a restructuring of Commonwealth departments, and a new Department of Employment, Education and Training was created under a new Minister, John Dawkins. In August 1987 he released a Green Paper, *Higher Education*

(Dawkins, 1987), followed a year later by the White Paper (Dawkins, 1988) which was not substantially different despite wide consultation and much opposition.

The Government, with an espoused commitment to 'excellence in higher education', forecast measures 'to encourage institutions to be efficient, flexible and responsive to changing national needs'. In particular there would be:

- measures to make more productive use of institutional resources and facilities, including institutional consolidations and more systematic credit transfer arrangements;
- greater targeting of resources at the institutional level and improved institutional management;
- increased flexibility and incentives for performance for both institutions and individual staff;
- encouragement of an environment of productive competition between higher education institutions (Dawkins, 1988, 27).

Main features of the White Paper were the proposal of a Unified National System (UNS) which would consist of fewer but larger institutions than hitherto. The Minister believed that students would benefit from studying in larger institutions where resources were concentrated to promote 'the highest quality of teaching and research'. At the same time institutions would have:

- more flexibility to determine the particular courses to be offered and areas of research to be undertaken;
- greater control over their own resources, enhanced revenue-raising options and decreased intervention by governments in internal funding and management decisions;
- guaranteed triennial funding bases on agreed priorities for institutional activity and performance against those priorities, rather than on an arbitrary system of institutional classification (Dawkins, 1988, 27).

In short and in practice this meant: the binary line was to be abolished. The 19 (pre-1987) universities and the 44 colleges were to amalgamate and join a Unified National System, under the direct control of the Minister. Institutions would negotiate their educational profiles with the Minister and his department; for this they would state their mission and responsibilities, and proposed activities to meet particular goals. They needed to provide a research management plan, an equity plan, and indicate in which areas they were expanding or consolidating teaching. The restrictions concerned those activities which the government funded – hence student numbers had to be negotiated, too. The government stipulated minimum institutional size to qualify for a range of teaching programmes. But the institutions were free to offer courses to and take in any number of overseas and local full fee-paying students.

The present phase of university foundations, then, is not a response to an increase in student numbers. Instead, new universities were established through amalgamations of colleges with universities and colleges with colleges. Among these new universities were a couple of former institutes of technology, which by State charter, had been changed to universities of technology, only to be forced to amalgamate with other colleges. It is expected that the number of higher education institutions will fall from 72 in 1988 to about 35 in 1990 (Dawkins and Duncan, 1989, 21).

The present amalgamated universities – and the few who are still holding out or negotiating – all offer bachelor degrees of generally three to four years' duration, and graduate certificates, graduate diplomas and course work masters degrees for advanced study over six months to two years. In addition, research masters and doctorates are being offered, which normally take from two to five years of full-time study following a bachelor degree. At the sub-degree level, several of the newer universities continue offering certificates and diplomas which were part of the offering in the college sector.

All Australian universities offer part-time study opportunities and some provide sandwich courses. Several universities provide co-operative education courses in engineering, accounting and computer-science, where the curriculum is developed jointly with industry or professional groups. Other universities have compulsory industrial experience semesters.

Universities are meant to retain diversity in course offerings and compete for students. But even within the UNS, universities will differentiate between themselves on the basis of research excellence. The pre-1987 universities, i.e. those institutions which precede the upgrading and amalgamations, were funded for research and most established an enviable research record. However, all of the pre-1987 universities now have components from the previous college sector. Clearly this must have a major impact on how universities see themselves, on how faculty staff see their role, and how society or government sees them.

Funding Arrangements

The Universities Council in its advice to the CTEC found it necessary to reaffirm the essential nature of universities. It defined universities, *inter alia,* as 'separate, distinctive and autonomous institutions, built around the notion of a self-governing community of scholars' (Tertiary Education Commission, 1981, 9). Individual and institutional autonomy are among the hallmarks of academic life, and they have been seen as threatened in the present societal context for nearly a decade now (Anwyl, 1982). Most of the funding for higher education is public – 97 per cent for universities in 1986–87 (DEET, 1990). The acquiescence of institutions to Government demands can be explained by this very strong dependence on one source of funds; only the oldest universities could have afforded to resist the Government, as they had substantial income from other sources. At the same time, institutions are being encouraged to find other sources of income, including from full-fee paying overseas students and Australian students enrolling for graduate professional courses. This will and already does make institutions less dependent on government and allows development of areas and programmes which do not need agreement by the government.

Over the past few years many universities and colleges had already adopted a modified 'strategic planning' approach. These measures were at institutional level. The federal government, however, also sought system-wide performance indicators which could be used eventually in the determination of funding allocations. The Efficiency and Effectiveness Review and the White Paper advocated the use of performance indicators for higher education institutions. The AVCC with its college counterpart thereupon decided to develop a system of indicators which would provide comparative data on all of the functions of a higher education institution. The Commonwealth Department of Employment, Education and Training is already collecting much data, and many of the statistics would be part of a set of the performance indicators which could eventually be used to aid decision making in funding. Performance indicators in research are already being used within institutions for distribution of some funds, and by the Australian Research Council (ARC) in its awards of Ph.D. scholarships. Performance indicators for teaching are presently being developed.

In the UNS, funding arrangements have changed. In the past, universities and colleges were funded in different categories, with only the universities being funded for research. Separate funds were made available for general recurrent expenditure, equipment, minor works, and special research grants. In the UNS, each institution receives a single block operating grant calculated on a particular formula. The government, now, through the negotiation of individual institutional profiles guarantees certain levels of funding, enabling universities to plan ahead over a triennium.

But of the total operating grants, 1 per cent is retained in a National Priority (Reserve) Fund. Institutions may bid for project funding in areas specified by the government. Among these areas are management reviews, and trial and pilot programmes for a longer academic year, summer terms, co-operative education programmes, measures to improve student access and completion rates, and staff performance assessment programmes and staff development. Clearly, all of these serve the government agenda of making institutions more efficient and of opening programmes to the community. New priority areas are in the curriculum and teaching areas – environmental and heritage studies, improving distance education, promoting multiculturalism, and improving access to Asian studies (Dawkins/Duncan, 1989, 8).

The government has increased its spending on higher education, planning to provide 49,000 new student places in the 1989–91 triennium and a further 14,000 in 1992. Much of the expansion in enrolments, however, is to be funded by the Higher Education Contribution Scheme (HECS), a graduate tax, introduced in 1989 (Dawkins/Duncan, 1989, 18,25).

Accountability

The concern for efficiency and effectiveness of the system is also manifest in the insistence on more public accountability of higher education institutions. CTEC had sponsored departmental reviews in institutions (Roe/Moses, 1986) and discipline reviews across the system; the AVCC has been examining honours degree standards in a number of disciplines. Several institutions now have regular departmental or faculty reviews. Regular appraisals of probationary staff are also quite common (Moses, 1988), and appraisal procedures for all faculty staff are being developed now in most institutions as a result of a wage agreement.

Accountability as a concept and obligation is accepted by both institutions and faculty staff. However, many of the measures introduced to ensure accountability like appraisal processes and sometimes reviews are seen by some faculty staff not only as intrusive and bureaucratic control mechanisms, but as essentially dysfunctional and anti-collegial and anti-scholarly.

The Impact of the Unified National System on Higher Education

The Changing Role of Higher Education

Higher education institutions change over time, in response to societal demands and values. The recent restructuring of higher education was based on the Minister's vision of the contribution higher education can make, and must make, to society. In his White Paper he stated his conviction that higher education is vital for the economic and social good of Australia.

> Higher education has much to contribute. It is a primary source of the skills we need in our cultural, artistic, intellectual and industrial life. (...) We want to be a society that aspires to excellence and that continually extends its skills and knowledge, rather than one that tolerates mediocrity and stagnation. (...) We want to be a society that understands its own political processes, enables all citizens to participate in these

processes and does not accept without question decisions made on its behalf. Higher education is the source of much of this understanding. (Dawkins, 1988, 7) These are values and goals which would be shared by the majority of Australians concerned with higher education. But many university staff, from lecturer to vice-chancellor, and particularly those concerned with the role of the humanities and social sciences and of pure research, see the above statements as rhetoric. The Government is generally perceived as assigning purely instrumental value to higher education and promoting a narrow vocational role for it. In this it is 'in tune' with the prevalent popular culture which is anti-intellectual and at the same time 'out of tune' with industry which while still assigning an instrumental role to higher education, is increasingly warning of too narrow a vocational focus.

Functions of Academic Staff

As noted, all university staff are expected to be active teachers and researchers. Selection procedures for new positions tend to focus on research ability and performance. As legitimated in the promotion and tenure criteria, university staff have as their primary functions research and teaching, and as secondary functions administration and service to the community and involvement in the professions. Several research studies on Australian university staff clearly demonstrate that the majority of Australian academics believe that involvement in research is necessary for advanced teaching and learning (Moses, 1988). A recent study[1] established that the majority of university academics in the survey were actively engaged in research and publishing. Indeed, academics in the disciplines surveyed published regularly in international journals, the main publication outlet.

In the college sector, faculty were appointed to positions and promotion was generally only possible if a position fell vacant or was newly created. Each grade had specific roles connected to teaching and administrative functions. Professional involvement and practice were encouraged; research was generally not until quite recently. Indeed, our survey showed that despite academic drift, there was less research-teaching synergy in colleges, as may be expected. Promotion rules required excellence in teaching and course development, leadership in institutional affairs, involvement in the professions. Research publications, however, became increasingly important.

Table 3: Academic staff 1989 in Victorian universities and colleges

	Pre-1987 Universities (n=4) % of staff	Colleges (n=17) % of staff
Teaching only	4.5	69.8
Research only	19.1	0.4
Teaching-Research	76.3	29.8

Source: Calculated from table 19, DEET, 1990a.

Table 3 shows the distribution of staff in the old university and college sectors in one state across teaching and research functions. Most of the teaching-research staff in the college sector were employed in a large metropolitan institute of technology, which, as similar institutes in other states, has much in common with universities.

---

1   A study funded by the Australian Research Council on Staff Attitudes and Characteristics in Australian Universities and Colleges.

Our research quoted above, shows quite conclusively that many college staff ranked themselves quite high as researchers; but that compared with university staff in the same disciplines they did not perform well on any of the performance indicators. Their main publication outlets, for example, were internal reports.

The new amalgamated institutions are seeking now to define academic functions anew. They need to make allowances for the background, qualifications and experiences of former college staff without devaluing the strong research orientation of the university.

For several years, there have been suggestions that promotions acknowledge excellence in any of the legitimate functions of academics. This view is shared by many university staff. However, more recent attempts to disengage the research from the teaching function for university staff have met with opposition.

The attack on the research-teaching nexus came already in 1986, and from unexpected quarters. The Department of Science in its Submission to the Australian Science and Technology Council argued that involvement in research was not necessary for effective university teaching in all disciplines and levels of study; that concentration on research may impede teaching excellence and that decoupling of teaching and research may well improve teaching performance and give teaching a higher profile (21–22).

University staff, in the past, have taken it for granted that their research be funded by their institution or, in competition, from external sources. Due to financial pressures, many universities for some time now have made only minimal research funds available on a per capita basis and have encouraged internal competition for research grants. With the abolition of the binary line, even the Australian Research Council is now arguing that not all staff should be expected to do research.

However, the academic unions oppose this view as leading to second-class academics. But with research as the distinguishing criterion in the new university system, faculty staff in all of the institutions try to establish research credentials. Already there is a new stratification in the system: pre-1987 universities which had been funded for research, and the former college sector. Institutions which had a high research profile and have staff with high qualifications try to maintain and better their positions. Several new universities, amalgamations of colleges without research tradition are at the bottom of the hierarchy.

The emphasis on research across the whole system must lead to a diminished role for teaching. A recent Senate Committee (Parliament, 1990) criticised Australian higher education institutions in their teaching role. The challenge now is to create and legitimate within the UNS a diversity of academic roles, so that excellence in teaching is promoted and is publicly acknowledged. Such suggestions are being made from within the system, from ARC, from the Committee and other sources. Yet the stratification and the reputation has been based in the past on access to and success in research and the provision of advanced professional education. There is no indication that this will change.

The new universities at the bottom of the hierarchy have little expertise in research, no research infrastructure, and also none of the high status professional courses like medicine, veterinary science, or law. Engineering, which has been part of the college sector, is the only professional course available in these new universities.

In the amalgamations, there was much anxiety among college staff about a possible devaluing of their past contributions and their present role. While several titles in the college and university sector were the same, e.g. lecturers and senior lecturers, functions were not. At more senior level there was salary parity, but the professorial title was reserved for university staff. Hence university staff in turn were anxious following the amalgamations about having their titles devalued by former college staff who were gaining professorial titles without having the research excellence normally associated with it.

Research

The UNS intended to and indeed has a noticeable impact on research. Research funding which had decreased over a number of years is being increased, the importance of research for the economy is being realised. But the research funding is more focused.

Research in (pre-1987) universities is funded through the operating grant. In the UNS some of the funds which used to be given to the pre-1987 universities are now accessible for competitive bidding (referred to commonly as the clawback) through the Australian Research Council, reducing the amount and proportion of research funds allocated to the older universities. However, the older universities despite their established infrastructure, quality of staff, and resources for research are fearful that their share of research resources will decline, while the newer universities are disillusioned that the abolition of the binary line has not meant that they will be funded for research like the older universities used to be.

As research grants are being distributed on the basis of excellence of proposals and researchers involved, older universities remain competitive. Newer universities are presently compensated for lack of past research funding by additional infrastructure grants for which they may bid. In addition, a 35 per cent infrastructure loading is awarded automatically to successful applicants for ARC grants from the former college sector. However, academic staff in the former colleges, indeed the institutions themselves, see themselves as disadvantaged with peer review favouring colleagues from the well-established universities.

The Government aims in its research policy both to select the best projects and to concentrate research expenditure in areas of both scientific strength and of national interest. Priority areas in the research grants programme of ARC for 1991, for example, are materials science and minerals processing; cognitive science; biological sciences in the management of the Australian terrestrial and marine environment; scientific instruments and instrumentation; and Australia's Asian context.

Since 1982 Special Research Centres have been funded which support 'high quality research in areas of importance to national economic, social and cultural development'. Currently, the Commonwealth is planning to establish 50 Co-operative Research Centres over the next five years which would be joint endeavours between universities, industry and the Commonwealth Scientific and Industrial Research Organisation (CSIRO).

Applications for grants from ARC and for research fellowships require that applications address how the research projects may benefit the Australian economy or society. The emphasis on applied research and directly economically exploitable research is of great concern to the pure sciences as well as to the humanities, and even though the funding for these areas has not decreased, there is a tendency of public devaluing of at least the humanities and little student demand for the pure sciences.

Universities and Manpower Development

Australia is striving to become a 'clever country';[2] in order to achieve this, most of the workforce should have undergone or be undergoing post-school education and training. In 1989, 10 per cent of the labour force (15 years and over) had a degree; twice as many had a certificate or diploma (sub-degree level), and 16 per cent had a trade or apprenticeship qualification. This leaves more than half of the labour force without any post-school qualification. Clearly, both school retention rates and access to higher education had to become political issues if the educational level of the labour force were to be increased. The retention rates to year 12 of secondary school and enrolments in tertiary education have increased substantially, encouraged by a variety of government measures.

The higher education system now is expected to provide the panacea for economic ills. Generally, expectations of the system are diffuse and contradictory: it is urged to address the needs of a very diverse student body for a variety of degrees which meet their vocational needs and educate them, which are academically rigorous and build on their (lack of) subject knowledge, life and work experience; to address the needs of the public and private sector for graduates with transferable skills, as well as for graduates with subject competence, and for graduates with specialised skills; and to address the needs of society and academia itself for more research scientists.

In response there are numerous new courses at undergraduate and graduate level, a confusion over the legitimate goals of higher education, more pressure for research skills training while at the same time the research training leading to Ph.D. is being questioned.

For some time now, many university staff have left the ivory tower and have worked with industry, commerce, the community and government. There are new links in the R&D area. The Australian Research Council (ARC) has made available fellowships in which academics work on specific problems in the private sector, supported by a company. There are also graduate research scholarships for students wanting to conduct research in industry.

Towards the end of the decade, Australia, like many other countries which expanded its higher education system at the same time, will be facing a retirement wave of academic staff. It needs to make research and academic careers more attractive so that a pool of suitable university staff will be available. As a first step the number of graduate research scholarships available each year has been increased and the stipend increased. ARC established a career structure for research fellows which will keep some of the best researchers in higher education.

There is or will be severe shortages in other professions. Computer science and engineering studies, but also studies in the pure sciences are therefore being promoted. In the period 1980 to 1989 the proportion of science students as a share of total student enrolment rose from 12.7 per cent to 13.8 per cent, with a large proportion of this increase in computing science. The increase in enrolment 1980–89 occurred mainly at bachelor degree level (49.8%), with only 18.6 per cent at graduate level (DEET, 1990b). In engineering, there is concern about the low proportion of Australian students enrolled in graduate degrees; at Bachelor level only 10 per cent of students are overseas

---

2   In November 1990 the National Board of Employment, Education and Training organised a
     national conference, *The Clever Country. Education and Training in Perspective*, where academics,
     bureaucrats, politicians and leaders from industry and the community interacted.

students, but at Ph.D. level, they constitute more than 40 per cent of students (DEET, 1990c).

New Agendas: More Equitable Access

Australia is committed now more than it ever has been to giving all its citizens 'a fair go' – one of the key concepts in Australia's self-image. Greater access to and equity in higher education have been actively promoted during the past few years. Traditionally, primary education was available to nearly all children, even those in remote communities. A full secondary education is being promoted now. Universities have been very selective in the past, and only in the last decade or so have admitted students who had not the traditional 'matriculation' credentials. Despite its long history of part-time and distance education, Australia drew in the past on those youths and adults who had formally qualified for entry to university. These were for decades in the majority young males (for full-time students) of Anglo-Saxon-Celtic descent.

In higher education there has never been open admission, and the selection of students is left to the institution. The college sector had been established to serve a different function and a different student group; hence colleges were more liberal than the universities in recognising a variety of qualifications as justifying admission, and TAFE institutions gave easiest and most access. In the 1970's, mature age students who had not matriculated were admitted to universities under a variety of schemes without lowering the qualifications barrier for school leavers. Since the mid-1980s, there have been active programmes in most institutions to enable students who had been disadvantaged in the past, to enter university and to participate as full students. Hence universities had to recognise that some of the students were under-prepared and had to provide bridging or complementary courses particularly in the sciences and maths. The ethnic composition of Australia and the presence of many non-native English speaking students from overseas also meant that students needed help at university with their English language skills. Thus the student population has become more heterogeneous in terms of academic ability and preparation.

The Federal Government, under its Higher Education Equity Programme has been financing many initiatives in institutions and has invited more. All institutions are required to develop equity plans as part of their negotiation documents for funds from the Government. A recent report from within the Department of Employment, Education and Training (1990), *A Fair Chance for All*, requires institutions to reach out into the community and to convince those school students (and adults) from groups with a low participation rate in higher education, that higher education may be within their reach. Such groups are people of Aboriginal or Torres Strait Islander descent, women, people from socio-economically disadvantaged or from non-English-speaking backgrounds, people with disabilities, people from rural and isolated areas. This requirement puts an additional resource strain on institutions – many of these students require special support programmes.

The composition of the student body has changed considerably over the past decades. In 1975 women's share of higher education enrolments was 40.6 per cent; in 1989 it was 52.1 per cent; part of the increase is due to nursing having been transferred from hospitals to higher education institutions. Women are still under-represented at graduate level, particularly doctoral studies, and in many disciplines, e.g. engineering, physical sciences, and economics.

Aborigines and Torres Strait Islanders were virtually absent in the higher education system until the 1970's. Since 1982 the number has nearly quadrupled to 3307 in 1989;

Table 4: Higher education students by gender and level of course, 1988

Level of course	Females		Males	
	No	%	No	%
Undergraduate				
Bachelor	139,030	64.6	144,433	70.2
Diploma	32,191	15.0	9,181	4.5
Other	9,278	4.3	12,489	6.1
Total	180,499	83.9	166,103	80.7
Postgraduate				
Ph.D., Higher Doct.	2,780	1.3	5,964	2.9
Masters	8,392	3.9	13,089	6.4
Diploma	17,476	8.1	16,279	7.9
Other	2,284	1.1	1,764	0.9
Total	30,932	14.4	37,096	18.0
Non-award	3,645	1.7	2,575	1.3
Total	*215,076*	*100.0*	*205,774*	*100.0*

Source: DEET, 1989b.

but proportionately, they are still under-represented at 0.7 per cent of total student enrolment (DEET, 1990d).

Rural students are another target group for access and equity actions. Most of the universities are in urban, largely metropolitan areas; a few are in rural, none in remote areas. The participation rates of students in remote areas is less than half for males, but somewhat better for females. Nearly 31 per cent study by distance education mode, with education counting for nearly a quarter of all enrolments (DEET, 1990e).

Market Orientation

Australia, for some time, has been offering student places in particular to South East Asians. Part of the new agenda is to regard education as a marketable good; hence university education in Australia is now marketed particularly in Asia on so-called education fairs. There is now a large number of overseas undergraduates and graduates studying in Australia. In some courses, overseas students form a significant minority, particularly at graduate level. In the period 1982–89, enrolment of overseas students in higher degrees by research increased by more than 900 per cent, enrolment in coursework masters degrees more than doubled, and in other graduate awards more than quadrupled (Higher Education Council, 1989, table 7.1; DEET, 1990a, table 12). Most overseas students now attend Australian universities as private full-fee-paying students or on scholarships.

Other aspects of the market orientation are evident in the research agendas and competitive funding, the management structures borrowed from business, and the involvement of industry and the professions in co-operative education programmes.

Prospects and Conclusions

As noted, the formerly Australian binary higher education system which allowed for a relatively uniform system of universities and a very diverse system of multi-purpose and single-purpose colleges and institutes of technology has been restructured to a Unified National System. There are several tensions inherent in this new model, two of which will be discussed, viz. diversity versus uniformity, and the notion of credit transfer.

Diversity vs Uniformity

It is recognised by the Higher Education Council, one of the advisory bodies to the Minister for Employment, Education and Training, that it is vital that diversity be maintained in the UNS. The Council noted in a recent draft of a paper:

> The system has to provide participants with real choices and this will happen if institutions develop unique strengths. No two institutions share naturally all the ground relating to their course and student mix, faculty composition, international concerns, links with industry and responses to labour market pressures; nor should they share, by definition, an identical philosophical approach to education simply because they share the title 'university' (Higher Education Council, 1990a, 30).

In the past, the newer universities certainly have organised their teaching and research activities differently from the old universities; they had multi-disciplinary schools, not single-discipline departments; they fostered multi-disciplinary and inter-disciplinary studies. But they were all staffed by similarly qualified faculty and all had the same function.

Australia's UNS will develop into a higher education system which is in itself stratified. The Higher Education Council noted,

> Only well-established institutions will have the resources and critical mass to support high quality teaching and research activity in a broad range of fields. Typically, relatively small institutions will need to limit their activities so that they excel in those which can be well resourced and competitive. The "new" universities particularly will have an opportunity to develop fresh profiles (Higher Education Council, 1990a, 30).

This will leave many of the newer institutions with the 'cheaper' courses like arts, education and business, disadvantaging students in those areas. The Higher Education Council proposes that Australian higher education institutions develop networks so that resources can be used efficiently for optimal student access to courses.

But there is a real danger that the academic drift will lead to endeavours to emulate the traditional, elitist, concept of university, sacrificing the diversity in course offerings from which students were meant to benefit. Already there is a drift to upgrade sub-degree courses to degree courses; to replace college teaching approaches with university teaching approaches. If Australian universities are to be truly comprehensive they need to retain the large mix of course types, of philosophies, of different entry and exit points.

Credit Transfer

The breakdown of the binary system also led to a re-examination of 'articulation' between the TAFE sector and the new higher education sector. In the past, some colleges and institutes (later universities) of technology had arrangements with TAFE colleges that certain diplomas and certificates were acceptable and would gain students entry to or advanced standing in specific courses. There was a degree of permeability in the system. The move now is to extend articulation arrangements across the curriculum. This must lead to a re-examination of necessary entry skills, of skills which students may acquire while studying for their degree, and of desirable outcomes of a university education.

There are concerns: articulation, course modularisation, easy transfer, agreed nomenclature and course length, could lead, but should not, to greater uniformity across the system with regard to curricular content and teaching. There is, for example, talk of a common first-year science course. Block credit for TAFE studies in science would lead to advanced standing in a university course. Less focus has been put, but will be increasingly put, on credit for competencies achieved through work experience, life experience, and in-house training courses or private courses. Australia might well follow the USA where higher education institutions only provide a little over a third of the organised learning opportunities for adults (Cross, 1987, 103). This demands generous and systematic cross-crediting criteria and arrangements for courses and experiences. The Higher Education Council certainly seems to favour more openness, more flexibility, a greater diversity of learning opportunities, and a greater acknowledgment of the value of life and work experience (Higher Education Council, 1990b).

Some of the issues related to these developments have not yet been fully discussed. Should there be courses offered by publicly funded institutions which are open only to students sponsored by particular companies? Will this accommodation to sometimes very specific curricular demands affect the courses offered to regular students? Do these co-operative courses provide new vocational straitjackets for students at a time when the workforce moves towards multi-skilling and transferable skills?

The Government, despite its heavy-handed restructuring of the higher education system, has to an unprecedented degree engaged in discussions about future directions with the wider community and the higher education institutions themselves. A stream of discussion papers examines priorities, trends, strategies. The demands on the new higher education system with its vertical integration of previously separate sectors and its horizontal integration across the binary line are largely instrumental. The expectations that the higher education system will cure the economic ills and prepare Australia for a prosperous future are high!

References

Anwyl, J.E. (ed) (1982) *University Government Relations. Proceedings of the Conference on University Governing Bodies.* Canberra, AVCC.

Cross, K.P. (1987) 'The Changing Role of Higher Education in the United States'. *Higher Education Research and Development* Vol 6, No 2.

CTEC (1990) *Review of Efficiency and Effectiveness in Higher Education.* Canberra: AGPS.

Dawkins, J.S. (1987) *Higher Education. A Policy Discussion Paper.* Canberra: AGPS.

Dawkins, J.S. (1989 *Higher Education. A Policy Statement.* Canberra: AGPS.

Dawkins, J.S. and P. Duncan (1989) *Better and Fairer. Achievements in Employment, Education & Training.* Canberra: AGPS.

DEET (1989b) *Female Students.* Higher Education Series, Report No 1, April 1989.

DEET (1990) *Education at a Glance.*

DEET (1990a) *Selected Higher Education Statistics 1989.* Canberra: AGPS.

DEET (1990b) *Science Students.* Higher Education Series, Report No 4, May 1990.

DEET (1990c) *Engineering Students.* Higher Education Series, Report No 6, July 1990.

DEET (1990d) *Aboriginal and Torres Strait Islander Students.* Higher Education Series, Report No 3, April 1990.

DEET (1990e) *Urban and Rural Participation.* Higher Education Series, Report No 8, September 1990.

Graduate Careers Council of Australia (1990) *1988 Australian Graduates in 1989.*

Higher Education Council (1989) *Australian Graduate Studies and Higher Degrees.* NBEET. Canberra, AGPS.

Higher Education Council (1990a) *Higher Education: The Challenges Ahead.* Working Draft, August 1990.

Higher Education Council (1990b) *Higher Education Courses and Graduate Studies.* NBEET. Canberra, September 1990.

Martin Report (1964–67) Committee on the Future of Tertiary Education in Australia, Report to the Australian Universities Commission, 3 Vols. G.P. Melbourne.

Moses, I. (1988) *Academic Staff Evaluation and Development.* University of Queensland Press.

Parliament of the Commonwealth of Australia (1990) *Priorities for Reform in Higher Education,* a report by the Senate Standing Committee on Employment, Education and Training. Canberra: AGPS.

Roe, E. and I. Moses (1986) *Departmental Reviews in Higher Education Institutions.* Canberra: CTEC.

Teichler, U. (1988) *Changing Patterns of the Higher Education System.* London: Jessica Kingsley Publishers.

Tertiary Education Commission (1981) *Report for 1982–84 Triennium,* 1 (2) *Advice of Universities Council.* Canberra: AGPS.

Trow, M. (1984) 'The Analysis of Status' in Clark, B.R. (ed) *Perspectives on Higher Education.* Berkeley: University of California Press.

Williams, B. (Chairman) *Education, Training and Employment,* Report of the Committee of Inquiry into Education and Training Vol 1. Canberra: AGPS.

CHAPTER 16

Structures and Functional Differentiation
Remarks on Changing Paradigms of Tertiary Education in Europe

Claudius Gellert

Introduction

Since the late 1960's and the early 1970's, much of the expansion of Europe's higher education systems has been accompanied or steered by a process of overall institutional differentiation, i.e. by the fact that the traditional university segments lost their positions as exclusive providers of professional training and that new forms of advanced education were implemented by most governments. Thus, for instance, in the UK the polytechnics were founded, in Germany the *Fachhochschulen* emerged, and in France the IUTs (*Instituts Universitaires de Technologie*) were established.

While some of the newly created institutional forms were somewhat short-lived and given up as a major conception in the meantime (like the German Comprehensive Universities; cf. Pritchard 1990), others were unable to gain more generalised paradigmatic influence within their systems (like the short-cycle provisions in France; OECD, 1973). And while yet other experiments, like the polytechnic sector in Britain, were perhaps 'too successful', insofar as they were overtaken by 'academic drift' (Pratt 1989, and Kogan in this volume), the whole development has by no means been brought to a halt. In fact, there are strong indications that the almost exclusive attention given to changes and issues in the public sectors, may be short-sighted and misleading; because, there is a rapidly emerging 'third sector' in higher education which is to a large extent privately organised and financed and which in many countries is already providing professional training for large numbers (OECD, 1991, 27f.). But also the main areas of public higher education continue to be subjected to reform debates and new legislative measures. The Mediterranean countries are prominent examples at present (Moscati, 1988).

Thus, we can observe, as some would say, a constant process of changing structures in European higher education. But what exactly does it mean to talk about 'structural' change (or 'institutional' change, for that matter) in the field of post-secondary education? Obviously it has to do with the kind of transformation of the system or the emergence of new forms of higher learning which we referred to above. Thus we may take the problem of differentiation or diversification as our area of investigation, since it is a phenomenon which occurs in almost all systems.[1] Apart from that, it is also well suited for demonstrating the need to understand related institutional modifications as *qualitative*, and not just quantitative or formal developments.

We, therefore, attempt to offer a 'functional' approach to the understanding of institutional differences in higher education, i.e. a methodological perspective in which the functions (or roles and tasks) of higher education are of primary importance. It will recur to historical dimensions as well as to more recent societal and political developments and influences. We will begin with the problem (which is a policy as well as an institutional one) that differentiation is often discussed in relation to quality distinctions between units (departments and universities) or sectors in higher education. A possible starting-point is a respective policy-debate in Germany. This will be followed by an overview on major historical university-models and a discussion of recent analytical attempts to throw some light on major structural issues in European higher education.

Quality Differences in Higher Education

In West Germany, as part of the conservative political turn since 1982, which has also affected all fields of education, there has occurred a debate on the presumed decline in the quality of research and teaching in higher education as a consequence of the development of a system of mass higher education. This has resulted in demands for more institutional selectivity and distinctiveness, for a strengthening of the role of university professors in decision-making processes, and generally for more quality orientation in higher education. Special measures were asked for, like particular support of gifted students and outstanding researchers, or the creation of centres of excellence in higher education (Gellert, 1984b).

However, the discussion has been inconsistent in several respects. For instance, the need of special research support for those who have already proven their excellence is not self-evident, since such academics and students usually get the necessary funding. Particularly, there has occurred a fundamental unclarity: on the one hand, there were frequent demands for individual support measures, while, on the other hand, and in order to underline those demands, references were often made to England and the USA, whose elite universities supposedly guarantee high academic standards. One suggestion in this context has been to introduce private universities. This was however rejected with the argument that it was misconceived to equate private universities with elite universities. Moreover, it can be argued that elite places as such do not guarantee overall high quality, but that they are the result of specific system mechanisms of the whole institution (Gellert, 1981, 1992a). The example of the USA will be referred to again further down.

In the German context, one consequence of the elite discussion has been a debate on measuring and evaluating the quality of research and teaching. The discussion comprises a whole range of methods of measuring quality differences by performance indicators, like citation indices, reputation, external funds (in Parsons' terms, the 'drawing power' of academic institutions; Parsons/Platt, 1973), prizes, *Rufe,* etc. The unit of analysis usually is the individual researcher, since only his or her out-put can be 'measured'. The political intention behind such efforts is often an attempt to find exact methods for qualitative differentiation in higher education, i.e. the aim of those engaged in the debate (academics as well as politicians) is to find an objective basis for differential treatment of researchers and/or departments by governments.

The objections to such attempts are well known, and can be summarised as follows:

---

1   The terms 'differentiation' and 'diversification' are used here as synonyms.

1. The number of publications is misleading; quantity does not necessarily reflect quality.

2. The emphasis of the debate is too narrowly on research. Teaching is usually left out. Even more so: service functions, extra-curricular activities, etc. hardly play a role at all.

3. Citation indices, leading roles in professional associations, editorial boards etc are sometimes mostly reflections of power-structures or friendship-networks in scientific communities.

4. Finally, external funding depends on the prestige of the academic institution (Gellert, 1988a).

A central point in this context is the following: Even protagonists of quantitative approaches usually acknowledge that in most cases we are not dealing with exact measurement of quality, but with the *evaluation* of it, i.e. with opinions. Thus, seemingly objective criteria like citation-indices turn out to be what they really are: Social constructions which depend on individual values. E.g., the works of well-known people or of people from well-known universities get cited more often than others. Of course, these differences in prestige and reputation normally also have something to do with quality distinctions. But they cannot be completely explained this way. While for instance it is at least an open question whether those academics who manage best to attract public attention, are also the best in their fields, a number of the very best neither have much inclination to attend conferences or other public meetings, nor do they care a lot about where exactly they publish (sometimes because they do not have much of a choice, which in turn may be a consequence of their refusal to participate in the general gamesmanship).

So we are dealing with a number of open questions, such as:

1. Is it really necessary to exactly measure quality differences between universities or departments, in order to achieve institutional differentiation?

2. What does quality differentiation mean anyway? Is it an institutional goal which the scientific community needs in order to do its best? Or is it a feasible political goal, which can be introduced to save money or to spend money more efficiently?

It is perhaps possible to argue that it is neither of the above. It is neither an institutional goal, because functionalist assumptions about fundamental societal needs or prerequisites are misconceived (Giddens, 1984). Nor is it a realistic political goal, at least not in the sense of a kind of government prescription or programme which could be imposed upon systems of higher education. And with regard to the first question, it may be suggested that exactly measuring quality differences is not necessary for achieving sectoral distinctiveness, even if we may concede that institutional differentiation is necessary (Gellert, 1988a).

This brings us back to the above-mentioned example of the American research universities. With regard to that institution it may argued that the mechanisms of quality differentiation are on all levels primarily sustained by the ongoing awareness of such differences by those actively engaged in the system (Gellert, 1992a). I.e. it is not exact measurement of such differences which brings about institutional differentiation and a permanent pursuit of excellence on all levels (between individuals, departments and universities), but the fact that most professors, students and administrators who work in these universities are constantly aware of real or imagined differences in quality and prestige between their own university and others. Of course, the media play an important role by reinforcing the perception amongst the audience of quality and prestige differences in the academic arena.

Historical Determinants in Higher Education

As we have seen, differentiation in higher education cannot solely be explained in quality and prestige categories, although the latter play an important role *within* a particular segment of a tertiary system. A more promising way to help us understand also present-day institutions of higher education in their basic tasks and purposes is to look at their development, i.e. how specific patterns within respective national systems have emerged. Of course, a historical picture does not necessarily reveal all of today's features and peculiarities. But it can, particularly in the field of such time-honoured institutions as universities, provide us with a fairly reliable and comprehensive first account of fundamental organisational and normative elements which are unlikely to disappear or to be totally modified overnight.

In this context it is for example possible to emphasise that English universities traditionally had a strong interest in the personality development of their students.[2] This does not mean to say that the other major functions of research and professional training play a less important role there than elsewhere. But it is probably correct to say that the function of 'character formation', as it was called at the time of the 'Oxford movement' of Cardinal Newman in the 19th century (Newman, 1852), or of 'liberal education', as it has been termed in recent times (Ashby, 1967), played, at least within Europe, a vastly more important additional role at English universities than in most other university systems. Therefore, we may, without wishing to reduce the scope of the system in any arbitrary manner, call the English paradigm the 'personality model'.

The German university, in contrast, has in modern times above all been concerned with the research function (Gellert, 1992b). Again this does not mean that the functions of professional training or personal development were not important there. The task of professional training has, as anywhere else, been of fundamental relevance since the Middle Ages. Nevertheless, it is true that in modern times the distinguishing characteristic of that model has been its strong preoccupation with research activities, not least with regard to the consequences for the teaching process. Here it is possible to point to the basic difference between the English and the German models. While they both were concerned with educating their students, this task was seen in dramatically different ways. For Humboldt and some of the Idealist philosophers, education through *Wissenschaft* was meant finally to enhance exactly that: *Wissenschaft* itself (Fichte, 1845/46; Humboldt, 1964). For Newman, research and *Wissenschaft* were not even necessary attributes of university life. In his opinion they could also be pursued in academies outside. What mattered for him, and what still matters for modern supporters of the 'collegiate ideal of education' (Halsey, 1961), is the institutional utilisation of socialisation mechanisms which only to some extent can be effectuated by academic means of knowledge dissemination. Thus we may refer to the German university system as the 'research model'.

In the USA, the German research example was adopted towards the end of the 19th century (Flexner, 1930; Diehl, 1978). But there, in contrast to England, the consequences for the organisation of university teaching and research were more radical.

---

2   In this context, it is more appropriate to concentrate on England, rather than to include the whole of the UK or Great Britain, since Scotland has always been much closer to the continental research tradition than England (Davie, 1961).

Apart from a complex process of differentiation in the overall system of higher education, the sector which is comparable to the European universities, i.e. the 'research universities', underwent a gradual process of organisational and functional segregation from within. The three major functions of the leading American universities today seem to correspond to a threefold structural segmentation: the function of liberal education, in many respects similar to its British counterpart (although more defined in terms of the academic requirements of interdisciplinarity) is almost exclusively reserved for the undergraduate level; the function of professional training is placed in specialised professional graduate schools; and the research function is exercised mainly within the academic graduate schools of arts and science (Gellert, 1988b).

The French system, finally, is often referred to as the Napoleonic model, because of its strict hierarchical state subordination (Neave, 1990). Other observers have correctly chosen the French system as the one which is characterised by a high degree of institutional segmentation between 'science in' and 'science out', i.e. the fact that much of the research activities happen outside the university sector, particularly in the Centre national de la recherche scientifique (CNRS) (Ewert/Lullies, 1984; also: Wittrock/Elzinga, 1985). Or, the French system can be regarded as being almost unique in yet another respect, viz. the existence of the elite-sector of *Grandes Écoles* besides the universities. From a functional perspective, the last two aspects are however also relevant in another respect. On the one hand, the existence of a strong element of 'science out' means that the university system itself is predominantly concerned with the function of professional training. And besides the often-referred-to aspect of being centres for elite recruitment, the *Grandes Écoles* also possess the major characteristic of being primarily places of teaching for top professional positions. Thus we may conclude that the French university system as a whole is, more than other systems, emphasising the function of professional training. We can therefore call it the 'training model'.

Of course, it would be a misunderstanding to assume that these national models can be reduced to the described paradigms. They are all, and always have been in their history, composed of several functional elements. But a historical analysis also teaches us that national systems differ in important respects, i.e. in some basic modes of defining and pursuing their tasks and purposes. And in this respect, the university systems of many countries have in the past shown an astonishing degree of inertia and continuity. This explains why some of the leading systems in the world still display major structural components of some centuries ago. The structural differences between these models therefore have to be located above all in the varying definitions and pursuits of their roles in state and society. But that in turn means that structures in higher education are much more than organisational or formal characteristics and have to be interpreted functionally.

In the following, we will attempt to further clarify the issue by looking at some methodological problems concerning the phenomenon of structural differentiation in higher education.

On the Concept of Structures in Higher Education

Analyses of systems of higher education are often concerned not only with structures, but also with such concepts as institutions, norms, values and models (for a general overview, see Gellert, 1984a). In several respects, however, the usage of such categories or concepts is frequently vague and ambiguous. Therefore, we will in the following analyse some of the related topics by looking at a recent account of structural issues in the analysis of higher education systems, which was offered by Ulrich Teichler (1988a).

Teichler refers to a long-lasting debate in the 1960's and 1970's in which three major approaches to structures of higher education were distinguished:

- The 'idiosyncratic' approach dealt with historically determined characteristics of higher education which remain stable over long periods (op. cit. 14).

- The 'functional' approach was concerned with the observation that 'all modern industrial societies are influenced by certain societal, economic, technological, cultural or educational factors more or less common at certain developmental stages of industrial societies'. (*ibidem*)

- And finally, 'political approaches' raised questions 'in what way and to what extent deliberate options shape higher education'. (15)

To start with the second aspect, it seems that the 'functional' approach in the above definition, although it is even broader, deserves the same kinds of criticisms which 'functionalist' conceptions in the social sciences in the tradition of Talcott Parsons were confronted with in the past (Parsons/Platt, 1973). In particular, it also contains the notion of latent or manifest general needs which can be detected in all societies. As has been pointed out before, our own usage of the term 'functional' is more narrowly defined, and simply means 'referring to the role or task of an institution', either at a given historical moment or at present.

Trow's developmental classification from 'elite' to 'mass' to 'universal' higher education, as the 'best known' model of that kind, to which Teichler refers in this context, is further confusing, since Trow's categories can at best be used in a descriptive manner, in order to account for broad quantitative changes (Trow, 1979). But they hardly lend themselves to a meaningful analysis of emerging qualitative patterns, unless the scope of analysis is reduced to the trivial insight that the 'class-function' of social institutions diminishes proportionally to the disappearance of a society's class-structure itself. The hidden evolutionist assumptions in Trow's scheme (and in Teichler's definition of the 'functional' approach itself) are also difficult to support, since they portray societal development in a deterministic, linear fashion.

Also, the third aspect of 'political approaches' is not really useful in explaining fundamental structural phenomena, since on this level structure is a programmatic concept, but not an analytical tool to discriminate reality.

The most important of the above approaches for the explanation of institutional structures is, from our point of view, and notwithstanding the curious terminology, the 'idiosyncratic' one. This approach comes closest to the one chosen here, insofar as we are attempting to demonstrate that only a historically informed vision of the grown tasks and roles of universities within differing cultural and socio-political contexts and traditions enables us to understand recent and contemporary modifications of such patterns (Offe, 1969).

Varieties and Similarities

More recently, Teichler has taken up this issue again by discussing the OECD's recent report on Alternatives to Universities (1991). On the question of the emergence of new institutional patterns, he passes the following judgement: 'I definitely disagree, however, to the OECD report's view that most variations can be explained "idiosyncratically", whereas most common elements can be explained as outgrowth of "functionally" oriented policies' (in this volume). This statement contains a threefold misunderstanding:

- First, the authors of the report did not intend to classify areas of change or inertia within a given conceptual framework. They did attempt to describe and analyse new institutional forms of higher education in Europe and elsewhere, with an emphasis on new tasks (functions) and organisational patterns.

- Second, to the extent that they were concerned with historical ('idiosyncratic') explanations at all, their conclusions were rather the reverse from what Teichler seems to suggest. This is because they took the existing traditional university systems in the countries included in the investigation as their starting point, in order to highlight differences of new forms of higher learning (and perhaps modifications in the traditional systems themselves). Thus, historical determinants were identified as the major cause for the inertia of established systems, whereas recently developed institutions were seen as the result of new needs and expectations.

That takes us, third, to the last misunderstanding: Because, the OECD report does in fact not explain 'most common elements... as outgrowth of 'functionally' oriented policies'. It does not see 'policies' as the only or major driving force of institutional change in higher education at all. The two most important pushes for the overwhelming tertiary expansion all over the world and therefore also for the large-scale process of institutional differentiation, are seen in the 'manpower requirement approach' and in the 'social demand approach'. Both concepts reflect societal (i.e. socio-economic) expectations. The 'policies' which programmatically formulate these expectations or needs, are also important, but should not be confused with them. Certainly, the OECD report does not support the view that it was just the arbitrary and contingent will of politicians which brought into existence the technical colleges in Japan, the polytechnics in New Zealand and Great Britain, or the community colleges in North-America.

Explanations of Higher Education Structures

But let us return to the problem of 'explanations' of higher education structures. As we have seen, at least if we take the approaches which Teichler has selected, most attempts so far were inadequate. Let us see whether this also applies to the four basic structural 'models', which according to Teichler played a central role in debates of the 1960's. They are the following (op.cit. 29f.):

- the 'elitist model', which aims at quantitative limitations of student numbers, and depends on estimates of future needs of both academics and highly skilled professionals;
- the 'vertical model', according to which tertiary expansion should be based on different qualification requirements in the form of structured and separated components;
- the 'unitary model', which aims to establish as great a uniformity in institutions and courses as possible, in order to reduce inequality in education;
- the 'recurrent education' model, which aims at a broad basis of competencies; the acquisition of occupational qualification takes place 'on the job'.

The main objection to these kinds of 'models' is that they mostly do not operate with analytical, but with normative categories, i.e. that they are no social scientific models. They may have been useful for political debates; but since they are too vague for empirical analyses, even their contribution to exact policy-making is questionable. In fact, they are not only vague, but also inconsistent as a classification. Because, the last one, the 'recurrent education' model, does not match the others. This is not even a general policy model of higher education, since it is not concerned with overall structures, but only with one particular functional aspect. And the 'unitary model' is also unsatisfactory, even within this categorial framework. Because it confuses two very different aspects of inequality. To enhance uniformity in institutions is one thing, and to reduce educational inequality quite another. While the latter is certainly desirable, the former, with almost equal certainty, is not. It would in all likelihood be counter-productive, because the total harmonisation of educational institutions can only lead to a general decrease in quality. Thus, even as a programmatic policy model, the 'unitary model' is unrealistic. This leaves the first two 'models' as the only ones with at least a vague empirical foundation in reality. But since they too are not meant to be analytical instruments, but serve solely as guidelines for the formulation of political programmes, they also in the end are useless for the analysis of structures in higher education.

The search for 'optimal structural models' however continued, as Teichler points out, and soon the debate centered on two 'extremes' the 'diversified model', according to which the:

> system of higher education... should be characterised by a multitude of somewhat permeable institutions... distinctive in their major goals as well as in their academic standards... The diversified model would – in contrast to a clearly segmented system – provide for corrections of educational careers where appropriate' and the 'integrated model' which:

> advocates the admission of students with different prerequisites and abilities to the same institutions, even to a certain extent to common courses of study. In the framework of an intra-institutional differentiation, students would share some common experience and finally acquire degrees, which would differ in academic standards to a lesser extent than in the case of a 'diversified' structure (Teichler, 1988a, 31).

In contrast to earlier writings where he was supporting the idea of a comprehensive university (e.g. Hermanns et al, 1983), Teichler now seems to favour the diversified model. But despite a fairly detailed ideal 'typology' of the diversified model (54–56), he never gets around to clearly stating whether in his opinion it applies for instance to the USA or not (a view that could well have been supported by many empirical findings, and that, if formulated, could have served as the basis for further empirically oriented discussions of the concept; Riesman, 1981). This difficulty in committing himself to analytical clarity is probably due to the fact that in the whole book he is in reality not dealing with analysing structures, i.e. empirically testable features of higher education systems, but only with political programmes and policy models.

The way in which Teichler finally concludes his account of structural debates in higher education, is therefore significant in our context:

> The debate as well as the corresponding research seldom focus convincingly on the major issue of controversy between the diversified and the integrated model, i.e. to what extent learning in higher education is most successfully promoted either by a relatively homogeneous or a relatively heterogeneous environment. (99)

This conclusion is highly interesting, because the functional aspect of learning (which of course is closely connected with the one of professional training), although it was hardly mentioned in his analysis until then, in the end turns out to be 'the major issue'. The reason why Teichler finally emphasises this aspect of learning is, from our perspective, the need to acknowledge functional aspects of structures which go beyond the formal or programmatic concepts he has been dealing with. Structures, also in higher education, are thus much more than the ideal-typical concepts and policy programmes. They are, as we will see in more detail further down, the action framework of institutions, i.e. the place where things are happening, or, more precisely, they are what is happening and what is being done. In other words, the understanding of institutions of higher education only begins here. At this point we have to analyse what is being done, by whom, for what purposes, and so forth. Only such an analysis will enable us to understand what universities and other tertiary institutions are about.

Teichler, at the end of the book, sums up with a rather relativistic remark on dealing with structural phenomena:

> To summarise, we note a broad range of interesting approaches in analysing the structural developments of higher education. They make us aware of specific aspects and provide interesting explanations of certain phenomena, but by and large they provide partial views, explain only some cases in a plausible manner and tend to overestimate the explanatory power of the individual approach. Thus, one has to draw upon a broad range of diverse concepts in order to examine their utility in explaining structural developments in higher education and their causes in industrial societies in the last few decades'. (107f.)

A pluralist conceptual approach may well be required. But this should not prevent us from realising that structures in higher education are not just formal categories, which can be used to classify systems of higher education. Indeed, it may be argued that precisely by attempting such classifications of overall systems of higher education in the first place, one obstructs a meaningful insight into what these structures really are.

Thus, Burton Clark has noted that differentiation of higher education institutions depends on 'legitimacy of institutional roles'. And, as he continues, 'to stabilise a role, a sector must have a separate set of tasks in which its personnel believe' (Clark, 1983, 221). This demonstrates well our point that structure has to do more with content than with form. And in this perspective the 1991 OECD report correctly points to the ever-growing importance of non-university sectors (NUS) in higher education which in many countries are characterised by similar functional features such as vocationally oriented curricula, responsiveness to industrial needs, narrow disciplinary offerings, and a concern with improving educational opportunities (Gellert, 1991c).

But Teichler does not share this fundamental insight into the growing significance of non-university sectors in higher education. Since he is predominantly concerned with formal aspects of higher education, he also in this context reaches a surprising conclusion when, in a study on the 'changing organisation of studies' in Europe, he states that 'terms such as 'university-type' versus 'non-university' higher education... continued to become more inappropriate in the 1980s' (Teichler 1988b, 170). For us, the just-mentioned functional features are, however, more important for an understanding of higher education structures in Europe than, say, the fact that the study periods in NUS-sectors tend to become longer.

Structures and Institutions

Sociologically speaking, structure is a sub-concept of institution. It refers to routinised social actions and their normative orientations. Institutions are relatively stable forms of reproduced social structures, in which 'knowledgeable agents' permanently create the conditions for their own continued social existence. We are thus dealing with a 'duality of structures' (Giddens, 1984, 297ff.). Applied to institutions of higher learning this means that the 'knowledgeable agents' of such systems (professors, students, etc) are reproducing their institutional frameworks according to the inherent functional requirements.

The definitions of the latter may vary. But the main point is that social actors of a particular institutional setting pursue and implement, within the framework of their institution, norms and values which are mostly historically determined and thus pre-given. Of course, there exist manifold normative overlaps, changes and external influences. Thus, the members of a scientific community are naturally and often concerned with problems of educational equality and social selectivity in society at large. But they cannot transform these general social and political concerns into primary institutional definitions of the rationale of academic institutions, without drastically changing their identity. The latter cannot resolve any kinds of societal injustice. Individual members of the institution are of course free to engage in theoretical and practical activities to overcome such societal insufficiencies. The institution at large, however, cannot but define its *raison d'être* in its own functional terms (Gellert, 1989).

Of course, there is always room for institutional modifications. And they do indeed occur, as we can observe everywhere in the field of higher education. But they always have to do with norms, values, goals, in brief, functional definitions. Recent trends towards more accountability or vocationalism of institutions of higher education are, to the extent that these aims do not only remain one-sided policy-objectives of governments, but become intrinsic concerns of the institutions in question, functional attributes (Gellert, 1991a, 1991b). Therefore, the main segments of tertiary education should, for analytical reasons, be kept separate. Otherwise it is impossible to identify and analyse differences in major objectives between the universities and the non-university sector or other forms of advanced training. Even if we wish to put our emphasis on the process of 'blurring of boundaries' between sectors which occurs in some systems, this makes only sense if the respective structures are understood as alluding to substantive aspects of roles and tasks (cf. Kogan in this volume).

Conclusion

As was suggested above, a functional approach to the classification of university models is useful for the understanding not only of the flagships of European higher education, i.e. the universities themselves, but also for a differentiated analysis of institutional variations as well as historical and political developments occurring in relation to European systems of higher education. The identification of the 'research model' in Germany, the 'training model' in France, and the 'personality model' in England did not mean to imply that there are such 'pure' systems. Since the described models are not pure and homogeneous structures, but a mix of different tasks and purposes, although with differing emphases in respective areas, they should be treated as ideal-typical concepts in the Weberian sense (Weber, 1972). They serve heuristic purposes, insofar as they make alternative developments within their own realms as well as differing structures and aims in other systems more transparent and easier to locate.

A major result from the above considerations is the methodological need of putting less emphasis in future analyses of this European research field on formal aspects of structural differentiation, and of concentrating more on functional, i.e. qualitative and historically informed features of tertiary education and research institutions. Particularly, it should be attempted to distinguish more rigorously the genuine characteristics of the institutions in question from outside societal functions, norms and values. This does not mean to say that such external political or social concerns are less significant. But it means that by confusing those norms with the functional requirements of universities and other institutions of higher education, the difficult task of analysing comparative higher education is becoming even more burdened.

The most important reason for using a functional and historically informed approach for the analysis of tertiary education, however, consists in the overall process of differentiation which almost all systems of higher education in the West have experienced during the last 20 or 30 years. Because it is only if we possess a fairly clear idea of what the historical origins of higher education, i.e. the university sectors, looked like, what their predominant features were, before the diversification processes began, that we can try and understand some of the shifts and modifications in the ways in which the European tertiary training institutions are performing their tasks.

Therefore, as was pointed out before, it is not useful to attempt to conceptualise complete systems of higher education in their functional respects. The (changing) differences in functions and societal expectations of differing sectors of higher education are of central interest. The notion of differentiation or diversification, however, is first of all a formal one. It either exists or it does not. This fact in itself is not yet of fundamental importance. But it is, for instance, significant that the emergence of non-university sectors in many countries was characterised by new and specific functional orientations (like curricular responsiveness to practical industrial needs). Structural modifications or processes of differentiation are therefore only relevant insofar as they signify the formation of new roles and tasks in higher education or the research system and the ways in which these are related to changing needs and expectations in the economy or in society at large.

References

Ashby, E. (1967) 'The Future of the Nineteenth Century Idea of a University' in *Minerva* Vol VI No 1 Autumn 1967, 3–17.

Ben-David, J. (1977) *Centres of Learning: Britain, France, Germany, United States.* New York.

Clark, B.R. (1983) *The Higher Education System: Academic Organisation in Cross-National Perspective.* Berkeley: University of California Press.

Clark, B.R. (1987a) *Academic Life in America: Small Worlds, Different Worlds.* Princeton, N.J.: Carnegie.

Clark, B.R. (1987b) *The Academic Profession in Europe and America. Berkeley: University of California Press.*

Davie, G.E. (1961) *The Democratic Intellect. Scotland and Her Universities in the Nineteenth Century.* Edinburgh University Press.

Diehl, C. (1978) *Americans and German Scholarship 1770–1870.* New Haven: Yale University Press.

Ewert, P. & St. Lullies (1984) *Das Hochschulwesen in Frankreich – Geschichte, Strukturen und gegenwärtige Probleme im Vergleich.* Munich: IHF.

Fichte, J.G. (1845/46) *Sämtliche Werke. Berlin: Veit & Comp. Vol VIII.*

Flexner, A. (1968) *Universities, American, English, German.* New York: Oxford University Press (first 1930).

Gellert, C. (1981) 'Institutionelle Status- und Qualitätsdifferenzierung von Universitätssystemen. Anmerkungen und Thesen zur Elitediskussion' in *Beiträge zur Hochschulforschung* No 4, 423–439.

Gellert, C. (1984a) 'Institutions- und Strukturforschung über das Hochschulsystem' in D. Goldschmidt, U. Teichler & W.D. Webler (eds) *Forschungsgegenstand Hochschule. Überblick und Trendbericht.* Frankfurt: Campus, 217–231.

Gellert, C. (1984b) 'Politics and Higher Education in the Federal Republic of Germany' in *European Journal of Education* Vol 19, No 2, 217–232.

Gellert, C. (1985) 'State Interventionism and Institutional Autonomy' in *Oxford Review of Education* Vol 11, No 3, 283–293.

Gellert, C. (1988a) 'Wettbewerb und institutionelle Differenzierung – Anmerkungen zur universitären Leistungsbewertung in den USA' in *Beiträge zur Hochschulforschung* No. 4, 467–496.

Gellert, C. (1988b) 'Andere Ziele, andere Zeiten. Der angloamerikanische Mut zur Erziehung wird durch kürzere Studienzeiten belohnt' in *Deutsche Universitätszeitung* No 19, 20–23.

Gellert, C. (1989) 'Zur Analyse der institutionellen Voraussetzungen der Wissensproduktion in den USA' in H.-J. Hofmann-Nowotny (ed) *Kultur und Gesellschaft.* Bern: Seismo, 453–456.

Gellert, C. (1991a) 'Andersartig, aber gleichertig – Anmerkungen zur Funktionsbestimmung der Fachhochschulen' in *Beiträge zur Hochschulforschung* No 1, 1–25.

Gellert, C. (1991b) 'Entwicklung der Hochschulsysteme als funktionale Differenzierung – Ein internationaler Vergleich' in *Plenum* (Austrian Rectors' Conference) No 2, 45–50.

Gellert, C. (1991c) 'Postsekundäre Bildungsgänge als internationale Herausforderung' in *EG-INFO (Arbeitsgemeinschaft Berufsbildungsforschung)* No 2, 2–5.

Gellert, C. (1992a) *Wettbewerb und Leistungsorientierung im amerikanischen Universitätssystem.* Frankfurt: Lang.

Gellert, C. (1992b) 'The German Model of Research and Advanced Education' in B.R. Clark (ed) *The Research Foundations of Graduate Education: Germany, Britain, France, United States, Japan.* Berkeley: University of California Press.

Giddens, A. (1984) *The Constitution of Society.* Cambridge: Polity.

Gieseke, L. (1987) *Aus Tradition in die Zukunft. Die Hochschulen in der Bundesrepublik Deutschland, Bildung und Wissenschaft* No 1–2.

Halsey, A.H. (1961) 'University Expansion and the Collegiate Ideal' in *Universities Quarterly* 16, I, 55ff.

Hermanns, H., U. Teichler & H. Wasser (eds) (1983) *The Complete University: Break from Traditions in Germany, Sweden and the U.S.A.* Cambridge, Mass.: Schenkman.

Humboldt, W.v. (1964) *Schriften zur Politik und zum Bildungswesen,* Werke Vol IV. Stuttgart: Cotta.

Moscati, R. (1988) 'Editorial: Higher education in Southern Europe: different speeds or different paths toward modernisation?' in *European Journal of Education* Vol 23, No 3, 189–194.

Neave, G. (1990) 'On Preparing the Markets: trends in higher education in Western Europe' in *European Journal of Education* Vol 25 No 2, 105–122.

Newman, J.H. (1965) *On the Scope and Nature of University Education* London: Everyman's Library (first 1852).

OECD (1973) *Short-Cycle Higher Education: A Search for Identity.* Paris: OECD.

OECD (1991) *Alternatives to Universities.* Paris: OECD.

Offe, C. (1969) 'Historische Aspekte der Funktion und Struktur der deutschen Universität' in UNESCO-Institut für Pädagogik (ed) *Faktoren und Zielvorstellungen der Hochschulreform in der Bundesrepublik.* Hamburg. 20–31.

Parsons, T. and G.M. Platt, (1973) *The American University.* Cambridge, Mass.: Harvard University Press.

Pratt, J. (1989) *Alternatives to Universities in Higher Education: Country Study United Kingdom.* Paris: OECD.

Pritchard, R. (1990) *The End of Elitism? The Democratisation of the West German University System.* New York: Berg.

Riesman, D. (1981) *On Higher Education. The Academic Enterprise in an Era of Rising Student Consumerism.* San Francisco et al.

Teichler, U. (1988a) *Changing Patterns of the Higher Education System: The Experience of Three Decades.* London: Jessica Kingsley Publishers.

Teichler, U. (1988b) *Convergence or Growing Variety: The Changing Organisation of Studies.* Strasbourg: Council of Europe.

Trow, M. (1979) 'Elite and mass higher education: American models and European realities' in *Research into Higher Education: Processes and Structures.* Stockholm: National Board of Universities and Colleges, 183–219.

Weber, M. (1972) *Wirtschaft und Gesellschaft.* Tübingen: Mohr (first edition 1914/18).

Wittrock, B. and Elzinga (eds) (1985) *The University Research System: The Public Policies of the Home of Scientists.* Stockholm: Almquist & Wiksell Int.

List of Authors

Poul Bache
Ministry of Education, Copenhagen

Patrick Clancy
Department of Sociology, University College, Dublin

Bruno De Witte
Law Faculty, Limburg University, Maastricht

Claudius Gellert
European Policy Unit, European University Institute, Florence

Leo C.J. Goedegebuure
Centre for Higher Education Policy Studies, University of Twente, Enschede

Jean-Pierre Jallade
European Institute of Education and Social Policy, Paris

Maurice Kogan
Department of Government, Brunel University, London

Emilio Lamo de Espinosa
Complutense University, Madrid

Jean Lamoure
École Nationale Supérieure d'Enseignement Technique, Paris

Jeanne Lamoure Rontopoulou
Comité Nationale de la Gestion, Paris

Erich Leitner
Department of Higher Education, University of Klagenfurt, Klagenfurt

Eduardo Marçal Grilo
Calouste Gulbenkian Foundation, Lisbon

Peter A.M. Maassen
Centre for Higher Education Policy Studies, University of Twente, Enschede

Roberto Moscati
Department of Sociology, University of Milan, Milan

Ingrid Moses
Centre for Learning and Teaching, University of Technology, Sydney

Einhard Rau
Institute for Sociology of Education, Free University, Berlin

Christos Saitis
Ministry of Education, Athens

Ulrich Teichler
Centre for Research on Higher Education and Work, Comprehensive University of Kassel, and Northwestern University

Johan L. Vanderhoeven
Centre for Comparative Education, Catholic University, Leuven

Don F. Westerheijden
Centre for Higher Education Policy Studies, University of Twente, Enschede

Willy Wielemans
Centre for Comparative Education, Catholic University, Leuven

Subject Index

References in italic indicate figures or tables.

Name Index